The Gypsies of Early Modern Spain, 1425–1783

The Gypsies of Early Modern Spain, 1425–1783

Richard J. Pym

palgrave
macmillan

First published 2007 by
PALGRAVE MACMILLAN
Houndmills, Basingstoke, Hampshire RG21 6XS and
175 Fifth Avenue, New York, N.Y. 10010
Companies and representatives throughout the world

PALGRAVE MACMILLAN is the global academic imprint of the Palgrave Macmillan division of St. Martin's Press, LLC and of Palgrave Macmillan Ltd. Macmillan® is a registered trademark in the United States, United Kingdom and other countries. Palgrave is a registered trademark in the European Union and other countries.

ISBN 978-1-349-54346-5   ISBN 978-0-230-62532-7 (eBook)
DOI 10.1057/9780230625327

A catalogue record for this book is available from the British Library.

Library of Congress Cataloging-in-Publication Data
Pym, Richard.
    The gypsises of early modern Spain, 1425–1783/Richard J. Pym.
      p. cm.
    Includes bibliographical references and index.
    ISBN –13:978–1–4039–9231–4

    1. Romanies—Spain—History. 2. Spain—Ethnic relations—History.
    I. Title.

DX251.P96 2007
305.891′4970460903—dc22   2006051019

10   9   8   7   6   5   4   3   2   1
16   15   14   13   12   11   10   09   08   07

Transferred to Digital Printing 2011

For Annie, Alex and Charlotte

Contents

Acknowledgements

I owe a considerable debt to the pioneering archival work on Spain's gypsies carried out by Bernard Leblon, Antonio Gómez Alfaro, and María Helena Sánchez Ortega, especially in relation to the eighteenth century, and additionally in the case of María Helena Sánchez Ortega, the Inquisition. Others whose work has been of fundamental importance for my own include Teresa de San Román and Amada López de Meneses, as well as Sir Angus Fraser, whose writings on gypsies, while by no means limited to Spain, provided a wealth of valuable information, especially about the late medieval period. More recently, a study by Lou Charnon-Deutsch, although concerned primarily with the nineteenth and twentieth centuries, has done much to help extend our understanding of how the culturally iconic figure of the Spanish gypsy has been constructed and represented by Spaniards and non-Spaniards alike.

I should also like to express my thanks to Jaume Riera, Head of Referencing at the Archivo de la Corona de Aragón, José María Burriaza at the Archivo General de Simancas, and other archive staff too numerous to mention individually there and at the Archivo Histórico Nacional in Madrid and Toledo for their professionalism, generosity, and patient encouragement. I am grateful, too, to the Arts and Humanities Research Council for the generous research leave award that enabled me to complete the book.

Special thanks are due to Alistair Malcolm of the University of Limerick's Department of History, who read the entire manuscript with the eye of a lynx, making many useful suggestions. Finally, I would like to express my profound gratitude to Melveena McKendrick of Cambridge University for her unfailing support, wise counsel, and remarkable generosity of spirit.

Some of the material in Chapters 2, 6, and 8 originally appeared in *Rhetoric and Reality in Early Modern Spain*, ed. Richard J. Pym (Woodbridge: Tamesis, 2006) and is reproduced here with the kind permission of the publisher.

All translations are the author's unless otherwise indicated in the endnotes. Where early modern sources are cited, the original spelling has been preserved in titles, though modern accentuation has been added here and there for the sake of clarity.

Introduction

A great deal has been written about Spain's Jewish and Muslim (or converted *morisco*) minorities in the early modern period. Its gypsies or *gitanos*, however, have been largely ignored by scholars of the period. Very few historians of early modern Spain, with the distinguished exceptions of Antonio Domínguez Ortiz, Henry Kamen, and the specialists mentioned in the preface, even accord them the briefest mention, preoccupied for the most part with centrist or more generally European or imperial concerns. Certainly, no full-length study in English of the early history of Spain's gypsies has ever been written. Yet there is much to be learned from such a study, not just about the fortunes of the gypsies themselves, but also about the larger society through which they moved. The purpose of this book is therefore to reconstruct the first three and a half centuries in Spain – the opening chapter covers the late medieval period when the gypsies first arrived there – of a people who have until now remained largely invisible to history in the English-speaking world. It will focus in particular on the late sixteenth century and the first four decades of the seventeenth, a crucial period of crisis for Spain and its minority *morisco* and gypsy populations alike. Such a project is not, however, without its difficulties. Before the work of Leblon, Sánchez Ortega, Gómez Alfaro, and López de Meneses began to appear, the little that had previously been written about Spain's gypsies had tended far too easily to buy into myth, uncritically re-cycling received wisdom, and lacking a solid evidential base. In the nineteenth century a much romanticized version of the figure of the Spanish gypsy even became for many non-Spaniards a virtual synonym for Spain itself. When Lou Charnon-Deutsch noted that her recent study was not about 'the real Romany', she was acknowledging precisely this fictive yet undeniably influential aspect of so many representations of 'the idealized and sometimes demonized figure of the Spanish Gypsy, conceived throughout hundreds of years as a foreign and exotic presence who stealthfully imported something of the East into the West'.[1]

Behind such romanticizing or demonizing distortions, which can be traced back at least to Cervantes's day, the gypsies themselves, history's real gypsies, inevitably remain somewhat elusive. Many social groups in history have been voiceless. The gypsies are not alone in that. But when to the profundity of that silence is added their always marginal and, for most of the period, unregistered status, the fact that, entirely illiterate, they left no written records, no works of art, no literature, no recoverable oral tradition, and that they had no distinctive religious liturgy or representative institutions of their own, then the task of writing about them is inevitably daunting. As to quantitative data, one should make it clear from the outset that these are virtually non-existent before the late eighteenth century. Even then, the census figures of 1783, for example, should not be regarded as particularly reliable in that they are unlikely to be comprehensive. That said, the eighteenth century is very much better documented than earlier periods, though there is almost certainly much early evidence still to be discovered in local or family archives, especially in southern Spain, where the greatest gypsy concentrations were (and still are) to be found and where they enjoyed some powerful protectors. If, then, as is sometimes claimed, written history is a jigsaw with some of the pieces missing, this one will inevitably lack more than most. But that does not mean that there is nothing useful to be said. Whilst our means of access to early modern Spain's gypsies are almost always indirect, except, perhaps, for the occasional defensive or dissembling voice meticulously reproduced in the records of the Inquisition, there remains nevertheless sufficient documentary evidence to allow much of this significant minority's early history to be reconstructed. Where that evidence is incomplete or allows only for conjecture, I have tried always to make this clear, and can only add that the reader's inevitable frustration at such moments is shared, acutely, by the author. In one sense, then, this book also represents a plea for further archival research. Many questions remain to be answered: there is, for example, the relationship between gypsies and *moriscos* during *and* after the expulsions of the latter in the early seventeenth century; or the little researched dynamics of interracial relations in the early modern period in areas like the *campiña* south-east of Seville and around Jerez de la Frontera; or, indeed, the true extent and nature of the protection against the civil authorities for so long extended to gypsies by the Church, the nobility, and ordinary Spaniards.

Even the gypsies' remote past remains shrouded to a degree in controversy, though today's consensus view, supported by linguistic analyses which have identified Sanskrit traces in the many different dialects of Romaní, points to an origin in the Indian subcontinent. From there, it is generally believed that the gypsies departed en masse, for reasons unknown, in the tenth century, moving slowly westwards before eventually arriving in western Europe early in the fourteenth. The gypsies in question are Roma, *calés* (dark-skinned) as Spanish gypsies call themselves. They are the subject of this study. Groups who found their way into Spain in later periods and who are nowadays usually considered *gitanos*, like the Portuguese *cinganos*, many of whom are probably not in fact of gypsy origin, and the *húngaros*, who are few in number, have no place in this narrative. Nor do the so-called *quinquis*, a shortened form of *quincalleros* (tinkers), another, almost certainly non-gypsy group, itinerant until the mid-twentieth century and possibly descended from peasants driven off the land and onto Spain's roads by hunger and disease in the late sixteenth century.[2]

Just as there exist significant differences related to economic status, sedentarization, and regional origin among Spanish gypsies of today,[3] so too it would be a mistake to think of the gypsies of early modern Spain as an entirely homogenous group. As we shall see, the authorities' conception of who or what a gypsy was tended anyway to evolve, and for most of the early modern period was determined much more by behavioural criteria than any narrowly construed notion of genetic descent. Such a notion would anyway have been of strictly limited utility, given the degree of miscegenation that had undoubtedly occurred down the centuries, *gitano* endogamy, then as now, being practised much more strictly in some patrigroups than in others. How, then, should we think of the term *gitano*? Max Weber wrote that ethnic groups are 'those human groups that entertain a subjective belief in their common descent because of similarities of physical type or of customs or of both, or because of memories of colonization or migration'.[4] More specifically, the social anthropologist Teresa de San Román has proposed five constituent features around which today's *gitanos'* sense of cultural or ethnic identity may usefully be considered to coalesce. First, in *caló* Spanish gypsies share at least the vestigial remnants of their own common language. Second, they share in Weberian terms a shared, disaffiliative and contradistinctive sense of ethnic identity vis-à-vis non-gypsy or *payo* society. This is based on language, the markedly patriarchal extended family or *raza*, respect for clan elders, often referred to nowadays as *tíos* (uncles), a profound reverence for the dead, the importance of virginity and fidelity in gypsy women, pollution taboos associated with the female lower body, especially in respect of menstruation, respect for the territorial claims of other patrigroups, and the conspicuously lavish and colourful celebration of weddings and baptisms. Third, their relationship with the authorities continues on the whole to be one characterized by conflict and distrust, and, one should add, a shared, if historically indistinct cultural memory of repression. Fourth, they have developed cultural strategies based primarily on a ready mobility designed to maximize access to scarce resources. And fifth, they benefit from an extremely flexible socio-spatial organization, frequently using endogamous marriage to cement alliances which enhance that flexibility.[5]

As suggested, I shall also argue that a study of this nature can provide useful insights into the attitudes and practices of important sections of early modern Spanish society, especially in rural areas. These relate not just to the often complex relationship between Spaniards of every estate and the gypsies, but also to the intractable problems encountered by the crown in its attempts, frustrated time and again, to impose its will via legislation on recalcitrant nobles, churchmen, and ordinary Spaniards alike. Such questions, related as they are to the continuing co-existence or *convivencia* in early modern Spain of different ethnic groups, also connect with a larger historical debate. Notwithstanding L. P. Hartley's much-quoted maxim, the past, at least as far as Spanish historiography is concerned, seems less another country where they do things differently than a battleground on which competing, and often radically different versions of nation and national identity, of 'Spanishness', are anxiously locked in struggle. I refer here not so much to the fact that for most of the early modern period 'Spain' was not a unitary state in any meaningful sense of the term, but rather to the way historians have long tended to propose very different versions of how this society or societies should be interpreted. One has only to think of the sharply antagonistic response of some Spanish historians to Henry Kamen's recent assertion that the creation of the Spanish empire was not in fact the exclusive preserve of Spaniards, but rather a distinctly collaborative enterprise involving many nations and peoples, including those subjected.[6] Such conflicting claims are not new, and can be traced back through much of Spanish history. Perhaps, though, their best-known modern manifestation is to be found in exchanges in the last century involving Américo Castro and Claudio Sánchez-Albornoz, discussed at greater length in my opening chapter. Elsewhere, partly with the general reader in mind, I have devoted some more general discussion to particular historical contexts, like the early reign of Ferdinand and Isabella, the crisis years of the early seventeenth century, or the changed political landscape of eighteenth century, Bourbon Spain, wherever, in fact, I felt this might throw a particular light on the situation of Spain's gypsies or where significant developments had specific, lasting implications for them.

Finally, one should perhaps explain very briefly why this book has nothing at all to say on the subject of flamenco, an art of course closely associated with Spanish gypsies, who remain among its most adept interpreters. The reason is simple. The very first reference to anything that can with a reasonable degree of confidence be identified as an ancestor of today's flamenco occurs only late in the eighteenth century in José Cadalso's *Cartas marruecas*, written in 1773–4. In this work the author, an army officer, describes gypsy women dancing in the country house of a young Andalusian nobleman with whom their leader, one 'tío Gregorio', quaffing jugs of wine, distributing lit cigars, and alternately cursing and clapping out the rhythms, appears to be on altogether familiar terms.[7]

1
The Early Years

> It seems that the gypsies were born into the world solely in
> order to be thieves: they are born of thieving parents, they are
> brought up with thieves, they study how to be thieves, and,
> in the end, they emerge thieves through and through. Stealing
> and the urge to steal are part and parcel of their very being, and
> are eradicated only when they go to the grave.

So begins Cervantes's novella *La gitanilla* (*The Little Gypsy Girl*), the tale
chosen by its author to open his 1613 collection of *Novelas ejemplares*.[1]
The passage's seven insistent references to theft famously epitomize the
common stereotype of the gypsy that had long since come to enjoy
widespread currency across Europe. In Spain, the continual attribution
to gypsies throughout the early modern period of transgressions ranging
from highway robbery and worse by the men, to sorcery, petty theft,
and various forms of deception by gypsy women, continued to fuel
their unenviable reputation. But a vicious circle was also at work. At
least part of the blame for the stubborn persistence of gypsy criminality there must lie with the very instruments repeatedly invoked to
control it. As draconian legislation increasingly demanded that the
gypsies abandon not just their few traditional occupations, but also in
many cases even their homes, what began as a response to specific,
delinquent behaviours quickly translated into wholesale stigmatization
and economic emasculation. Framed by men of the centre with little
real knowledge of those at the outermost margins of society against
whom they were directed, the laws unsurprisingly reflected the short-
comings of the simplistic, demonizing stereotype of the gypsy on which
they drew, and which, of course, they further reinforced. As they did

so, the few economic options available to gypsies became ever more limited, the crown eventually demanding that they work only as agricultural labourers, as casual employees, that is to say, of non-gypsy landowners. Little wonder, then, that many continued to resort – or reverted – to the very behaviours the legislators had set out in the first place to curb. Yet even the universal assumption that gypsies could be relied upon to be inveterate thieves seems hardly sufficient in itself to explain the disproportionately prominent place they eventually came to occupy in certain Spanish minds of the period.[2] For most Spaniards, the spectre of the thieving gypsy owed at least as much to hearsay and demonizing myth as it did to direct experience. Yet by the early seventeenth century, this otherwise distinctly marginal figure had come, for some Spaniards at least, centrally to represent many of the ills that now beset the nation. The facile pathological displacement of Spain's perceived woes onto this despised pariah group reflected the acute crisis of confidence that had by now begun to affect important sections of the nation's intellectual and religious élite. After a series of debilitating setbacks, Spain, or more properly in this context Castile, the very heart of a vast empire that now stretched half-way across the world, had, it was feared, at last begun to falter. Unless appropriate remedies could be found, some now saw decline as inevitable. How and why all of this came about and how, in particular, such fears were to impact on Spain's gypsies will be central concerns of this book, as will the role played by the institutions, society, and culture of an early modern Spain that now seems more complex, more pluralistic, in some ways more dysfunctional, and yet in others more robust than has sometimes been allowed. As to the gypsies, or *gitanos* the word is a corrupt version of the Castilian term *egipcianos* (Egyptians) – marginal they may have been, yet by the time Cervantes was writing they were well established in Spain. In fact, some two hundred years had passed since the first groups to penetrate south of the Pyrenees had crossed what nowadays represents Spain's northern border. As we shall see, the first contacts with these newcomers were far from being marked by the official hostility later to be visited upon them in their adopted land. Indeed, in what must qualify as one of history's smaller ironies, among the very earliest historical documents we possess relating to Spain's *gitanos* is an order dated 26 May 1425 and issued by King Alfonso V of Aragon – Alfonso the Magnanimous, as he was known. In it, he instructs the townsfolk of Alagón, near Zaragoza, to return to 'Count Thomas of Egypt' two dogs, a mastiff and a greyhound, which they had stolen from him.[3]

Newcomers in western Europe

The earliest reliable reports of the arrival in western Europe of gypsies date to the second decade of the fifteenth century. An anonymous German chronicle recorded the presence of these strange newcomers at Augsburg in late 1417. It also made the astonishing claim that they had come equipped with letters authorizing them to steal from anyone refusing them charity.[4] Improbable enough, one might think; yet a number of remarkably similar claims were reported elsewhere. At Bologna, an Italian chronicle recorded the arrival on 18 July 1422 of some one hundred gypsies led by a 'Duke Andrea'. They carried with them an order issued, so they said, by the king of Hungary which authorized them to steal with impunity during the seven-year term of the 'pilgrimage' on which they insisted they had embarked some five years earlier.[5] The king, their story went, had confiscated Duke Andrea's territories as a punishment for his apostasy, and, when he and his followers subsequently accepted baptism and returned to the Christian faith, had exiled them to wander the Earth for seven years to expiate their sin before presenting themselves to the Pope in Rome. Certainly, if the Italian chronicle is to be believed, they seem to have taken full advantage of the king of Hungary's vicarious (and presumably invented) largesse. It reports that the gypsy women in particular busied themselves stealing anything on which they could lay their hands in Bologna before the group finally left two weeks later in the direction of Rome, despite one of them having given birth to a child in the market-place just three days earlier.[6] As to the letters they presented, whatever their provenance, and however they were obtained, it is worth noting that the Emperor of Germany, Sigismund, who had been king of Hungary since 1387, is known to have been at Konstanz in 1417 and 1418, not far from Lindau where the letters seem to have originated.[7]

Numerous other encounters with gypsy groups are mentioned in chronicles of the period, at Lübeck, Rostock, and other north German towns in 1417, Colmar in Alsace and Berne in Switzerland in 1418, St Laurent near Mâcon in 1419, Brussels in 1420, Bruges in 1421, Tournai and Basle in 1422, Regensburg in Bavaria in 1424, and Paris and Amiens in 1427. As well as recording various versions of the story of the seven-year pilgrimage, now ordered by the king, now by the pope, many of these reports also coincided in other ways in their descriptions of these foreign arrivals: they noted the gypsies' habit of travelling in groups of between ten and a hundred or more, each led by its 'count' or 'duke', or sometimes both; their encampments set in open country; their dark-skinned, unkempt, and unappealing appearance; the ear-rings worn by both women and children; their fortune-telling; their claim to have originated in 'Egypt' or, as several reports had it, 'Little Egypt'; and, not least, their marked propensity for thieving. It is significant, too, that on at least two occasions, 1422 in Tournai and 1424 at Regensburg, reference is made to their claim to privileges giving those who led them the exclusive right to administer justice among their own kind.[8] However implausible they might seem now, the stories they told, repeated time and again in this place or that across western Europe, must have helped these roaming groups to subsist. Certainly the distinguished Dutch historian Johan Huizinga long ago thought it perfectly likely that the tale told by the gypsies who arrived outside Paris in 1427 would have fallen on credulous, even sympathetic ears:

> The familiar image of Fortune's wheel from which kings are falling with their crowns and their sceptres took a living shape in the person of many an expelled prince, roaming from court to court without means [. . .]. It is not surprising that the people of Paris should have believed in the tale of the Gypsies, who presented themselves in 1427, 'a duke and a count and ten men, all on horseback', while others, to the number of 120, had to stay outside the town. They had come from Egypt, they said; the pope had ordered them, by way of penance for their apostasy, to wander for seven years, without sleeping in a bed; there had been 1,200 of them, but their king, their queen, and all the others had died on the way.[9]

One notes, though, that having thus enlisted the pope, the gypsies were quick to extract the maximum advantage, adding that he had also ordered 'that every bishop and abbot was to give them ten pounds *tournois*', to help alleviate their sufferings.

Into Iberia

The earliest document indisputably to indicate the presence of gypsies south of the Pyrenees is a letter of safe-conduct issued in Zaragoza on 12 January 1425, once again by Alfonso V, to 'Don Johan of Little Egypt' ('Egipte Menor'), as he is described.[10] The letter does not refer to him as a count or a duke, but the use at that date of the honorific *don*, derived from the Latin *dominus*, nevertheless suggests that his noble status was taken for granted.[11] Valid for three months, the letter required that he be allowed to travel unmolested through different parts of the kingdom of Aragon along with 'those accompanying him, with all their mounts, clothing, possessions, gold, silver, saddlebags and any other items they might be carrying with them'.[12] There is no indication of how many people were travelling with him, but the strangers seem to have been received amicably enough by their Aragonese hosts, who treated them as pilgrims. As far as the fifteenth century is concerned, the rather sparse documentation relating to gypsies in Spanish state archives consists primarily of such royal safe-conducts, some 30 of them in all. Many of these, like those presented elsewhere in Europe, refer to the gypsy leaders as 'counts' or 'dukes' of 'Egypt' or 'Little Egypt'. Often, like the three issued at Seville in March 1491 to the gypsies Jácomo, Felipo, and Luis, respectively, the letters noted that the latter were intending to journey along with those accompanying them to the shrine of the apostle St James at Santiago de Compostela as a penance.[13] In an age of faith when the provision of assistance to pilgrims was regarded as a Christian duty, the claim by these groups of exotic foreigners to be undertaking such a pilgrimage would have served the gypsies well, not just as a means of obtaining food and perhaps shelter, but also as a way of explaining their presence in the peninsula (the Spanish word for a pilgrim, *peregrino* itself derives directly from the Latin *peregrinus*, 'foreign' or 'strange'). More importantly, it would also have served to disguise and familiarize a nomadic habit otherwise likely to arouse suspicion or even outright hostility among the settled indigenous population. Similarly, the translation of their traditional respect for and allegiance to male clan elders into terms likely to be more readily accepted by their hosts – into the vocabulary, that is to say, of a hierarchical, and patriarchal European social formation in which status meant nobility – would have represented a similarly sensible stratagem. They may have been helped, too, in their attempts to achieve some degree of chameleon adaptation to the larger environment through which they were moving by the fact that in the fifteenth century a new breed of foreign travellers, typically men of noble blood, had taken to plying the traditional pilgrim routes. Often accompanied by sizeable retinues of armed men, these men used pilgrimage largely as a pretext to sample foreign courts, display their prowess abroad, and otherwise seek adventure.[14] We have no way of knowing how the gypsies' embassies to the rulers from whom they sought favour were conducted, though it has been suggested that money may have changed hands between gypsies and court officials during such transactions.[15] Such suspicions belong, though, to the realm of conjecture, and such evidence as there is suggests that gypsy leaders were for much of the fifteenth century accorded by their aristocratic Castilian and Aragonese hosts a treatment generally in keeping with their frequently reiterated claims to noble blood.

Certainly, this was the experience of the earliest groups of gypsies to arrive in Andalusia. When Thomas and Martin, 'two Counts of Little Egypt', along with 'up to a hundred women and children, their compatriots and vassals', arrived in Jaén on 22 November 1462, they were accorded a magnificent welcome there by no less a figure than the Constable of Castile, Don Miguel Lucas de Iranzo. The one-time favourite of Henry IV of Castile, it had been rumoured four years earlier, when he was first appointed to this high office, that he might also be awarded the militarily and financially powerful role of the mastership of the Military Order of Santiago.[16] Don Miguel, who was also governor of the northern Andalusian town, proceeded with his wife Teresa de Torres to entertain his guests in the lavish, indeed pointedly courtly style that was the hallmark of the ambitious aristocrat of his day.[17] They stayed with him for 'fifteen or twenty days', and were provided with 'bread, wine, meat, poultry, fish, fruit, straw and barley in abundance'.[18] The gypsies, for their part, claimed to be penitents, re-cycling the old tale of pilgrimage ordered by the pope and adding that their sin had been to deny the faith after being conquered by the Turk. When they eventually left, amply provisioned by their host with clothing and other goods for their journey, Don Miguel honoured them further by accompanying them for half a league before finally bidding them farewell. Similar events occurred in 1470 at the Constable's residence in nearby Andújar. This time he entertained 'Count Jacob' of 'Little Egypt', 'his wife the Countess, whom they called Loaysa', and 50 or so persons travelling with them.[19] They stayed in Andújar for five or six days and, just over two weeks later, were replaced by one 'Duke Paul' and company, also of 'Little Egypt'. Paul arrived bearing letters 'from our lord the king and from the king of France and other dukes and great lords, as he was travelling the world as a pilgrim and penitent' (his travels would eventually take him in May of 1471 to Murcia, where the town council granted him 1000 *maravedís* to help him on his long journey home).[20] Once again, the Constable displayed considerable largesse towards his guests, 'demonstrating that generosity which he never denied to anyone', as his chronicle put it.[21] As centuries to come would show, he would not be the last member of Spain's nobility to adopt a liberal, even protective attitude towards the gypsies.

Yet Don Miguel's generosity may also have been his undoing. In what was to prove an ominous sign of the times, he met his death just three years later on 21 March 1473, the feast of San Benito. He was murdered by a hooded assassin who, using the butt of a crossbow, dealt him a fatal blow to the head as he knelt at prayer in Jaén cathedral. It is likely that he was killed because of his support for and protection of *conversos* there. These were Spaniards of Jewish blood who had converted, often under pressure, to Christianity, but who continued to be regarded with deep suspicion, jealousy, or worse by many of their neighbours. That year and the next saw outbreaks of anti-*converso* rioting, first in Córdoba, then in Jaén, Seville and elsewhere.[22] The widespread urban unrest was sparked initially by the soaring food price inflation of the preceding four years and then fuelled, as the humanist chronicler Alonso de Palencia pointed out, by simmering resentment of the relative wealth of many of Spain's Jewish community.[23] The question of racial origins and religious affiliation was one that had cast its shadow intermittently over the peninsula for centuries, erupting periodically in outbreaks of extreme violence, as in the massacres of Jews carried out in the summer of 1391 in Seville, Toledo, Burgos, Logroño, Valencia, Girona, Barcelona and a number of other towns.[24] Then of course there was the question of the affront to Christendom represented by continuing Muslim rule in the Nasrid emirate of Granada; and then, too, there were the suspicions nursed by many about the *mudéjares* (the word derives from the Arabic for 'tributaries'), free men and women of Moorish origin who had chosen to remain and live under Christian rule in those territories which had been re-occupied as the Christians pushed south. For over a century now, internal strife and the virtual collapse of public order had preoccupied Castile's rulers as they struggled to contain the ambitions of a turbulent nobility who at times seemed bent on anarchy. True, cross-border skirmishes with Muslims continued sporadically to occur in the southeast: but final completion of the long project of the *Reconquista* had for many years now not been pursued with the vigour or focus that such an enterprise demanded. No doubt the continuing payments of tribute, the *parias*, extracted by Castile's monarchs from Granada's Muslim rulers served very considerably to sweeten this otherwise bitter pill:[25] but now, as the fifteenth century wore on, times were about to change, and questions of race and religion soon looked set to take centre stage once again.

As to the gypsies, few in number in both relative and absolute terms they may have been, but they too were soon to feel the effects of the gathering change in climate. Many Spaniards, like other Europeans, continued for almost two centuries to assume that the gypsies' ultimate origins lay in Egypt, as the earliest arrivals in western Europe had themselves so often claimed. In his *Examen de ingenios* (*Examination of Wits*) of 1575, the physician Huarte de San Juan, setting the date of their arrival in Spain some 50 years earlier than had actually been the case, observed that over the 'more than two hundred years since the first gypsies [*gitanos*] came from Egypt to Spain, their descendants have not yet lost the sharp wits and cunning their forebears brought out of Egypt, nor their tanned colour'.[26] Nor were such assumptions in the least discouraged by what one writer has described as 'the protoracism inherent in Christian biblical genealogies':[27] thus the gypsies had been condemned to roam the earth as a punishment for their refusal to aid the Holy Family during the flight into Egypt, as the Franciscan Melchor de Huélamo insisted in 1607;[28] or they might be Ezekiel's Egyptians, scattered by God among the nations; or perhaps they were the remnants of Pharoah's hosts who had expelled the Hebrews from Egypt. In 1619, Sancho de Moncada, professor of theology at the University of Toledo, added that 'most people believe they came with the Moors, when Spain was lost' – in the year 711, that is to say, – though no evidence beyond the assumed north African connection spiced with malicious rumour was ever adduced to support such claims.[29] In his *Memorial de el hecho de los gitanos* (*Report on the Gypsy Question*), written a year or so earlier and addressed to Philip III, the genealogist and chronicler Pedro Salazar de Mendoza rejected such notions, observing that no mention of this had ever been made in the histories of Spain. For Salazar the gypsies themselves lacked even the crudest sense of their own history, and he asked rhetorically, 'what other misfortune could be like that of a people who do not know their own origin or homeland?' Widespread the belief in an Egyptian origin may have been, but there was no shortage of authorities prepared to venture a different view. Salazar went on to enumerate the various hypotheses advanced by those who had written of such matters: Pope Pius II had thought the gypsies to be from the Caucasus; the Erasmian humanist, Juan Lorenzo Palmireno, in *El estudioso cortesano* (1573) had argued that they had come from Bohemia, as had Sebastian Münster in his *Cosmographia universalis* (1550), and others, including Andrea Alciato, Francisco Fernández de Córdoba, Aldo Manuzio, and the lexicographer Sebastián de Covarrubias, had variously identified them as of Chaldean, Syrian, Turkish, Hungarian, Bulgarian, Walachian, Circassian, Nubian, or Tunisian origin. An uncharacteristically sceptical and matter-of-fact Salazar noted, finally, that the gypsies themselves, 'in line with traditions handed down by their elders, say that some of them are from Egypt, and others from Greece: and that is why they are called Greeks and Egyptians'. Just a few lines earlier, after citing Palmireno, he added almost as an afterthought that the latter had pointed out that the gypsies 'speak the Greek of the Morea, and do not understand the Egyptian vernacular'.[30]

In fact, the 'Little Egypt' so frequently mentioned in the gypsies' earliest letters of safe-conduct across Europe, and which was interpreted in England in the early sixteenth century as gesturing imprecisely towards Asia Minor,[31] seems rather more likely to have referred to certain parts of Greece, and perhaps specifically to part of the southern Peloponnese – known in the medieval period as the Morea – where gypsies spent some considerable time on their centuries-long journey westwards from the Indian sub-continent.[32] The port of Modon in the southwestern Peloponnese, half-way between Venice and Jaffa, was a popular staging point for pilgrims bound for the Holy Land. As such, it would have provided a regular supply of travellers upon whom the gypsies – reported by a number of pilgrims from as early as 1384 to be present there outside the city walls – could exercise their particular talents.[33] Perhaps, too, as Fraser has suggested, these contacts, which continued through the fifteenth century, may have suggested to the gypsies the likely advantages of adopting a pilgrim identity as they moved through the Balkans and into western Europe. Given the widespread acceptance in fifteenth-century Europe of the legend of their Egyptian origins, it is even possible that the name 'Little Egypt' may first have been coined by Europeans passing through Modon, and only then adopted by groups of gypsies moving west, rather than the other way round.[34]

But whatever the truth of such matters, what can be said with certainty, at least as far as the Iberian peninsula is concerned, is that from the late 1480s a second wave of newcomers arrived there, this time declaring themselves to be Greeks, not Egyptians, and presenting themselves from the outset both as pilgrims and as refugees in flight from the Turk. Both waves, the earlier 'Egyptians' and now the 'Greeks', arrived speaking Romaní, albeit thoroughly mixed with many words from other countries through which they had travelled.[35] Thirty years earlier, in 1453, the Ottoman Sultan Mehmed II had finally overrun Christian Constantinople, and, in an ominous gesture of intent, had immediately declared its great church of Hagia Sophia a mosque.[36] By 1461 the Turks had occupied Serbia and the Peloponnese, before seizing Bosnia and Herzegovina in 1463. Other Turkish successes in the Balkans followed, and, as Ottoman pressure continued to build, the threat to western Europe – and to Christendom itself – now became palpable.

Of *convivencia* and conflict

Any attempt to describe the society the gypsies found in Spain during their first seven decades there must inevitably engage with certain fundamental problems attaching to Spanish historiography. The term *convivencia* (co-existence) has sometimes been used to describe the relative racial and religious tolerance that characterized relations between Spain's Christians, Moors (as Spain's Muslims were known), and Jews during certain periods of the middle ages. As one might expect, the degree of *convivencia* varied significantly from place to place, and from century to century, as did the population mix. In Aragon and Valencia, for example, by the fifteenth century *mudéjares* comprised over a quarter of the population, while in parts of Navarre the figure exceeded 50 per cent. In Aragon, the *mudéjares* enjoyed royal protection, the right to rule their own communities, the freedom to take up the trade or profession of their choice, and, on the whole, peaceful relations with their Christian counterparts, at least until the later sixteenth century when economic tensions between lowland *moriscos* and the 'Old Christians' of the mountainous areas finally erupted in violence.[37] Navarre's numerous *mudéjares* enjoyed a similarly wide range of privileges. Those in Valencia, on the other hand, unlike those of Aragon, spoke Arabic, by far the most telling mark of their unassimilated status – and one that helps to explain the sack of the *mudéjar* quarter there by a Christian mob in 1455. Nor was this an isolated event. In the late thirteenth century, a number of other towns there had also seen rioting directed against the *mudéjares*. Yet there were other places where relations approached the cordial. In Castellón de la Plana, for instance, *mudéjares* were actively, even eagerly encouraged to settle in the town by its Christian inhabitants.[38] And in Murcia, although Alfonso X of Castile had ordered a wall to be constructed in the thirteenth century to separate *mudéjares* from Christians, this signally failed to prevent them forming a joint Brotherhood or *Hermandad* in the fourteenth.[39] By the fifteenth century, Muslim jugglers and musicians were accepted as routine participants in Christian religious festivities there.[40] And of course the earlier legacy of *mudéjar* architecture in Christian churches built by *mudéjar* craftsmen, churches with decorations that sometimes even incorporated Arabic script, bears eloquent witness to the spirit of tolerance and real appreciation that had once existed. By the later decades of the fifteenth century, however, tensions were once again on the rise. In Castile itself, the *mudéjares* had always been much less numerous and more widely dispersed than in Navarre, Aragon or Valencia. Indeed, of their approximately 120 communities, only seven could boast of more than one hundred households. Ever more restrictive legislation there, intended primarily to regulate the kingdom's Jews, who were increasingly the butt of popular vitriol and resentment, inevitably touched the lives of its *mudéjares*, too, notwithstanding the dispensations repeatedly granted to them by the crown. Almost everywhere some degree of discrimination was the norm: *mudéjares* were taxed more heavily than their Christian counterparts; and they, like the Jews, were usually held to be officially ineligible for public office, though *conversos*, Jews who had converted to Catholicism, often came to occupy positions of very considerable influence; and contacts, beyond those required for the intercommunal trade in which most *mudéjares* were permitted to engage, were generally discouraged.[41] In frontier towns, unsurprisingly, cross-cultural interactions were rather more common, both Jews and Muslims sometimes attending Masses and, on occasion, *mudéjar* musicians even being contracted to play in the churches, much to the consternation of the Church authorities.[42] Meanwhile, the counterparts of the *mudéjares* on the other side of the frontier, the *mozárabes*, Christians living under Muslim rule, also enjoyed considerable freedoms, as did the Jews. Indeed, in the mid-fifteenth century, Alonso Fajardo, one of the Christian nobles to whom border campaigning had largely been left by the crown, could even chide Henry IV of Castile, threatening to change sides, hand over the territories he held to Granada's Muslims, and, having metamorphosed into a vassal of the Emir, 'live as a Christian there as others do'.[43]

But it is what has been made subsequently of the fact that any *modus vivendi* existed at all that goes to the heart of a centuries-old historical anxiety. In its modern form, this dates to the mid-twentieth century and, broadly speaking, concerns attempts to appropriate Spain's always historiographically unpredictable past to one or other of two, essentially mythopoeic narratives. The peculiar intensity of the debate is explained by the fact that one of the main issues at stake was (and is) the energetically contested notion of 'Spanishness' itself. The first line of argument was set out by the literary historian Américo Castro in 1948 in his *España en su historia: cristianos, moros y judíos*:[44] the second, which repudiated Castro's interpretation, was expounded in Claudio Sánchez-Albornoz's *España: un enigma histórico*, published eight years later.[45] Both have attracted their supporters. Castro advanced the view that the Moorish invasion of 711 represented in effect a paradigm shift in the evolutionary history of Spanish culture, which, together with the splendid contribution provided by its Jews, especially evident in literature, had marked the nation's cultural identity in the most profound and enduring way. He used the term *convivencia* to encompass the acculturative processes, both mimetic and contradistinctive, which, he argued, had inexorably served to forge a unique Spanish identity after the arrival of the Moors. But while Castro accepted that reaction *against* Muslim influences had an important part to play, it is worth pointing out that the term *convivencia* is itself positively inflected, suggesting quite distinctly, as the most authoritative of Spanish dictionaries puts it, as 'people living together in considerable harmony' ('buena armonía').[46] One does not therefore have to disagree with Castro's conclusion to suspect that it may nevertheless always have tended to precede his argument. As it was, the more obvious, if relatively prosaic examples of lasting intercultural influence, such as the many Arabisms that entered the Spanish language from the eighth century on, seem to have interested Castro rather less than necessarily more speculative notions. He thus suggested that Castilians' preoccupation with purity of blood, especially evident from about the mid-sixteenth century, shadowed Hebrew preoccupations with genealogy and endogamous marriage, or, to take another example, that Spain's martial Catholicism represented a mimetic institutionalization of Islamic religious militancy.[47]

Sánchez-Albornoz, on the other hand, preferred to stress unity, seamless, indeed occasionally invisible continuity, and the allegedly unwavering, teleological character of Iberian resolve to recover the peninsula exclusively for the banner of Christendom. Some of his arguments are rather reminiscent of those advanced around the turn of the twentieth century by members of the so-called 'Generation of 98', and especially of Miguel de Unamuno's notion of *intrahistoria*. Thus Sánchez-Albornoz's assertion of an uninterrupted, if periodically latent substratum of inherited and unchanging Spanish temperament stretching back to the Hispano-Romans and Visigoths inevitably recalls Unamuno's image of history – especially where this involved events inimical to the idea of Spain he wished to imagine – as merely waves rolling across the surface of an ocean in whose undisturbed depths could be found the eternal verities of Spanishness (*casticismo*). Collapsing the diachronic into an 'eternal' present, Unamuno asserted that it is in the 'depths of the sea, beneath history, where the true, eternal tradition lives, in the present, not in the past'.[48] As Hillgarth has pointed out, while neither Castro's nor Sánchez-Albornoz's views can be said to be innocent of myth, Castro's seems at least to approximate more closely to the complex realities of Spanish history (the line he cites in what follows is from Sánchez-Albornoz's *España*, volume II, p. 366):

> Myth for myth, the myth that Spain was created by the *convivencia*, the productive tension, of three religions, is undeniably truer to the facts than the idea that the Islamic conquest of 711 represented no more than 'a step backwards — unparalleled in the West — in the progress of an historical community towards its national unity'.[49]

Hillgarth concludes that,

> Despite many outbreaks of intolerance and the extent to which fusion was always incomplete, Christians, Jews, and Muslims did coexist for centuries in Spain – unlike the rest of Western Europe – and the Islamic model, according to which Jews and Christians were subject but tolerated communities ruled by their own authorities, was largely (though imperfectly) adopted in Spain down to 1492.[50]

As the fifteenth century advanced, whatever interracial and interfaith tolerance had existed previously had begun to break down. Growing anti-Jewish sentiment in Spain was essentially based on a volatile mix of religious zeal – often, ironically enough, articulated in its most vituperative forms by *conversos* eager to demonstrate publicly the sincerity of their faith – and popular envy of Jewish financial successes coupled with deep resentment of some of their accustomed roles as money-lenders, rent collectors, and tax-farmers. The situation was not helped by the kind of power struggles between influential *conversos* and Old Christians which in 1449 provoked disturbances in Toledo amid bitter accusations that King John II's favourite, Álvaro de Luna, himself of *converso* origin, had shown intolerable bias towards Jews.[51] Attitudes towards the *mudéjares* and Granada's Muslims, on the other hand, had rather more to do with fear. The Turkish advances in the eastern Mediterranean in the mid-century had by now given a new urgency to persistent concerns that Spain might once again be vulnerable to attack from North Africa, especially since continuing Muslim control of Granada seemed to offer an open door into the peninsula for any such attempted incursion. In this gathering atmosphere, some inevitably saw the *mudéjares*, too, as representing a potentially dangerous enemy within.[52] Yet such suspicions only represented part of the story. Despite the fluctuating religious and cultural tensions, pragmatic considerations, not least in respect of commercial exchanges, must in many places still have ensured a certain level of civility in intercommunal relations at the local level. After all, both Muslims and Jews had an important economic role to play, the Muslims as labourers, especially on the land, and the Jews as physicians, artisans, textile producers and financial agents.[53] However uncompromising the rhetoric of intolerance, it is hard to believe that ordinary human sympathies would not frequently have made themselves felt across racial and faith barriers in such day-to-day contacts between the communities.

This, briefly then, was the culturally complex and increasingly turbulent fifteenth-century society through which gypsies, too, were now moving, still, one should add, with relative ease. Indeed, I argue, as have others of the relations between the *moriscos* and their Old Christian neighbours,[54] that throughout the early modern period local relations between gypsies and non-gypsies were on the whole characterized, especially in the south, not so much by hostility as by a form of *convivencia*, intermittent, geographically patchy, and sometimes distinctly uneasy, but *convivencia* nevertheless.[55] But one must be careful. What has been described by a number of commentators as a honeymoon period for the gypsies in the early years after their arrival was in fact far from devoid of signs of conflicts to come.[56] Indeed, the claim by later arrivals to be 'Greeks', their leaders usually now demoting themselves to 'captain' or 'gentleman' rather than count or duke, may have been designed to deflect aggression directed towards them by Spaniards who had by now become increasingly antagonistic towards their 'Egyptian' forerunners.[57] A safe-conduct issued at Valladolid in 1489 to 'Greek merchants' who had arrived from Sicily having earlier abandoned Negropont (now Khalkis) in the Euboea with the Turkish onslaught of 1470, as had other gypsies arriving in Spain,[58] suggests that the stratagem was not always effective, since the local populace immediately took them for Egyptians and abused them anyway.[59] In Lérida on 30 September 1482, the 'Bohemians' 'Johan Gil', 'Nicholau', and 'Antoni' were denounced to the authorities by one Pere Soldevila, who accused them of relieving him under threat of death of the money he was carrying. The three were captured when local people, hearing the victim's cries, came to his help. Despite their subsequent attempts to place the blame on a woman and an old man, presumably in the hope of eliciting a token sentence, they were judged guilty, condemned to 100 lashes each, and then expelled from the area. Two years later, on 2 September 1484, the authorities in Castellón also ordered 'Bohemians' there to leave forthwith, noting that they were responsible for 'great damage in the town and surrounding area', and adding that force should be used to expel them if necessary.[60] But some of the friction was internal. Even before the arrival of travellers calling themselves 'Greeks', a safe-conduct granted by John II of Aragon and Navarre on 16 September 1476 at Logroño to 'Count Juan of Little Egypt' to enable him to travel to Santiago had also revealed the enmity existing between him and Counts Martín, Miguel, and Jaime, from all of whom he required physical protection.[61] In a letter dated 1 July, a year later in Barcelona, the same monarch ordered the punishment of Juan Fetó 'from the said land of Little Egypt', who four years earlier as the group passed through Tortosa, had knifed and killed Jorge Serpa, another gypsy, the assailant taking refuge thereafter in that town's castle. The letter was written at the request of 'Don Martín, Count of Little Egypt'.[62] Another document dated 23 April 1484 in Toledo contains a pardon granted to Givio, 'a native of the kingdom of Greece' for having occasioned the death of Lucas Nantel, another 'Greek'.[63] But the gypsies also had their own, traditional ways of arbitrating disputes, a fact acknowledged in the early seventeenth century by Salazar de Mendoza, who noted that 'the gypsies have their count, to whom they go with their disputes, not recognizing any other superior'.[64] Indeed, some of the safe-conducts issued by John II between 1460 and 1476 contained passages conceding to gypsy leaders the right to administer justice within their own communities. The studiedly convoluted vagueness of the Latin wording suggests, however, that the invitation to police themselves should not be read as extending to any formal relinquishment by the king of his own royal prerogatives in the matter.[65] It is not difficult to see the potential advantages of such an arrangement for the monarch, when attempts to enforce his will were regularly frustrated as those accused went to ground, claiming sanctuary with a range of more than willing protectors. Indeed, in 1480 in Toledo, Henry IV of Castile found it necessary to reiterate legislation first enacted by his father John II in order to address precisely this problem. It ordered anyone sheltering malefactors or debtors fleeing their creditors to hand them over to the authorities, regardless of whether they had found sanctuary in 'fortresses, or castles, or noble residences, or villages under seigneurial or abbatial jurisdiction', and notwithstanding historical privileges or previous custom and practice.[66]

Internecine strife among gypsies is not uncommon; but related in particular to their traditional social formation and way of life are kinship-reinforcing 'blood feuds' and occasional territorial disputes.[67]

While it is true that rural society in early modern Spain cannot properly be described as wholly sedentary, since economic pressures, marriage, and housing needs ensured that migration into and out of the village was common,[68] most people's lives were nevertheless bound up in cycles of production of one kind or another. The gypsies, though, almost constantly on the move, produced relatively little of their own. They almost certainly engaged opportunistically in the kinds of marginal, traditional occupations often associated with nomadic or semi-nomadic groups, such as basket-weaving, blacksmithing, and livestock trading, shearing or clipping, all of them trades typically associated with gypsies right up to the modern era. And, as we shall see, some were occasionally contracted as performers. But they clearly also relied, in Spain as elsewhere, on begging, fortune-telling, and, as their many accusers were quick to attest, theft. If one thinks of these as forms of predation on what was an at least relatively settled indigenous population – gypsies were commonly compared to wolves or raptors[69] – a predatory habit requires sufficient space to allow a prey-to-predator ratio, or, to put it another way, potential market share sufficiently favourable to ensure on average a reasonable chance of success. As the numbers of gypsies increased to levels sufficiently troubling to encourage the crown to legislate to curb their activities (as it soon did), so too, then, may territorial tensions between different gypsy patrigroups (*razas*), especially where the latter happened to coincide on their travels in smaller settlements offering limited resources to exploit. Even in recent decades, such tensions have been identified as a source of friction between gypsy kinship groups.[70] One must add, though, that as far as fifteenth-century Spain is concerned this must remain conjecture: little or nothing in the sparse documentation that has so far come to light can be adduced to support it, not least because quantitative data is conspicuous by its complete absence.

The question of gypsy numbers may be unanswerable – though one assumes they were still relatively low – but it does nevertheless raise another important issue. By the 1470s, the first glimmer of evidence was beginning to emerge of just how slippery a term 'Egyptian' or *gitano* was eventually to become. Writing almost a century and a half later, Pedro Salazar de Mendoza sought to draw some distinction between the 'Egyptians' and the 'Greeks':

The Greeks, for the most part, are blacksmiths, and they rely on deception using language and trickery more than on theft. The Egyptians are idle, and fond of travelling on horseback, and they rely more on theft than on deception and fraud.[71]

But for Salazar and his contemporaries they were all, first and foremost, gypsies, and he was quick to add that 'what all writers are agreed on, without exception, is that the gypsies are people of wicked and abominable ways'. For by the time he was writing, the whole notion of who or what a gypsy might be said to be had become problematic. Even the early evidence suggests that it was already believed that others – outsiders – were from at least the 1470s, and for reasons unspecified, beginning to join the gypsy groups roaming Spain.[72] And, as later chapters will show, the widespread and abiding conviction that this was the case would be an important factor contributing to the increasing stigmatization of gypsies during the early modern period proper.

However, as with the *mudéjares* and Jews, whilst relations between gypsies and non-gypsies had certainly deteriorated during the fifteenth century, the picture nevertheless remained mixed. In 1484, for example, the municipal council of Madrid awarded a visiting 'gypsy count', whose name has not come down to us, a not inconsiderable grant of 1000 *maravedis*. And in 1445, when the gypsies Martín, Luis, and Felipe complained to Prince Henry of Aragon, Lieutenant-General of Catalonia and the Balearics, known as 'Prince Fortune', that the local population was reluctant to provide them with anything other than the most miserly assistance, frequently humiliating them into the bargain, he took them under his wing and offered them protection.[73] But one of the earliest and certainly best-known examples of the favour extended to gypsies by certain members of the ruling class concerns Don Diego Hurtado de Mendoza, third Duke of the Infantado. Don Diego, who was born in 1461, was, as Luis Astrana Marín put it, 'a man of excellent taste and very noble qualities', but one who 'nevertheless lacked the will, even when old and ailing, to overcome the appetites of the flesh'.[74] Of his seven or more illegitimate children, one, Martín, was the result of an amorous liaison between the twenty-eight year-old Don Diego – at that time still Count of Saldaña – and María Cabrera, one of a troop of gypsies who had danced in Guadalajara, the ducal seat, for the Corpus Christi celebrations of 1488. Don Diego later provided María with a home, 'so that she might live without travelling as a pilgrim', as the contemporary source cited by Astrana Marín put it, adding that the gypsies of her group would for many years thereafter return to visit the ducal palace.[75] Meanwhile, Martín de Mendoza, 'el gitano', as he was dubbed, was destined by his father for a career in the Church. After some ducal intercession, including a successful 1514 appeal to the Queen, Doña Juana, requesting that his son be recognized and thus eligible to obtain ecclesiastical benefices and enjoy the other fruits of legitimacy,[76] Martín went on to occupy a range of ecclesiastical posts, accumulating some wealth in the process. These culminated, just after his twentieth birthday on 22 December 1509, in his appointment as Archdeacon of Guadalajara, a role whose higher purpose nevertheless failed to deter him from embarking on an affair in 1529 with María, the daughter of an official, Juan de Cervantes, who had been appointed two years earlier to the Duke's council.[77] The result of their union was a daughter, Martina. Many years later, Juan de Cervantes's grandson, Miguel, would never refer directly in his writings to this remote family connection to Spain's gypsies via his cousin Martina.[78] Indeed, one cannot even be quite certain that he knew about it, though it is possible that his novella *The Little Gypsy Girl*, discussed briefly in Chapter 4, owes at least something to this attenuated family link between Spain's nobility, its gypsies, and its greatest writer.

Of course, to write of Spain's gypsies at all in the late medieval period is a form of shorthand, a convenient enough device, to be sure, but one which is strictly speaking quite inaccurate. The Iberian peninsula of the early fifteenth century in fact comprised a number of independent kingdoms: Aragon, Castile, Portugal, Navarre, and, in the south east, the Muslim emirate of Granada, the last foothold of the Moors in the peninsula they had all but overrun some seven hundred years earlier. Castile, by far the most extensive of these realms, included not only today's Castilla-La Mancha and Castilla y León, but also the whole of northern Spain from the western Pyrenees to Cape Finisterre in Galicia, as well as most of western, southern, and northern Andalusia. The Kingdom of Aragon, roughly a third of the size of Castile, included all of present-day Catalonia and the region of Valencia as well as Mallorca, Sardinia, and Sicily. But before a nation even beginning remotely to resemble modern Spain would finally come into existence, a number of changes would first be necessary: the marriage of Ferdinand and Isabella in 1469; the accession of Isabella to the contested throne of Castile in 1474 amid a civil war which even then lasted another five years; the dynastic union of the Crowns of Castile and Aragon in 1479 with the death of Ferdinand's father; the monarchs' subsequent expulsion of the Moors from Granada in 1492; and, finally, the annexation of the Kingdom of Navarre 20 years later. Even then, Spanish officials would continue for two centuries and more carefully to refer in documents of state to 'these Kingdoms'. But for the peninsula's minorities, its Moors, Jews, and now its gypsies, the reality was that the Catholic Monarchs' determination to impose their authority on their kingdoms and restore order in Castile was to leave little room for difference, little space for those who could not or would not fit the newly exclusionist religious and cultural template that was being forged. It is to these developments that I now turn, and in particular to a brief excursus on those institutions which for almost three centuries to come would impinge directly to one degree or another on the lives of Spain's gypsies.

2
Under One God

The Spaniards, whose nature it is (as Pompeius Trogus said) when they lack foreign enemies, to seek them instead at home. (Fernández Navarrete)[1]

Changing the rules: royal authority, law and order, and faith

Under Ferdinand and Isabella, Castile, Aragon, and Navarre remained, *de jure* and *de facto*, independent kingdoms, and continued to be governed in accordance with their own jealously guarded statutes and traditional privileges and charters. Yet it soon became clear that something quite fundamental had begun to change with the union of crowns. The new monarchs were determined from the outset to assert and consolidate the personal authority of the crown throughout the disparate territories over which they now jointly presided. The late fifteenth and early sixteenth centuries thus saw a concerted effort by them to relegate to history the decades of destabilizing political strife and violence that had so recently beset Castile and from which the constituent parts of the Crown of Aragon, especially Catalonia, had themselves been by no means exempt. The *Cortes*, a representative, though not itself legislative assembly convened by Ferdinand and Isabella in late April of 1476 at Madrigal de la Altas Torres marked the beginnings of a new bond, effectively one of co-dependency in the early years, between monarchs and towns that would help to underpin the crown's authority and begin finally to erode the much abused power of an overweening Castilian nobility. Further measures, including the definitive assertion of royal control over the powerful Castilian Military Orders of Santiago, Calatrava, and Alcántara, acknowledged finally by a papal bull of 1523, served further to reign in the power of the aristocracy. Meanwhile, the year 1476 also saw the restoration of the *Hermandad* or 'Brotherhood' first established by Henry IV,[2] an organization tasked with curbing the lawlessness and banditry that had for years plagued the Castilian countryside. The royal chronicler and councillor of state, Hernando del Pulgar, painted a vivid picture of the parlous state to which things in Castile had come during the reign of Henry IV:

> In those times of strife, justice suffered, and could not be brought to bear on those malefactors who robbed and tyrannized people in villages, on the roads, and generally throughout the kingdom. And no one paid what he owed unless he wished to: no one thought twice about committing any sort of crime: no one dreamt of obeying or subjecting himself to another, greater man. And so it was [. . .] that people became accustomed to so much disorder, and that a man who eschewed violence was held a coward. And townsfolk, country people, and men of peace were no longer masters of their own possessions, and had nowhere to turn, faced with the robbery, violence and other evils they suffered at the hands of governors of fortresses and other thieves and robbers. And every one of them would willingly have contributed half of what he owned to see himself and his family safe.[3]

The *Hermandad*, a rural police force, based locally but answerable to a central *junta* or Supreme Council, was empowered through its unpaid *alcaldes* (justices of the peace) both to pronounce and execute sentence on those it apprehended for robbery, murder, or any of the other offences – including rebellion – carefully stipulated as falling under its jurisdiction. Its reputation for the gruesome and decidedly exemplary punishment of malefactors, whose arrow-riddled bodies would frequently be left by the roadside *pour encourager les autres*, began soon enough to achieve the desired effect, not least as tangible evidence of the extension of royal authority throughout Castile.

The benefits it brought were, however, restricted to Castile, whereas in the much smaller Crown of Aragon, where Ferdinand's attempt to introduce the *Hermandad* had failed, banditry and internecine strife continued for many years to represent a serious problem.[4] Indeed, in 1567 the Venetian ambassador Antonio Tiepolo observed of both Old and New Castile that 'few crimes are committed in this kingdom', whereas 'in the three kingdoms of Aragon, Catalonia and Valencia, where his Majesty does not enjoy absolute power, the most atrocious crimes are committed and travellers have no security whatsoever because these regions are everywhere infested with bandits'.[5] Even in Castile, despite the advantages the *Hermandad* had brought in terms of the ready availability to the crown of large numbers of armed men for the Granada campaign,[6] the eventual abolition of the Supreme Council in 1498 in response to protests from the towns at the cost of its upkeep inevitably saw the organization's cohesiveness and impact much reduced.[7] By 1479, in another move designed to extend their authority and restore order, the monarchs had appointed *corregidores* (the word puns on 'correctors' and 'co-rulers') to the larger towns of Castile. These men, whose role was broadly gubernatorial, were responsible not just for keeping the peace, but also for the defence and maintenance of royal jurisdiction in the towns to which they were assigned, their individual success or otherwise being assessed via a formal process known as the *residencia* at the end of their term of office. It remained the case, however, that large expanses of the lands over which Ferdinand and Isabella nominally ruled still remained firmly under the jurisdiction of the nobility or the Church.

Finally, at the *Cortes* of Toledo in 1480, the monarchs, once again looking to the medieval period for a precedent that would ensure some sense of continuity, or at least of restoration, remodelled the *Consejo Real* (Royal Council) as the main advisory body on government in Castile as well as its supreme court. In so doing, they took pains to ensure that its voting membership was constituted in such a way as to take account of the legal expertise of university-educated *letrados*, while severely limiting the influence of the higher nobility in its workings.[8] As part of their reform of judicial administration, which had previously centred on the peripatetic monarchs themselves, in March 1489 at Medina del Campo they fixed upon Valladolid as the permanent location of the *Chancillería*, a civil and criminal tribunal outranked only by the *Consejo Real* itself. In 1505, they relocated a second *Chancillería*, originally established at Ciudad Real nine years earlier, to Granada, the Tagus marking the boundary between northern and southern zones of jurisdictional competency.[9] Other, lesser courts or *Audiencias* were established in Santiago de Compostela in the north and Seville in the south. As to Aragon, far from seeking to impose central control there, Ferdinand contented himself with the appointment of viceroys in Aragon, Catalonia, and Valencia. Preoccupied for much of the time with Castilian matters, he spent only six and a half of his 37 years on the throne in Aragonese territories, though he did establish an advisory Council of Aragon in 1494. And while Ferdinand and Isabella did seek to extend their authority in the sphere of finance, no concerted attempt was ever made by them to create a unitary state in constitutional or legislative terms – a point either ignored or overlooked by most other Europeans, who tended on the whole to regard and advert to their realms simply as 'Spain'.

Yet there was one cause that might still serve to unify their kingdoms, or at least to unite as perhaps nothing else could the martial energies of their subjects – above all certain bruised and rebellion-prone elements of the Castilian aristocracy. Its promotion would rely on a continuing appeal by the monarchs not just to their subjects' sense of a common identity as Christians, but also to readily aroused fears that the Catholic faith itself might increasingly be under threat, both from without and from within. Both monarchs hoped that the pursuit of religious homogeneity – undertaken with a single-mindedness as devout as it was determined, notwithstanding Ferdinand's Jewish blood on his mother's side – might help finally to overcome factionalism and discord in Castile. Needless to say, their success was purchased at a price, one that would continue to be paid for well over a century by Spain's increasingly beleaguered minorities. For this would be more than simply a question of the military completion of the Reconquest with the expulsion of the Muslims from Granada, achieved finally in 1492: it would also take the form of an increasingly febrile determination to root out the less tangible, but still keenly intuited threat of heresy represented by those others, the perennially suspect *conversos* and *mudéjares*, who continued to live out their lives among Castile and Aragon's 'Old Christians'.[10] Faced with seemingly incontrovertible evidence of backsliding and Judaizing practices among the *converso* population, Ferdinand and Isabella turned yet again to a medieval precedent for a solution. They found it in the papal inquisition that had been introduced in the Aragonese territories, though not in Castile, in the thirteenth century to investigate claims of heresy and which, never very vigorous, had by the fifteenth fallen into a state of virtual desuetude. In 1478, the monarchs requested Pope Sixtus IV to issue a bull establishing the Holy Office of the Inquisition in Castile. Its primary task would be to root out heresy among New Christians and in particular to investigate reported cases of Judaizing practice among *conversos*. It began operations in the south in late 1480, though formal papal approval was only rather grudgingly secured in 1483, and, over the next two decades in particular, many *conversos* and others were executed for heresy.[11] The Inquisition soon enough turned its attentions to other groups such as Muslim converts to Christianity, Illuminists, Protestants, bigamists, homosexuals, and even followers of Erasmus, though it had no jurisdiction over those not baptized into the Christian faith, like the Jews. The latter were accordingly required by a royal ordinance of 31 March 1492 to convert to Christianity or leave, resulting in the departure of some 50,000 of their number from Castile and Aragon.[12] A similar ultimatum was presented in 1502 to Castile's *mudéjares* and extended in 1526 under Charles V to include the Kingdom of Aragon. Of these, most, lacking the funds or, indeed, the inclination to go into dangerous and quite possibly fatal exile on North Africa's Barbary coast, opted for baptism rather than expulsion. They were thereafter dubbed *moriscos*, a permanent, demeaning and, as their descendants would later learn, ominous reminder that conversion could not change their racial and religious origins, still less place them beyond suspicion.

Finally, the Inquisition also investigated gypsies, many of whom had never been baptized, but whom it seems anyway to have regarded as legitimate, if relatively unimportant quarry, people who, lacking any other religious persuasion, might justifiably be treated as lost sheep and therefore Christians by default, albeit bad ones. The first such case occurred only in 1539, when the gypsies Juan de Escalona and his wife of Palomares de Huete in Cuenca were brought before the inquisitors accused of superstition.[13] But it was three decades earlier, in 1499, still bent on strong governance and the imposition of civil order, that Ferdinand and Isabella, the 'Catholic Monarchs', as Pope Alexander VI had dubbed them in 1496, enacted the very first legislation designed to curb the activities of the gypsies. Elsewhere in Europe, too, the closing decades of the fifteenth century saw similar legislation, together with the rescission of letters of safe-conduct granted previously, in the Duchy of Milan, the Swiss Federation, and the Holy Roman Empire.[14]

The Catholic Monarchs' 1499 ordinance and its reiterations

The royal ordinance promulgated by Ferdinand and Isabella at Medina del Campo on 4 March 1499 was addressed to 'you, the Egyptians who wander our realms with your women and children and dwellings'. It announced itself tersely as follows:

> Know that we are informed that you have for many years wandered from place to place lacking trades or any other means of supporting yourselves apart from begging for alms, stealing and bartering things, deceiving people, and engaging in sorcery, fortune-telling, and other activities which are neither proper nor decent.[15]

Growing concerns about the gypsies' reliance on alms had already figured in later letters of safe-conduct, which had begun to focus less on the duty of subjects to assist them than on the gypsies' right to take up honest trades.[16] Noting that the behaviour it described was not only offensive to their subjects but that it also represented a 'bad example', the ordinance now ordered the gypsies to take up settled residence and 'recognized occupations', find a master to serve who would provide for them, or leave the kingdoms, giving them 60 days to comply. For those failing to do so, a first offence would merit 100 lashes and banishment for life, a second, notching of the ears – a device intended to facilitate identification of recidivists who moved on to offend again elsewhere[17] – and confinement in chains for 60 days followed by banishment. Those apprehended for a third time were to become the slaves of their captors. The ordinance also rescinded with immediate effect all letters of safe-conduct previously issued by the monarchs. In his classic 1920 study of the *Mesta*, the powerful Castilian sheepowners' organization, Julius Klein claimed that 'the expulsion of gypsies and of the Moors after the capture of Granada had freed the country of many roving peddlers'.[18] Klein's implicit assumption that the promulgation of an edict also presupposed its more or less effective implementation is one that others have shared, to be sure; but it is not borne out by the facts, either in this case or, to take another obvious example, that of the *moriscos*, whose expulsion early in the seventeenth century is now known to have been not nearly as 'definitive' an event as once thought.[19] Even the fact that Charles V found it necessary to reiterate the 1499 ordinance against gypsies on no fewer than three occasions, in 1525, 1528, and 1534, bears witness to its at best partial efficacy.[20] The primary aim of the ordinance seems anyway to have been assimilation via dispersal-dilution rather than expulsion. Having specifically forbidden the gypsies to wander the kingdoms in groups, it added that the penalties it set were to be applicable to those found after 60 days 'without an occupation, or without masters, *or together*' (my italics). This, broadly speaking, would continue to be the tenor and force of most subsequent legislation, at least until the eighteenth century. Klein observed additionally of the gypsies that the *Mesta* 'was largely instrumental in securing the decree which expelled them from the country'. This seems perfectly possible in principle – the *Mesta* certainly had occasion to complain about gypsy depredation on its flocks in the seventeenth century, for example[21] – though one should add that the document he cited as evidence of this influence seems to have disappeared at some point over the last century.[22] This is unfortunate, but it is not difficult to see how such legislation would anyway have been likely to find its way onto the monarchs' agenda as part of their continuing project to restore order in the countryside. To have ignored the gadfly, if increasingly irksome activities of the gypsies would have been to concede that certain of the crown's subjects were beyond the reach of the royal writ, and the promulgation of such an ordinance would have served to restate to those around the monarchs and elsewhere that no such *de facto* exceptions would be countenanced, 'Egyptian' or otherwise. Such a reminder would doubtless have seemed all the more apposite at a time when another, real challenge to royal authority was building among the recently subjected Muslims of Granada, who finally rose just eight months later in November 1499. The rebellion began in Granada's Albaicín district and then spread across the whole of the mountainous Alpujarras region between Granada and the Mediterranean and was finally suppressed in 1500 after much brutality on both sides.

The relative scarcity and particular nature of sixteenth-century documents concerning gypsies in Spanish state archives means that any attempt to extrapolate from them to more general conclusions about the wider state of relations between gypsies and non-gypsies across Spain at the time must inevitably be tentative. In addition to various royal ordinances and their reiterations, these archival sources consist in the main of denunciations by non-gypsies, usually for theft or deception, records of criminal investigations, documents relating to the always problematic manning of the oars of Spain's Mediterranean galley squadrons, and, in the second half of the century, the meticulous records of the Inquisition's proceedings against gypsies, to which I return in a later chapter. As one would expect, the picture of Spain's gypsies offered by such sources is essentially negative, though some records, especially those of the Inquisition, do suggest that there was also another side to the story. In fact, there is reason to believe, partly on the basis of seventeenth- and eighteenth-century evidence, that while gypsies were widely regarded as a nuisance, their relations with the society through which they moved were not always and everywhere nearly as antagonistic as the bulk of documents would suggest, depending, of course, on where and when one looks. As already suggested, perhaps the closest comparison to suggest itself is the geographically fluctuating state of relations between Old Christian Spaniards and the *moriscos*, although no one saw the gypsies as a threat to the state in quite the same way as some saw the *moriscos*. It is with all of this in mind, then, that one reads of the theft by gypsy women of clothing and money from the home of Inés de Ojinaga in Oñate in the Basque province of Guipúzcoa in 1523; or of the accusations of theft levelled in September 1556 at the gypsy Cristóbal Maldonado and his confederates, who had set up their encampment in Marchamalo just to the north-west of Guadalajara; or of a jurisdictional dispute in 1543 between the town council of Madridejos and Pero Díaz de Toledo, the *alcalde mayor* (chief magistrate appointed by the Council of Castile) of Consuegra, over the right to sentence some gypsy prisoners; or of gypsies in Jerez in 1541 selling *menudo*, a kind of mutton stew based on offal.[23] One reads, too, of graver incidents like the murder in August 1529 of an unnamed gypsy by the non-gypsies Juan Sánchez and Andrés Martínez in Torreperogil near Úbeda in the south. The latter had come upon the gypsy one night as he grazed his animals in one of their fields sown with wheat. When they attempted to remove the beasts and take them to the local magistrate to demand compensation for the damage caused, 'the said gypsy seized a sword and cape and attacked' one of them to prevent them doing so'.[24] The ensuing fight resulted in the death of the gypsy, whereupon the villagers immediately claimed self-defence. Although the gypsy was deemed to have been the aggressor, the matter was eventually resolved through the payment to his widow and children of 9000 *maravedis*, a not inconsiderable sum which would have represented at least a year's income for a labourer at the time.[25] Once it was paid, the gypsies disappeared with other members of their band and Sánchez and Martínez duly appealed to the king for a pardon. It is also evident from a petition presented to the king by the *Cortes* at Toledo in 1525 that some gypsies were still continuing to use the letters of safe-conduct supposedly rescinded by the 1499 legislation:

> Your Majesty should order that the royal ordinance which requires the Egyptians to desist from wandering around the Kingdom be implemented, along with the penalties contained therein, notwithstanding any letters of authorization from your Majesty they may possess to that effect; and no such letters should henceforth be granted to them, because they steal from the fields and ruin productive land, and kill and wound those who defend them, and in the villages they rob and defraud those who trade with them and have no other means of making a living.[26]

As Amada López de Meneses pointed out, Juan Lorenzo Palmireno claimed in *El estudioso cortesano* that gypsies were even continuing to use letters of safe-conduct purporting to be from the Emperor Sigismund in Spain as late as 1540, though Palmireno was quick to accuse them of lying, adding that 'the life they lead is not one of penitents, but rather of dogs and thieves'.[27] Similar petitions were received at the *Cortes* of Madrid in 1528 and 1534 and in each case Charles V responded by reiterating that the provisions of the 1499 ordinance should be respected.[28] But another concern had also been exercising the *Cortes* for some years now, for the gypsies were by no means the only footloose, mendicant groups wandering Spain. The 1534 *Cortes* also requested not just that that all healthy beggars be expelled, but that foreign vagabonds and beggars be required to depart the kingdom along with them.

Vagabondage and the gypsies

The concern with vagabondage in Castile can be traced back at least as far as the poor law enacted by Juan I in 1387. In some respects, this represented a precursor of the Catholic Monarchs' anti-gypsy legislation of 1499, though it of course pre-dated by almost half a century the gypsies' arrival in Spain. Nonetheless, it foreshadowed some of the principal concerns found in that later ordinance and which were to preoccupy monarchs and commentators for the next 250 years:

> Great damage is done to our Kingdoms by the presence here of many vagabonds and idlers who could work and live from their labours and do not do so. These people not only live on the toil of others, without working or deserving to do so, but they are also a bad example to others who see them living in this way. And so they too stop working and take up the way of life of these people: and that is why no one can be found to work the land, which goes uncultivated.[29]

The shortage of people, especially of those prepared to devote themselves to agriculture; more general concerns about the utility value or otherwise of the subject, especially of healthy beggars as opposed to the structural poor, the orphans, the physically disabled, the very old; the bad example set by vagabonds, and in particular, of course, by gypsies: all were issues anxiously raised time and again throughout the sixteenth century and well into the seventeenth. The *Cortes* of Valladolid in 1518 and again in 1523 wanted the poor to be prevented from moving around, swelling as they were the already worrying numbers of vagabonds and supposedly work-shy individuals already in circulation in Castile.[30] Little allowance was made for the fact that the seasonal nature of much work on the land in the early modern period left many with little to sustain themselves and their families once the crops were in; and the vagaries of the weather could easily reduce people to ruin and send grain prices soaring, as in Segovia in 1546, Toledo in 1558, or La Mancha in 1584–5.[31] In 1585, famine forced entire families to abandon their villages and take to the roads, swelling the population of Toledo with those who now found themselves reduced to begging for their food.[32] Behind the *Cortes*'s demands lay another motive, too, since Spain's textile industry found itself increasingly unable to meet demand because of labour shortages which, some thought, the indigent poor might be used to fill.[33] The legal mechanism through which this might be engineered had already been prefigured in the 1387 legislation, which had provided that healthy vagabonds could be drafted into service watching flocks or carrying out other menial work for one month without pay, the only obligation on their masters being to feed and water them.[34] The poor law of 1540, introduced after the disastrous harvest which followed the drought of the previous year, accordingly allowed vagabonds to be put to work without pay, though opposition to it by members of the Mendicant Orders ensured in the end that it was rendered relatively ineffective.[35] While the problem of vagabondage was by no means limited to Spain, it was nevertheless set to become particularly acute there, exacerbated in part by a significant influx of foreign vagrants keen to derive what benefit they could from the Spanish Church's traditional encouragement of charitable assistance to the needy.[36] The later sixteenth century in particular saw rampant price and rent inflation, the result of increases in the money supply and unsustainable structural changes to the rural economy of central Spain associated with the rise of Madrid.[37] These inevitably drove many Spaniards off the land altogether, serving further to swell the ranks of the destitute as they trudged their way across wide Castile eventually to descend on towns woefully ill-equipped to provide for their needs.

As to the gypsies, even in the fifteenth century suspicions had been voiced that other, non-gypsies were beginning to travel around with them. Now such claims began to surface once again. In 1539, the *Cortes* held at Toledo on 24 May noted that large numbers of foreign vaga-bonds and other Spaniards had begun to accompany gypsies roaming Castile and had 'adopted their language and dress and way of life'.[38] Charles V responded by reiterating the 1499 ordinance and increasing the penalties provided by it. Once again, the insistence was on sedent-arization. All gypsy males aged between 20 and 50 found without a 'recognized occupation' or a master were to be condemned to the oar for six years in Spain's Mediterranean galley squadrons. Gypsy women, on the other hand, were to be flogged, though it was then felt necessary to add 'and even if they are not, if they go around dressed as gypsies, then let them be whipped as the foregoing law provides'.[39] Similar suspicions were voiced elsewhere in Europe, too. In Germany, Albert Krantz had claimed in his widely read *Saxonia* that the gypsies accepted into their companies other men or women who wished to join them.[40] And when the authorities in England in 1554 introduced the death penalty for 'Egyptians' who refused to leave the country, the measure was met by indignant cries from the latter that they were Englishmen born and bred. The compelling logic of this argument duly prompted a more judiciously worded extension of the death penalty in 1562 to those found 'in any company or fellowship of vagabonds, commonly called, or calling themselves Egyptians', as well as any persons passing themselves off as Egyptians by 'counterfeiting, transforming or disguising themselves by their apparel, speech or other behaviour'. Half a century later, arguing that the assumption of an exotic identity made it easier for them to deceive simple people, a pamphlet of 1610 claimed that such groups even resorted to 'causing their faces to be made blacke, as if they were Egyptians'.[41] A similarly extravagant claim – this one involving the application of a plant-based brew 'which makes their skin go black' – was made in Spain in 1631 by Juan de Quiñones in his lurid *Discurso contra los gitanos*, in which the author, an *alcalde de casa y corte* (a magistrate with responsibility for law enforcement in and around Madrid), boasted of having hanged five gypsies he had apprehended in the Sepúlveda area for robbing the mails from Flanders, leaving their quartered remains by the road to discourage others who might be disposed to commit similar acts. He also cited, second-hand, a case in which two 'gypsies' confessed that they were in fact 'Moors' before being baptized and then hanged.[42] Whether or not such claims had any substance to them – Quiñones is not a reliable witness – the increasingly widespread assumption that others were masquerading as gypsies was eventually to evolve into the frequently stated conviction, in part politically or propagandistically motivated, that Spain's gypsies, far from being ethnically distinct, were in fact nothing more than a domestic underclass, recalcitrantly delinquent, to be sure, but emphatically home-grown. And, once established early in the seventeenth century, this view, frequently repeated by those who for one reason or another had occasion to comment on such matters, would continue to inform attitudes and, indeed, policy towards Spain's gypsies for centuries to come.

That Charles V's 1539 ordinance had at least some immediate effect is suggested by the events reported by Pierre Leblon to have taken place on 14 May 1545 on the galley *San Ginés*, when a number of gypsies, three of whom were technically due for release, having served the sentences handed down to them six years earlier, managed to overcome their guards, free themselves from their chains and escape.[43] Certainly, completion of sentence offered no guarantee that a man would be freed.[44] Even the original ordinance put its money on hope rather than experience, appealing as it did to the good conscience of galley captains and enjoining them to honour due release dates.[45] Whatever its short-term effect, like its predecessors, the 1539 ordinance had to be reiterated four years later in 1542 in Valladolid, once again in response to a request from the *Cortes* that the order be properly enforced. The way this request was couched is of considerable interest in itself, since, even as it exhorted the monarch to enforce the law, it employed a version of a curious formulation not infrequently used by Spaniards during the early modern period to acknowledge royal authority on the one hand, whilst simultaneously contriving to frustrate, or at least delay its actual exercise on the other. 'Let it be obeyed, but not put into effect' ('obedézcase, pero no se cumpla'), went the usual wording. Delays in implementation were supposed, at least in theory, to be finite, subject to reiteration of the order after due consideration had been given to objections raised by individuals affected, whose right to engage with the legislative process in this way was taken to be the inalienable birthright of the Spaniard.[46] In fact, a similar phrase had already been used by Charles V himself in Toledo in his reiteration of the Catholic Monarchs' original ordinance at the request of the *Cortes* held there in 1525.[47] The 1542 *Cortes* duly cited verbatim that part of his response to the earlier petition: Furthermore, we request your Majesty to order the implementation of the ordinance forbidding the gypsies to wander around or enter these kingdoms, and they should not be granted licence to do so, and if they are, then such licence should be obeyed but not put into effect ('que sea obedescida y no cumplida'), and the said law should be enforced.[48] Paradoxical as it may seem from a twenty-first century standpoint, failure or even refusal to comply with certain laws – even, as time was beginning to tell, laws against gypsies – was not for Spaniards of the early modern period necessarily oppugnant to their theoretical conception of royal authority, even if it did effectively limit the practical application of the monarch's power at a local level. For all the grand rhetoric and external trappings associated with the unifying 'absolute' authority that Spain's monarchs and their ministers sought so assiduously to arrogate to the crown, the day-to-day reality of their relationship with their subjects remained, even under the later Habsburgs, fundamentally pragmatic. It was, that is to say, always liable to be tested against the criteria of benefit, moral acceptability, and traditional arrangements and privileges.[49] And despite the occasional inclusion in statutory instruments of clauses evidently designed to derogate the contestatory rights Spaniards had long taken for granted, it is clear that these had relatively little practical effect on the ground. As Henry Kamen has noted, the renowned jurist Jerónimo Castillo de Bobadilla, who had himself been a *corregidor* in Badajoz, Guadalajara and Soria, specified in his 1597 *Política para Corregidores y señores de vasallos en tiempo de paz, y de guerra* (*Policy for Corregidors and Lords and Vassals in Time of Peace and War*) that 'laws made by the king were not binding if they went against conscience, or faith, or natural law, or accepted laws. The idea of *raison d'état* [. . .] existed only in tyrranies and not in Spain.'[50]

But even Castillo de Bobadilla railed against vagabondage and idleness.[51] And a year later, Cristóbal Pérez de Herrera, a man of *converso* origins who had been Royal Physician to Spain's galleys for nine years in the 1580s, added his voice to the argument.[52] Echoing the refutation of Machiavellian reason of state advanced by the Jesuit Pedro de Rivadeneyra in the prologue to his 1595 *Tratado del príncipe cristiano* (*Treatise on the Christian Prince*), Pérez de Herrera argued in *Amparo de pobres* (*Protecting the Poor*) that 'true reason of state consists in princes carrying out works which serve and are pleasing to God, and seeking to cleanse their realms of vagabonds and wayward people who corrupt the moral character of the nation'.[53] The decades that followed would see many others identify the figure of the healthy vagabond, pilloried in print time and again as idle, useless, and corrosive, as a veritable contagion threatening the body politic. What made things worse for men like Pérez de Herrera was that the genuinely needy were so often left to fend for themselves. In 1594, it was reported in Seville, for example, that 'beggars, cripples and the sick [. . .], having nowhere to shelter, nor anyone to care for them, were dying in the streets, an evil as great as it is an affront in such an opulent city'.[54] Under the circumstances, it is hardly surprising that the gypsies in particular, for most Spaniards the very type of the healthy vagabond, came to be enlisted by some as convenient scapegoats for the complex and intractable socio-economic issues that lay behind the problem.[55] Indeed, the tendency to assign them to this role was already evident in Pérez de Herrera's treatise, as he accused both gypsies and *moriscos* of breeding like rabbits while Castile's 'Old Christians' either left for the Indies or succumbed to war, pestilence, or, especially in Madrid where he was writing,[56] the relative material attractions of the religious life.[57] Concerned nonetheless that Spaniards should provide for the genuinely needy, among whom he included soldiers wounded in or too old for war,[58] he reserved his strongest condemnation for those, especially the gypsies, whom he considered wantonly to have chosen mendicancy as a way of life:

As to genuinely poor and needy people, whom we should help with our alms, there are two kinds: some are publicly acknowledged and are given shelter and wear the distinguishing signs and apparel of the licenced beggar; and there are others, honest poor people, who are registered and recognized as being in need in their parishes; and these we protect – as is only right – along with those in gaol, captives and orphans, and those in the hospitals.[59] And if we do this, and we put an end to the waywardness and indolence of the gypsies – your Majesty is already attending to this – and other suspicious people who live here or come to these kingdoms, then your Majesty's kingdoms, well hoed and free of weeds, will enjoy abundance and repose.[60]

In 1551 in Madrid, the *Cortes* once again petitioned the king requesting that laws against gypsies be enforced, claiming that 'many' of them were still going around with letters of safe-conduct and committing all manner of offences made worse by the fact that they were committed against the poor.[61] The petition elicited the customary referral to existing legislation and a reminder that this should be upheld. However, in 1552, further legislation against vagabonds was introduced by Charles V at Monzón in Huesca in response to the deteriorating situation in Castile and the burgeoning criminality born of desperation in the face of increasingly difficult economic conditions on the land.[62] Directed not just at vagabonds, but also at ruffians, thieves and their accomplices, this ordinance did not mention non-sedentarized gypsies specifically, though it clearly applied to them, too. It provided new penalties for those apprehended: for males aged over 20 a first offence would henceforth attract a sentence of four years in the galleys, while second and third offenders would receive 100 lashes and serve eight years or life at the oar, respectively. This legislation was reiterated in Madrid in 1566 by Charles's son, Philip II, who now stated explicitly that gypsies, too, were to be considered vagabonds for the purposes of the said law. The royal ordinance of 1566 'concerning Vagabonds, Thieves, Blasphemers, Ruffians, False Witnesses, Confidence Tricksters, and Bigamists, and Other Matters' cited Charles V's 1552 ordinance and, in what was by now becoming a familiar lament, deplored the failure thus far to enforce the laws against such individuals. It duly reiterated the earlier ordinance, but increased the length of the sentence to be applied to thieves by two years, so that it now matched the six-year sentence at the oar already stipulated for itinerant gypsies in the 1539 legislation (which had itself been reiterated in 1560 by Philip II). It also reduced the age limit for galley service for males, at least for those whose health permitted it, from 20 to 17 years, and added unequivocally that 'we declare the Egyptians and foreign tinkers, whose expulsion has been ordered by the laws and ordinances of these realms, to be vagabonds for the purposes of the said sentence'.[63] In 1597, in his professional advice to *corregidores*, Castillo de Bobadilla confirmed once again that the term 'vagabond' should be understood to include both gypsies and healthy beggars for the purposes of the law, defining it as 'anyone who is not settled in an area, and with neither property, nor trade, nor a master, nor work, wanders idle and suspect, and liable to steal or commit other crimes'. *Corregidores* should do everything in their power to exclude itinerant gypsies from their jurisdictions. They should prevent them from selling anything and ensure that the laws of the land, so 'badly enforced in the past', were upheld. Moreover, he added pointedly, this was one of the items assessed as part of a *corregidor*'s end-of-term report (*residencia*), a requirement introduced by Philip II in 1586.[64] This could in theory result in financial penalties, especially the payment of compensation by the incumbent to the victims of any injustices imputable to him whilst in office.[65] Castillo de Bobadilla must have been aware that the *Cortes* had some years earlier expressed concern that the powerful connections enjoyed by most *corregidores* meant that the *residencia* had in practice become little more than a formality.[66] Undaunted, however, he insisted that special commissioners were now being appointed by the Council 'across the entire kingdom' to pursue gypsies 'at the expense of *corrigidores* deemed to have been negligent in this respect'.[67]

3
The Road to the Sea

Castillo de Bobadilla's advice to *corregidores* on gypsies echoed similar policies of exclusion adopted elsewhere in the peninsula and, indeed, the New World. The success of such policies, discussed below, was however mixed, with the large tracts of territory under seigneurial or ecclesiastical jurisdiction typically serving as convenient bolt-holes for gypsies on the run from the authorities in the *corregimientos*, the 66 administrative areas under royal jurisdiction as Castillo de Bobadilla was writing.[1] The frontiers between the peninsula's different kingdoms served a similar purpose, the border between Castile and Aragon being exploited in this way by gypsy and other bandits until at least the mid-seventeenth century. Meanwhile, the tendency, evident from an early stage, to identify gypsies with vagabonds or criminal elements was reflected in legislation which consistently defined them via reference to their dress, speech, and behaviour, though never at any stage in terms of race. In Castile itself, from the 1570s Philip II would seek to press gypsy males into service as much-needed oarsmen for his Mediterranean galley squadrons. If successful, this policy would of course amount to another form of exclusion, at once removing undesirables from Castile and separating them from their women, while also offering the additional benefit of cheap manpower.

Exclusion

In 1561, Philip II had fixed his court in Madrid, which thereafter became a powerful magnet for all manner of individuals, ranging from those seeking favour and fortune in the glittering orbit of the monarch to others whose ambitions perforce extended to little more than scraping a living as best they could at the margins. Some gypsies were by that time already living at least relatively settled lives there, even though an order of that same year forbade them to reside in the town.[2] Such orders were repeated time and again, though they seem to have had relatively little lasting effect in a town whose population was now growing exponentially, rising from some 30,000 in 1563 to 130,000 in 1617, a figure that did not include a transient population estimated by the social historian Antonio Domínguez Ortiz to have numbered some 20,000.[3] Pérez de Herrera suggested in 1598 that there were as many as 150,000 vagabonds in Spain as a whole,[4] though it is possible that this may have been something of an overestimate, based on what was in fact a predominantly Castilian problem and the disproportionate numbers of foreign and home-grown vagabonds who were attracted to Madrid.[5] Gypsies could anyway only have represented a relatively small percentage of those living at Madrid's social margin. As I have suggested, however, so representative of the problem of fraudulent mendicancy had they become for men like Pérez de Herrera, that the very term *gitano* had by now become slippery. Ostensibly denoting a racially distinct group of eastern origin, it was nevertheless now beginning to be applied, especially by those in authority, to others living a similarly suspect, itinerant, or disordered life.[6] Indeed, a most striking feature of Spanish legislative instruments and other official documents relating to gypsies throughout the early modern period is their formulaic and frequently repeated references to 'those who are known as Egyptians' or *gitanos*, virtually no other attempt being made to point up racial distinctiveness as one of their defining characteristics.[7] Instead, it was invariably the gypsies' dress, their language, usually referred to as *jerigonza* (gobbledygook) and taken by the authorities to be a form of thieves' cant, and, most importantly, their reputation, irreligion, and scandalous, footloose, and unregulated way of life that were invoked in order to define them for the purposes of the law. Consequently, the focus of legislation against gypsies in Castile turned increasingly to the outlawing of such signs of difference amid repeated attempts to oblige them to assimilate as agricultural labourers to the mainstream rural economy.

Just what precisely it was that constituted 'gypsy dress' remains somewhat unclear.[8] It is evident, however, given the many references to it throughout the period, that there were certain features that served immediately to distinguish it from the clothing of other Spaniards. As noted earlier, Pedro Salazar de Mendoza refers to some gypsy women wearing shawls and wide-brimmed hats (*rodelas*),[9] while Fray Melchor de Huélamo noted their fondness for adding embellishments to their clothing.[10] In 1592 a town crier in Madrid announced that 'women who are called gypsies are not to wear gypsy clothing or dress using coloured cloths as *gitanas* do, or as they have been used to do until now, either on their heads or in their dress, but rather they should adopt the dress and hairstyles commonly worn by Castilian women'.[11] In Gonzalo de Céspedes y Meneses's novel *Varia fortuna del soldado Pindaro* (1626), an episode involving gypsies paints a picture of a gypsy woman with dishevelled hair and many trinkets on her fingers and cites the language, demeanour (unspecified) and dark skin of the gypsies as features marking them out from others.[12] In 1719, the *alcalde mayor* Don Bernardo Ventura de Capua took a sworn deposition from a resident of Zalamea, who described the arrival there of 'a troop of gypsies, which you could tell they were from their faces'. He had also, he said, heard them converse in their *jerigonza*, and described the silver buttons and other silver ornaments on their clothing as well as the 'very good horses' they were riding.[13] And much later, in 1784, the gypsy Pedro Vargas, arrested on three counts in Fregenal de la Sierra 'for having exchanged two donkeys, neither of which was his, for failing to apply himself to work, and for failing to change his style of dress', was described as wearing 'a short jacket in black serge, a red satin waistcoat, and breeches of brownish-grey cloth'.[14]

Among the repeated attempts made by the authorities to expel gypsies from the capital was an order of 1585 instructing those without a trade or a master to serve to leave Madrid on pain of 100 lashes and condemnation to the galleys.[15] And on 13 August 1609, a decree was issued in response to a request from the *Sala de Alcaldes* the previous day instructing all gypsies, men and women, to leave Madrid and take up work on the land.[16] Despite the official antagonism, however, it is clear that relations with non-gypsies in Madrid were not always nearly as hostile as the official line would suggest. Even mixed marriages were not unknown, despite the gypsies' normal practice of endogamy, which was, and still is, stricter in some patrigroups than others. In 1611, for example, the Council of Castile received a request on behalf of a gypsy woman, Catalina Pérez, wife of the non-gypsy, Juan Bautista, 'who is an Old Christian and works as a water-seller to support her', asking that she be exempted as a matter of natural justice from the requirement to leave Madrid as the 1609 decree had demanded.[17] It is worth noting, too, that in Cervantes's novella *La gitanilla*, the gypsy women of the capital are described as always returning at night to the outskirts of Madrid accompanied for safety by the many peasant women on their way back to their villages. Even when one takes account of the obvious caveats attaching to a tale that moves between earth and ether to the extent that this one does, the passage in question has about it a ring of life observed at first hand.[18]

In the Kingdom of Navarre the policy from the mid-sixteenth century on had been to expel or, preferably, deny entry altogether to gypsies. The 1549 *Ordenanzas Viejas* of the kingdom had ordered that gypsies might not 'enter, be present in, or pass through' Navarre on pain of 100 lashes; but the prohibition evidently met with little success, since at the *Cortes* of Estella in 1556 and then later in 1569, 1572, and 1580 further attempts had to be made to expel them – after, the *Cortes* demanded, they had been separated from the other vagabonds and poor people with whom they were associating.[19] In 1602, the viceroy ordered all vagrants, including gypsies, to be sent to the galleys, and in 1678 the *Cortes* of Navarre passed a law excluding gypsies from the kingdom in perpetuity.[20]

In the Kingdom of Aragon, where the first gypsies to enter Spain had been granted safe-conducts to travel to Santiago, gypsy bandits had subsequently made much use of the frontier, moving from one jurisdiction into the relative safety of another. Such activities had, however, been policed by the Aragonese authorities with increasing rigour, especially in the second half of the seventeenth century, after en expulsion order of 1646.[21] By the middle of the eighteenth, a document originating there could observe of Aragon's remaining gypsies that it was no longer necessary to treat them with particular severity, since their numbers had been greatly reduced in previous periods of repression. 'It has been many years', it noted, 'since they have been accused of the kinds of outrages still perpetrated in Castile', though it added that vigilance was still necessary in order to ensure that the region did not for these very reasons attract gypsies in flight from the authorities elsewhere in Spain.[22] In 1749, the Governor of the Council of Castile, Gaspar Vázquez de Tablada observed more generally of the distribution of gypsy populations that it was in north-east and eastern Spain in 'the kingdoms of the Crown of Aragon [. . .] where the least number dwell'.[23]

In 1549, the *fueros*, or regional laws of the Basque regions of Vizcaya and Guipúzcoa, had forbidden gypsies to enter their territories. In this case, however, a marked insistence upon strict compliance suggests that enforcement may have been rather more rigorous than elsewhere in the peninsula. So, too, does a letter sent to Philip II in September 1573 in which the *corregidor* reported laconically of Guipúzcoa that gypsies 'do not come here'.[24] Another letter of 20 February 1589 requested the king to show mercy to the gypsies Antón, Martín, and Domingo de Ramus and another named simply as Baltasar, all of whom had indeed gone there and who had subsequently been sentenced to ten years in the galleys by Jerónimo de Aitamarrén, *alcalde ordinario* (locally elected magistrate) of the small village of Segura in Guipúzcoa. They all had homes in the village, it said, where they lived with their wives and 12 children, and had been sentenced 'without there being any evidence to suggest why they should deserve the said sentence except for the accusation that they are Egyptians and vagabonds, whereas it is clear from the proceedings against them that they practise trades as locksmiths and shoemakers'. The response merely stated, 'let them complete their sentences'.[25]

But gypsies were only ever present in small numbers in the Basque Country, demonstrating a clear preference for Old and New Castile and, above all, Andalusia, where their eventual numbers suggest that they found conditions much more amenable to their needs than in certain areas further north.[26] In a letter written from Porcuna in Jaén in northern Andalusia in 1674, Manuel Montillo, a priest and lawyer, protested that 'there is not a village or its surrounding land which is not populated by gypsies, who must have come from other parts'. He also claimed that the numbers of 'this useless race of gypsies' in Spain had increased significantly over the previous 40 years, 'in particular here in Andalusia because it offers richer country where those in flight from populated areas are able to live off the land'.[27] Attractive, too, may have been the relative security offered by the sheer extent of the territories under seigneurial control in the south, where in the medieval period the nobility, whose military service in the vanguard of the *Reconquista* had been indispensable to the crown, had amassed vast estates on land recaptured from the Muslims. Such evidence as there is suggests that noble families frequently extended their protection to gypsies in the south, even at the risk of invoking the displeasure of the crown.

Rural Catalonia, too, offered certain advantages to those with reason to fear the authorities in Castile. Certainly it provided an even less easily regulated environment, and resistance by the Catalan nobility to what was essentially regarded as unwelcome judicial interference from Castile made it virtually impossible for the viceroys to gain control over the banditry and lawlessness that flourished there, often with the connivance of these same nobles.[28] Indeed, it was only in 1616 with the arrival there of a new viceroy, the Duke of Alburquerque, who determinedly rode rough-shod over the privileges and exemptions of nobles who had been complicit in or supportive of such activities, that these seigneurial abuses were finally – and to popular approval – brought under some semblance of control, even though banditry itself remained an endemic problem.[29]

At any event, a significant number of gypsies remained in Catalonia, an almost certainly incomplete 1785 census recording some 935 sedentarized individuals there, mainly in the *corregimientos* of Tarragona (320), Gerona (200), and Barcelona (121), this despite an earlier expulsion order of 1715.[30]

In Valencia, as elsewhere, repeated attempts were made to expel the gypsies, and there is some later, eighteenth-century evidence to suggest that these may have been at least somewhat more effective than those made in Castile. On three occasions, in 1564, 1585, and 1604, The *Corts* there forbade gypsies to reside in Valencia and successive viceroys issued expulsion orders in 1576, 1581, 1586, 1624, and 1695,[31] while the regional *furs* simply rejected as invalid the royal letters of naturalization without which gypsies were forbidden to live in the realm.[32]

Attempts were also made to deny gypsies access to Spain's possessions in the New World. In July 1568, Philip II ordered the *Audiencia de Tierra Firme* to expel all gypsies and Portuguese found without a royal licence in mainland Central and Caribbean South America.[33] And in 1570, he forbade gypsies to travel to the New World altogether.[34] However, tacitly acknowledging the difficulty of enforcing the ordinance in the main port of embarkation, Seville, a city described by St Teresa of Avila in 1576 as wholly deserving of its reputation for double-dealing, corruption, and injustice,[35] he added that those who contrived to do so anyway should be returned forthwith to Castile. The Laws of the Indies noted that not only had gypsies and vagabonds travelled to the Indies, but that they continued to do so, finding it easy, once there, to exploit the 'natural simplicity' of the indigenous peoples for their nefarious purposes.[36] Henceforth, all those 'going around in gypsy dress, speaking their language, professing their arts, and guilty of bad conduct, theft, and inventions' should be put on the first available ships and sent back to Spain. Early in 1581, a royal decree drew the attention of Martín Enríquez, viceroy of Peru and President of the Lima *Audiencia*, to the fact that gypsies were continuing to cross the Atlantic and once again demanded that they be sent back. A marginal note records that similar instructions had been sent to *Audiencias* and governors across the New World.[37] In a letter of 25 February 1587, Francisco de Anuncibay, *oidor* (judge) of the Quito *Audiencia* informed the king that a number of gypsies had been returned to 'their places of origin', while another letter of 30 March that year reported that six gypsies had been arrested and would be sent back to serve in the galleys, where oarsmen were sorely needed.[38] None of this, however, prevented the gypsy blacksmith Jorge Leal, a resident of the Triana district of Seville, from obtaining a licence to travel to Havana in 1602 with his wife Magdalena Hernández and their children Fabián and Sebastián de Heredia. They did so in the company of the newly appointed Governor of Cuba and Knight of Santiago, Pedro de Valdés.[39]

Philip II and the manning of Spain's galleys

The introduction by Charles V in 1539 of a six-year sentence in the galleys for gypsies found without a master or a 'recognized' occupation was not without its precedents. It was the Catholic Monarchs who had introduced forced labour at the oar as a form of corporal punishment which, since it saved the crown the cost of hiring oarsmen, offered benefits to the exchequer that traditional, visually exemplary punishments such as flogging or the more permanent expedient of mutilation could not provide. Nevertheless, price inflation ensured that the one ducat per month cost of hiring an oarsman in 1538 had by 1571 risen to an altogether prohibitive eight ducats, so that the closing decades of the sixteenth century saw *forzados* (prisoners sentenced unpaid to the oar) virtually replace volunteer oarsmen in the galley squadrons.[40] As early as 1501, the city of Seville had petitioned the crown to commute to galley service the sentences of prisoners condemned to the lash or the amputation of feet, hands or ears 'so that the city might be free of malefactors'.[41] Royal ordinances of 1530, 1552, and 1566, the last of which specifically included gypsies, made service at the oar mandatory for vagabonds and thieves, together with their accomplices or protectors and – the charge would often be added for good measure – anyone resisting arrest.[42] The 1539 ordinance was reiterated by Philip II in Toledo in 1560, noting that the earlier legislation had not been enforced,[43] while the *Cortes* held there a year earlier had noted that the appeals routinely lodged with the *Chancillerías* by those condemned to the galleys were taking so long to be heard, 'since these are poor men who have no one to represent them', that execution of sentence was effectively being delayed for two or three years. Meanwhile, those sentenced, far from languishing passively to await the results of their appeals, were said to be responsible for other crimes and violent disturbances in the gaols where they were held. The king's response was to order the courts of appeal to hear at least one such case every week.[44] In the end, as delays grew worse, many such prisoners were simply sent to the galleys anyway, pending the outcome of appeals that could now sometimes take up to six years, during which time many became unfit for service, escaped, or, as was reported in Granada in 1617, managed to bribe their way out of gaol.[45]

The need for oarsmen increased as the sixteenth century wore on, especially after about 1550, when changes to the rowing system employed on Spanish galleys came into effect. Thereafter, all the men on a given bench handled a single oar, with only the one positioned furthest inboard, who controlled its operation, needing now to be an oarsman of several years' experience. The change made the widespread use of gypsies and others who might quickly be trained in what was required of them an altogether more feasible proposition than it had been previously. While the change allowed for the construction of bigger galleys, experiments earlier in the century by the Italians suggested that the greater hydrodynamic drag produced by increased hull displacement would require a geometric increase in the number of oarsmen if a galley's maximum speed of about seven knots, considered vital to the Spanish fleet, were to be maintained, even if only over short distances.[46] The result in terms of the number of oarsmen required on ordinary Spanish galleys was a 21 per cent increase from 144 per vessel in the mid-1550s to 174 by 1571, while for larger vessels like the *Capitana*, the requirement could rise to 375.[47] The destruction of 30 galleys at Djerba in 1560, and the loss in 1561 of seven more at the hands of the Barbary corsair Turgut Re'is, known to Spaniards as Dragut, was followed just a year later by the wrecking on 19 October of a further 25 when a sudden, vicious squall blew up off La Herradura on Spain's south-east coast.[48] Some four thousand lives were lost in this last incident alone, and although Philip II managed by the end of 1564 to reconstitute and even expand the fleet, replacing the lost crews continued to prove problematic.[49] Meanwhile, rising maintenance costs coupled with an ever impecunious crown's failure to fund the galleys adequately ensured that malnutrition, disease and neglect continued to take their lethal toll on the rowing benches.[50] In the 1566 ordinance referred to earlier, Philip was once again obliged to demand, as had his father in 1552, that sentences for crimes considered sufficiently serious be commuted forthwith to galley service for a period deemed by the judges to be commensurate with the gravity of the offence.[51] With the formation in 1571 by Spain, Venice and the Papacy of a Holy League, the defeat of the Turks at Lepanto that same year, which created the expectation thereafter of an aggressive Ottoman response, and, of course, the continuing need to reserve some galleys for the protection of Spain's vulnerable Mediterranean coastline, the requirement for greater numbers of *forzados* became even more critical.

Philip II's response was to write in December 1572 to all those responsible for the maintenance of law and order across Castile. He asked to be informed within 20 days of the number of men being held in gaols who had been condemned to death or the galleys, who were awaiting the outcome of appeals, or who were still to be sentenced and who 'could well be condemned to galley service, like thieves, ruffians, vagabonds, and those guilty of other types of crime'. The reports were to include full details of the crimes these men had committed. Citing the great number of *forzados* needed for the war against the Turk, 'the common enemy of Christendom', Philip noted that there were more galleys now than ever before and that he wished these to be fully crewed, armed and ready for action by early summer the following year. The letter continued:

> and since we are informed, notwithstanding the provisions of laws and ordinances old and new in respect of those who are known as gypsies, that there are great numbers of the latter in many parts of these Kingdoms, you will order your chief magistrates to endeavour with great diligence to apprehend and hold in custody those found in your jurisdictions . . .[52]

This demand was understood by most – though not all – of those to whom it was sent to refer to vagrant rather than sedentarized gypsies, in line with previous legislation, though the fact that the letter made no attempt to suggest that magistrates might operate outside their own areas of jurisdiction drew some frustrated comment here and there. The *corregidor* of León, for example, reported promptly on 20 December 1572 that he had no gypsies in custody and noted that, while they had in the past entered the city and the area it administered, they tended to limit their range to villages under seigneurial jurisdiction. Some might be apprehended, he added, were the king to grant him power of arrest in such areas.[53] A similar request was received from the Campos district, where the *alcalde mayor* Alonso Fernández de Córdoba reported the arrest of Francisco de Alvarado, 'count and leader' of a marauding band of gypsies, the remainder of whom had managed to evade their pursuers by crossing into another jurisdiction. The letter noted 'the crimes they commit, the extortion and molestation for which they are responsible in the villages' and added that 'since the said villages are small and they are great in number and heavily armed, with many of them mounted on horses, the inhabitants do not dare to resist them'. He added that the 60-year-old Alvarado had been sentenced to death for these crimes, but had immediately appealed his sentence to the Valladolid *Chancillería*.[54] Another report, this time from the *corregimiento* of Olmedo, complained about the failure of judges to enforce the law in villages under seigneurial or ecclesiastical jurisdiction, as well as in northern Castile's *behetrías*, towns whose inhabitants were free to elect and even negotiate conditions with their lord. It was dereliction of duty on the part of judges like these, claimed the letter, that explained the presence in such areas of so many vagabonds and gypsies, 'who stick mainly to villages under seigneurial control, avoiding and keeping their distance from those under royal jurisdiction, where there are *corregidores'*. Having suggested that the king impose severe penalties on those failing to do their duty, the letter went on to explain that some judges were anyway reluctant to imprison such individuals because once appeals were lodged with the *Chancillerías*, as they invariably were, these took so long to be heard that the expense of ensuring that the prisoners were fed and of trying to prevent their escape was simply unsustainable.[55] Complaints about these delays – one non-gypsy prisoner in Betanzos had been waiting over five years for his appeal to be heard – were a common feature of the responses to the king's request.[56] In some cases, as in La Coruña, it was the prisoners themselves, starving in detention, who requested to be sent to the galleys before their appeals were heard, so that they would at least be fed standard daily rations.[57] Then there was the additional cost, theoretically borne by the crown but loudly lamented by the authorities in Campos and elsewhere, of conducting the *galeotes* securely to Toledo, one of the designated distribution points.[58]

It is hardly surprising that escapes were frequent. Respondents reported recent breakouts from gaols in Alburquerque, Lorca, and Cebreros, in Andújar and Badajoz, in both of which towns the escapees immediately sought sanctuary in the church, and in Hornachos, where the prisoner was quickly recaptured. In La Coruña, a group of prisoners who had been held there for two months had broken out 'on two or three occasions'.[59] In Betanzos, proceedings were initiated against a gaoler who failed to prevent the escape of one of two prisoners sentenced to six years in the galleys; and in Laredo, the escape of two thieves who had been similarly condemned resulted in their gaoler himself being sentenced to three years at the oar plus a fine of 100 ducats to be used to purchase a slave, a replacement, that is, who would serve in the galleys for life.[60] Meanwhile in Cuenca, where 19 gypsies had been apprehended for vagrancy, theft, and extortion – others had managed to avoid capture – the *corregidor* begged the king as a matter of urgency to expedite their dispatch to the galleys, observing, as did other towns, that 'this city's gaol is insecure and they may succeed in breaking out'.[61] From Vélez Málaga, where of eight prisoners condemned to the galleys three were gypsies, came a similar request for further instructions, 'because they [the gaolers] have nothing for the prisoners to eat and they [the prisoners] will not receive their daily rations from your Majesty until you have told me what to do with them'.[62] The seven gypsies arrested in the *corregimiento* of Ronda and Marbella were reported by the *corregidor* to be in a state of 'great need and wretchedness' in gaol and he again requested urgent instructions, adding that their womenfolk were intending to make an appeal directly to the king.[63] From Plasencia, the *corregidor* reported on 4 February 1573 that 12 of the gypsies held in gaol had been there for over seven weeks and he asked the king, as he had already done once before, to tell him what to do with them. He did so, he said,

> so that they might go where they have to go and so that we might get them away from here, for I pity them, and were it not for some good people who give them alms, I believe they would go for many days without any food at all; and what they are given is insufficient, because there are so many of them.[64]

Of the twelve, nine were Andalusians, four being described as residents of Alcaudete, three of Utrera, and two of Luque, near Córdoba, the very distance of these towns from Plasencia being cited as sufficient evidence of vagrancy to justify their arrest. The other three, all of them blacksmiths, long a traditional gypsy occupation, had however been residents of Plasencia itself for seven years, though the evident ambiguity of Philip II's order, which is referred to in the same letter as 'instructing me to apprehend all the gypsies in this city', doubtless prompted the *corregidor* to have them detained anyway. Two of the 12, old men of 80 and 85 years of age, were subsequently released on bail.[65] In Mérida, on the other hand, the governor reported that there were five gypsies who were residents of the city, living there in their own homes with others; and there were more in surrounding villages, who, because they too were resident there and not vagrants, he had not yet arrested, pending further clarification of the king's wishes.[66] Sanlúcar de Barrameda reported that a 48-year-old gypsy blacksmith detained there in accordance with the king's order, one Blas Greciano de Bustamante, had been living in the town for six months with his pregnant Portuguese wife, by whom he had already had seven children, of whom only three had survived.[67]

Yet it is clear from other reports that residency in a particular town did not necessarily indicate the kind of settled existence envisaged and demanded by the crown. Medina del Campo, for example, declared that a number of gypsies were resident there, though none of the men had been seen for the past month. The letter added, 'but they have their houses and wives' in the town, and asked the king what should be done were they to return.[68] It is worth noting, however, that in all but one of these cases (that of Blas Greciano de Bustamante) the gypsies in question are described as *vecinos* or as being *avecindados* in the towns and villages where they were resident. The word *vecino*, whose literal meaning is 'neighbour', usually denoted a quite formally construed status as resident or householder in the early modern period, and it seems unlikely that it would have been used loosely in the legalistic context of the letters in question. One social historian put it as follows:

> the term was applied to a person who had the rights of citizenship (*vecindad*) in the municipality, or federation of municipalities, where he resided. Normally, the *vecino* was an adult family head. As a local citizen, a *vecino* had a series of rights and obligations. Each municipality had its own norms regarding citizenship, but the basic effect of being a *vecino* was to fall under the local juridical system, and to enjoy the protection of the local *fuero* [. . .].[69]

It is clear enough from the reports cited that some of Spain's gypsies had complied with previous legislation, accepting, perhaps even embracing, sedentarization, or relative sedentarization; but it is equally evident that their continuing marginal status and the suspicion they invariably attracted ensured that the mere fact of being able to claim that they were *vecinos* of a particular town or village offered little guarantee that they could in every case expect to be afforded much protection under the law.

All in all, the number of gypsies detained and sent to the galleys was probably significantly lower than the crown had been anticipating. Where gypsies had been apprehended at all, the 19 gaoled in Cuenca, the 12 in Plasencia, or the seven held in Ronda must be balanced against figures for other towns and villages, which rarely exceeded five and, more often than not, represented just one or two prisoners. Of Sanlúcar de Barrameda's surprisingly low figure of eight prisoners, only one was reported to be a gypsy, while of 17 men condemned to the galleys in Galicia's Cárcel Real, and 40 others awaiting sentencing or the outcome of appeals, none were – though the list did include seven Englishmen accused of stealing a boat and then wounding four Spaniards as they resisted arrest.[70] Many gypsies had simply melted away, managing to avoid capture, while those who remained were often far too old or unfit for galley service. Some of those who fled almost certainly had advance warning of what was in hand. It was, after all, virtually impossible for the authorities to arrange co-ordinated action on a specified date across the whole of Spain. Indeed, the difficulty of maintaining secrecy in respect of such initiatives was from time to time cited in the councils of state as one of the reasons for their failure.[71] Meanwhile, Burgos noted reports of gypsies in the neighbouring hills, though none had been apprehended; in the marquisate of Adrada, three were captured, though one of them had only one hand and others had succeeded in getting away; in Comares, of five arrested, two were too old to be of use to the authorities; and in Caravaca, of the two apprehended, one was 90 years old and crippled, while four of those detained in Cuenca were also described as 'crippled and useless for the galleys'.[72] Philip II may indeed have been informed that large numbers of gypsies were wandering Spain, but a surprising number of respondents claimed that there were none at all in their areas, still less in their gaols. Alcántara reported that 'there are no gypsies', and Palencia wrote that there were none in the area 'at present', as did Oviedo, Huelva, Bolullos, Almonte, Murcia, Lorca, Bayona, and Alcaraz, among others, though one gypsy gaoled two years earlier in Alcaraz and sentenced to hang for theft was reported by the Granada *Chancillería* still to be awaiting the outcome of his appeal.[73] Madrigal noted, perhaps a touch pointedly, that while all necessary investigations into vagabonds, ruffians, and gypsies had been carried out, 'no one who should have been imprisoned has emerged'.[74] Others, like Alburquerque, merely said they had no gypsies in their gaols, whilst in others gypsies simply did not figure – or at least were not mentioned – in the lists of prisoners presented to the crown. The Count of Benavente reported that 'no gypsies have been found at present in any of my lands', whilst Don Enrique de Guzmán, second Count of Olivares, replied in a letter so untypically short as to qualify as curt that 'in no village in my territories are there any gypsies, vagabonds, or other persons sentenced to serve in the galleys at present'.[75] As to the Count of Buendía's response, Philip II's secretary Juan Vázquez summarized it tersely on a coversheet with the single word 'nothing'.[76] Some were minded to offer the king alternative advice. The Duke of Medina Sidonia, for instance, suggested that Andalusia's abundant mulatto population might be rounded up wholesale to serve at the oar.[77] The *corregidor* of Ávila, on the other hand, proposed that Philip should consider using the almost wholly unassimilated Granadine *moriscos*, who in 1570 had been forcibly dispersed throughout the kingdom after the second rebellion of the Alpujarras. Among them, he claimed, there were those who were willing and able to serve in the galleys, though he thought only single men should be used, adding that 'there are very many of them, lost and idle and with no work to do'. The *corregidor* of La Coruña and Betanzos reported one such case, a man he had had arrested and imprisoned, 'a vagabond [...] who in my judgement and based on the nature of his confession seems to me to be a *morisco*'. It was subsequently ordered that he should be released and his 'gold chains and doubloons' restored to him. The *corregidor* noted that the man was still in the city and asked whether the king would like to see the prisoner's statements, since in his opinion, he had been released unjustly.[78] More ominously, from Murcia came a complaint that these same *moriscos* were now wandering around Spain, having abandoned the villages to which they were sent, sometimes with licences granted by judges, and trying, it was suggested, to get close to the Mediterranean coast, presumably with the intention of offering clandestine support to their supposed confederates threatening Spain from North Africa.[79] Certainly some of those apprehended who attempted to return to what they regarded as home were treated with extreme severity, as in Loja (Granada), where it was reported that two 'Moors' had been sentenced on 9 November 1570 to life at the oar, for most men a virtual death sentence, handed down to them in this case merely 'for having returned to this kingdom'.[80]

The crown's demands that gypsies should forcibly be enlisted for galley service were repeated on a number of occasions under subsequent monarchs. This, however, was less a reflection of an expanding requirement than of the very limited success of previous attempts, as the legislators themselves were the first to admit. As to those detained in the wake of Philip II's order of 1572, the task of quantifying them is complicated by the fact that although it was normal practice to append the word *gitano* to the surnames of gypsies listed, this may not have been done in every case. Improbably enough, in a list of over 130 prisoners with appeals pending in the Granada *Chancillería*, a list compiled by a number of different hands, only one prisoner is specifically identified as a gypsy, though elsewhere in the list the appearance together of family names like Maldonado and Malla raises at least the possibility that they too may have been gypsies.[81] It is also impossible to know how many of the gypsies apprehended actually ended up at the oar. Certainly escapes on the open road are known to have occurred, and the makeshift overnight gaols often employed as *forzados* were conducted to Cartagena, El Puerto de Santa María, Málaga, or any of a number of other ports on Spain's south and south-eastern coasts were often anything but secure. The loss at some point in the last 75 years of the relevant galley registers at Cartagena, which were anyway incomplete, makes any attempt to quantify the gypsy component of the body of *forzados* in the late sixteenth century a hazardous enterprise at best.[82] There is, however, some slightly later evidence on which we can draw. An undated document in the General Archive at Simancas, penned by a secretary in Philip II's service, referred to two subsequent orders of 24 February and 11 August 1573.[83] These, like yet another decree issued in 1575,[84] had once again ordered all vagrant gypsies suitable for the oar to be arrested and conducted to the galleys. It also reported that Philip II had requested Don Álvaro de Bazán, the Marquis of Santa Cruz, a hero of Lepanto who had been appointed Captain-General of the Galleys of Spain in 1576, to inform him of the total number of gypsies serving at the oar. The Marquis's response, delivered via a letter signed by the inspector and comptroller of the galleys, informed the monarch that there were just 59, 27 of them serving six-year sentences dating back to March and April of 1573. The sentences of the remaining 32 were not specified, though the letter insisted they had been delivered to the galleys as a result of those same orders. An accompanying note dated 21 December 1578 added that the Council of War, in discussion with Rodrigo Vázquez de Arce, the distinguished jurist and future President of the Council of Castile, had agreed to ask the king to sign a document 'in accordance with the law' authorizing the release of the said gypsies.[85] The prisoners would have been about to complete their six-year sentences, and Philip, deservedly described by one historian as a man 'who never erred in his life on the side of mercy',[86] felt obliged on this occasion to agree. A grudging note written in the margin read, 'approved, even though gypsies are the kind of people we know them to be; but if they do anything in future to warrant it, they must be returned to the galleys'.[87] Certainly, the king was aware that there were legal, moral, and practical concerns about the treatment that gypsy captives had received. Perhaps he even recalled the letter written to him from the galley port of Cartagena on 17 April 1575 by Don Juan de Austria, which had pointed out that many gypsies serving in the galleys were there simply because of the pressing need for oarsmen, not because of any crime they had committed. Might it not be possible, Don Juan had asked, to pay them something, since their plight had reduced their families to destitution, forcing them to return to a life of vagrancy?[88] At any event, the men now released were soon replaced. I. A. A. Thompson has estimated that by 1586–9 there were 158 gypsies at the oar, though he added that this figure would even then have represented under 3 per cent of the total number of oarsmen nominally available to the crown. They took their places beside the numerous other, non-gypsy vagrants sent to the galleys, Thompson going on to point out that another, anonymous memorandum of 1589 claimed that such men made up 'the greater part' of the numbers of men conscripted to the rowing benches.[89]

The closing decades of the sixteenth century, troubled times for Castile, saw a significant harshening both of the repressive measures adopted against Spain's gypsies, and of the tone of the increasingly strident rhetoric directed against them by those in positions of authority. From the 1580s, too, the question of what was to be done about Spain's *moriscos* seemed ever more urgently to demand an answer. Increasing numbers of Spaniards, reacting to the events of the Alpujarras rebellion a decade earlier, felt now that the continuing presence in Spain of a people they regarded as a potential enemy within could no longer be sustained, this amid suspicions, vindicated by modern scholarship, that material support for the rebels had been supplied from North Africa.[90] By the turn of the century, the crusading spirit of post-Tridentine Spain, newly emboldened by the great victory at Lepanto, had for a variety of reasons begun to give way to a more pessimistic outlook. Events now conspired to plunge Castile into what for men whose perspective and focus was both circumstantially and ideologically centrist would become a long period of crisis and self-questioning introspection, though many of Spain's problems were in fact endemic to much of Europe. Some, though, thought the body politic infected, and argued that it should be purged, while others argued that if part of the remedy lay in the expulsion of the *moriscos*, then the moment should also be exploited to rid Spain of what they regarded as that other contagion, its gypsies.

4
Years of Crisis

War, famine, and pestilence in late sixteenth-century Castile

In 1631, in his treatise *Restauración de la antigua abundancia de España*, Miguel Caxa de Leruela, a retired official of the *Mesta*, described war as an 'horrendous beast, worse than hunger and pestilence, for it is the cause of both these things, and swallows up honour, lives and fortunes'.[1] As they looked back over their nation's recent history, Spaniards had good reason to appreciate his sentiments. Debilitating conflict in the Netherlands from the late 1560s; interventions by Spanish troops in the French civil wars of the 1590s; the sack by the English in 1586 of Santo Domingo, Spain's principal city in the New World; their humiliating defeat of the Armada in 1588; and the occupation and sack of Cádiz in 1596 by the Earl of Essex, all had helped to sap Castile's confidence and exhaust both its human and material resources. Despite increased contributions to the royal purse from the Indies and significantly higher tax revenues, at least from Castile, the financial burden of so many military commitments had finally proven overwhelming. In November 1596, Philip II had been forced to suspend payments to his creditors, just as he had done twice previously in 1557 and 1575. Signs of serious disaffection in Italy and Portugal served further to darken the horizon.[2] Food prices were meanwhile soaring and famine years, while not frequent,[3] were nevertheless particularly acute in Castile in 1585 and Andalusia in 1599, serving further to exacerbate the sense of crisis and malaise; and as if all this were not enough, from 1596 to 1602, plague swept through Castile from north to south, taking with it some 600,000 lives, roughly 10 per cent of the population.[4] On 13 September 1598, after a long illness, Philip II died, to be succeeded by a son whose own father feared him incapable of managing adequately the burden of responsibility that

51

had now fallen to him.[5] Once great Castile, it seemed to some, was limping into its new century. In his *Memorial de la política necesaria y útil restauración a la República de España* (1600), Martín González de Cellorigo, a lawyer in the *Real Chancillería* of Valladolid, became the first to observe – he was writing as plague ravaged the city – that Spain might now be facing the kind of decline experienced by so many other great nations before it.[6] For Cellorigo, the time was out of joint, the instrument of state dissonant. Drawing on Platonic ideas, he argued that Spain now lacked the required 'proportion in all parts' that gave rise to the harmony necessary if kingdoms were to remain 'unchanging and firm'.[7] Among his primary concerns were the devastating effects of plague on a nation that could ill afford such a grievous demographic reverse, a nation which, he argued, had long lacked a sufficiently abundant population for its needs. In Cellorigo's pre-Malthusian day, it was widely believed that the greater the size of a nation's population, the greater, in theory, its prosperity. Greater numbers would thus, it was assumed, help to alleviate rather than exacerbate the acute difficulties faced by Castile in providing for the population it already had. The population deficit had been noted in 1589 by Giovanni Botero in his *Reason of State*, a work very familiar to Spanish commentators in the early seventeenth century.[8] Now, however, Cellorigo complained that of those who had been spared far too many were reluctant to devote themselves to the vulgar business of working for a living, so incompatible with the obsession with appearances and display that had increasingly come to pass for 'honour' among his contemporaries. 'The wealth that should have enriched us', he wrote, 'has instead brought impoverishment, because it has been used so badly that it has led merchants to give up trading and those who work the land to cease doing so'.[9] Cellorigo saw idle hands everywhere, and would heartily have agreed with the Augustinian priest Pedro de Figueroa, who, re-cycling the old proverb in his 1623 prescription for Spaniards, the *Médico espiritual*, described indolence as 'the mother of all vices'.[10] In such a climate, amid such perceptions of incipient decline, it was little wonder that Spain's gypsies, almost automatically regarded as work-shy idlers wholly dedicated to fraud or theft, came for some to symbolize a moral cancer which, they feared, had begun to eat away at the nation.

Nor is it surprising that in a year of subsistence crisis in Castile like 1585 there should have been yet another petition in the *Cortes* of Madrid requesting action against them, especially since their alleged depredations on those who could least afford it had already elicited complaints from the towns over 30 years earlier.[11] The petition was duly followed in 1586 by yet another royal ordinance, this time bolstering previous legislation against gypsies by adding a requirement that before they trade anything, either at fairs or elsewhere, they must first provide an affidavit signed by a public notary. This document must list their place of permanent residence and their right to reside there (their *vecindad*), together with the horses, mules, donkeys, and any other livestock, clothing or other items they were intending to trade, including any distinguishing marks that might help to identify such items. Should they fail to do so, yet still continue to trade, then the law would simply assume the animals or goods in question to have been stolen and the gypsies would be punished accordingly.[12] Severe restrictions were thus imposed on the kind of economic activity in which gypsies had traditionally engaged for generations and which represented a source of income that they would have found difficult or impossible to replace as an impoverished Castile approached the *fin de siècle*. Such orders merely sharpened the anxieties already experienced by those struggling at the economic margins of society.[13] As the avenues open to gypsies became ever more restricted, it is hardly surprising that some should have opted to take their chances outside the law, especially since the law seemed anyway to be proving difficult to enforce. For one should add that in the text of the 1586 royal ordinance the crown was much more explicit in its condemnation of the continuing and widespread failure to implement previous legislation than in its earlier reiterations thereof, which had typically represented little more than a formulaic reminder to Spaniards of their obligation to uphold the law.

A decade later at the *Cortes* of Madrid of 19 March 1594, Don Jerónimo de Salamanca and Don Martín de Porras, respectively first and second *procuradores* (delegates) for Burgos, together proposed a particularly bloodless piece of social engineering designed to solve Spain's gypsy problem once and for all. The gypsies, they argued, were 'lawless people [. . .] full of vice and without virtue'. None of these vagabonds worked for a living or had a trade; instead, they relied on theft and trickery, deceiving simple folk into believing they could foretell the future by reading palms. Nor did they marry within the Church, simply ignoring the prohibited degrees and neglecting to seek the requisite dispensations. None of them confessed, received the Holy Sacrament, or attended mass. 'Pray God', wrote the *procuradores*, mindful of Castile's continuing tribulations, 'that to have permitted such public sinfulness has not been the cause of part of our punishment'. Their proposal continued as follows:

> It would be of great benefit to root out altogether this word gypsies and ensure that no memory of this sort of people remains hereafter. And it seems that the remedy might be to separate the men from the women and send them to provinces very distant one from the other, preventing them from using either the dress or language of gypsies, and punishing them severely if they leave the villages to which they are assigned, because in this way they would marry people who work on the land and who live as other God-fearing folk do.[14]

Anxious nonetheless not to neglect the devil in the detail, they added that all children under ten years of age would be removed from their parents and installed in orphanages, where they would be instructed in Christian doctrine until the boys were old enough to be taught a trade, and the girls could be put into domestic service.[15] The joint stand taken by the two *procuradores* on this issue was somewhat unusual, given the frequently inimical positions occupied by them at other times, especially when it came to the crown's frequent and increasingly desperate tax-raising initiatives. For while Porras could usually be relied on to back such measures, the same could not be said for the more sceptical Jerónimo de Salamanca. Over the six and a half year period (1592–8) when the *Cortes* were in session, he became the key figure in what was effectively an organized parliamentary opposition to the political interests of the king and his ministers.[16] Fortunately, however, as far as the *procuradores'* joint proposal on gypsies was concerned, wiser counsels were to prevail. It was agreed to defer a vote on the matter until the following Tuesday in order to allow others not present on that occasion to examine the proposal and have their say. What was subsequently agreed on 22 March by a majority vote was that two delegates should be appointed to look into the matter further. These men, Juan Vaca de Herrera (Toledo) and Hernando Arias de Saavedra (Córdoba), would communicate the proposal to 'persons of knowledge and conscience', so that in due course, after a suitable period of consultation, the best course of action might be adopted. This time-honoured delaying manoeuvre did what it was designed to do, effectively pushing the scheme into the long grass, so that little came of it in the short term, at least directly.

The *moriscos* and the gypsies

With Philip III's accession to the throne in 1598, some Spaniards saw an opportunity to press home their growing conviction that the solution to the problem of Spain's *morisco* population must now lie in its total expulsion from the peninsula. Something similar had, after all, already been suggested in 1582. Then, a special *junta* comprising the Duke of Alba, the Count of Chinchón, the jurist Rodrigo Vázquez de Arce, Juan Delgado, Secretary to the Council of War, Juan de Idiáquez, and Fray Diego de Chaves, Philip II's confessor, had after three months of consultation suggested the possible expulsion from Spain of Valencia's *moriscos*, the most numerous and, together with the dispersed Granadines, troublesome group in the peninsula. The reasons then advanced were not just that the *moriscos'* continuing presence challenged religious orthodoxy and public order, but also that their suspect political allegiances might even be turned to tactical advantage by the Turks. However, the practical difficulties involved in implementing the proposal, especially the shortage of manpower, ensured on that occasion that nothing came of it.[17] The hardening of attitudes towards the *moriscos* had first begun to develop in the 1550s. Around that time, increasing frustration at the reluctance of certain elements of the *morisco* population, like those of Granada, to abandon their cultural and linguistic heritage began to evolve into a generalized denunciation of all *moriscos* and a growing conviction that these people could never be brought convincingly to the Christian faith. Even populations which had over many generations assimilated to the point of near invisibility in terms of cultural difference, like the *moriscos* of the Campo de Calatrava,[18] were eventually to suffer as a result of other Spaniards' inability or refusal to acknowledge their long-standing naturalization to Old Christian culture. In the Spain of Philip III there developed an even more virulent rhetoric of demonization, as anti-integrationists like Fray Blas Verdú and Damián de Fonseca argued in essence that those who had once followed Islam, and indeed their descendants, were fundamentally and irredeemably different. Much though they might nominally accept conversion, such people, they argued, could never be considered true Catholics.[19] For men of such persuasion, the rebellion in the Alpujarras in 1568 had merely provided proof for prejudice, marking out all *moriscos* as potential fifth-columnists. The forcible dispersal across Spain thereafter of up to 80,000 unassimilated Granadine *moriscos*, while diluting one problem, nevertheless created another, as communities which in many cases had never known *morisco* neighbours were now faced with what to many seemed a quite alien presence in their midst.[20] This, moreover, was still Counter-Reformation Spain, whose messianic sense of its imperial duty, whose ruling sense of itself, was thoroughly invested in a mission to defend the faith and convert the unbeliever far beyond its own borders. How, then, could it continue to tolerate the presence within those borders of a people who, some argued, could never be relied upon sincerely to embrace the faith? 'It is very strange', wrote Pedro de Valencia, 'that it should be Spain, which straddles sea and land, and which goes to the ends of the earth, east and west, to Chile, China and Japan, to convert the infidel [. . .] that fails to ensure the conversion and confirmation in the faith of these people it has at home'.[21]

Yet Valencia took a more moderate line than some others. Indeed he rejected expulsion as a solution, just as González de Cellorigo had done six years earlier, notwithstanding the Moriscos' suspect loyalties and fears that their population growth rate was outstripping that of Spain's Old Christians.[22] 'Among such great numbers of people', Valencia suggested, 'however misguided the community as a whole, it may be that there are many who are not only innocent of heresy and disloyalty to the king, but who are also good Christians and even saints'.[23] He opted instead for a more thinly spread dispersal of the *morisco* population across the entire peninsula. The evident failure of a similar policy over 30 years earlier after the second rebellion in the Alpujarras had, he argued, been due to the fact that too many *moriscos* had been allowed to remain together and form ghettos in the villages to which they were sent.[24] Still, though, hardliners convinced by the evangelical argument continued to argue for expulsion, with rumoured *morisco* treachery of one sort or another helping to ensure that the issue remained alive. On 14 May 1605, for example, the historian and courtier Luis Cabrera de Córdoba reported that many *moriscos* had been imprisoned in Valencia as rumours flew that they had requested English help to support a planned rising in the city.[25] And on 11 April 1609, just two days after considerations of political expediency finally persuaded the crown that the expulsions should indeed go ahead, he reported rumours that 'certain *moriscos* had crossed to Africa with an embassy from their fellows to Muley Cidán, offering him 60,000 armed men in Spain and a great quantity of money'.[26] As this would have represented rather more than 40 per cent of all of Spain's imperial forces at the time,[27] the figure illustrates nicely the heady mix of paranoia and alarmist propaganda out of which, on the whole, it was conjured.

Meanwhile, a similarly condemnatory rhetoric was routinely coming to be applied to the gypsies, not least by those who hoped that it might now be possible to expel them on the coat-tails of the *moriscos*. Increasing, too, were reports of others joining up with, or simply masquerading as gypsies. On 12 April 1603, the *Cortes* meeting at Valladolid, having heard a submission on the gypsies' continuing 'excesses' in Castile, had asked the *procuradores* Don Luis de Guzmán and Don Gonzalo de Cáceres to prepare a memorandum for Philip III requesting action and outlining the remedial measures that might be adopted.[28] Their report was discussed by the *Cortes* on 7 July. It noted the failure of previous legislation 'which forbids both those who falsely claim to be gypsies, as well as those who actually are, to live or speak as such'. Without expanding on the reasons for this failure, it went on to recommend expulsion, adding optimistically, 'because apart from ridding us of the abuses of the gypsies, many of those who make use of the name for their own wicked purposes will refrain from doing so in order not to have to leave their homeland'.[29] The report is interesting because it continues to assume an essential difference between 'true' and 'false' gypsies, an increasingly problematic distinction which, within two decades, would be manipulated by the crown to propose a 'solution' to the gypsy problem which, while politically expedient, would in fact amount to little more than a fudge. Meanwhile, however, the pressure for action continued to build. At the *Cortes* held in Madrid on 12 August 1607, the *procurador* Don Jerónimo de Aguayo Manrique raised concerns about the theft of horses, mares, and mules, all vital to the rural economy, by people who, having stolen them, would take them to other villages in other areas in order to sell them. He did not mention gypsies specifically, though the term he chose, *cuatreros* (horse or cattle thieves), was counted a virtual synonym by many;[30] and since the offences described matched precisely the *modus operandi* of which gypsies routinely stood accused, it is at least likely that many of his fellow delegates would have understood him that way.[31] A year and a half later, Don Alonso de Ulloa proposed with evident rhetorical exaggeration in the *Cortes* that both tillage and animal husbandry in Spain would benefit greatly if the gypsies were forced to take up fixed residence in certain villages which would be assigned to them. There, he proposed, they would be required to learn trades and would on no account be permitted to leave. A roll would be taken and checked twice yearly to ensure compliance and the civil and ecclesiastical authorities would investigate the gypsies' marital status and ensure that they confessed, received the sacraments, and baptized their children. He further proposed that they should be forbidden to trade, either directly or via intermediaries, in horses, mules or donkeys, or even to ride such animals. Any found in their possession should be regarded as stolen, which, he argued, they undoubtedly would be, for how else could 'people who neither breed nor purchase them' bring such large numbers of these animals to the fairs where they were traded? This, he noted, was very damaging to poor country people, who, reluctant to put their stock out to graze for fear of theft, were forced to bring their animals in and provide them at great expense with feed.[32]

Three months later, on 14 May, and then again on 3 November, he and Don Pedro de Vesga were asked by the *Cortes* to prepare recommendations as to how best the problem might be addressed.[33] Their report was finally presented to the *Cortes* a year later. After the now formulaic prefatory remarks about the failures of previous legislation and the irreligion and scandalous lives of the gypsies, it once again cited the damage done to agriculture and livestock as a result of their illicit activities. Again it drew attention to the plight of wretchedly poor country dwellers who lacked the resources either to feed stock brought in as a protection against theft by gypsies, or, indeed, to replace animals lost to starvation as a result. For such people, the loss of horses or mules to theft by gypsies effectively meant ruin. Moreover, they claimed, when herdsmen or shepherds grazed their stock on remote pastures or in the mountains, the gypsies would 'stalk them like wolves' and had been responsible for the deaths of many such men, leaving the animals in their charge abandoned and far from home.[34] In an ominous sign of the times, the report also noted of the gypsies that 'they are such bad people that they are incomparably worse than the *moriscos*, because while they resemble the latter in not being Christians, they eclipse them as thieves'. It therefore demanded that 'a way should be found to rid these kingdoms of the gypsy name and language' and recommended expulsion or death for gypsies who refused to accept sedentarization.[35]

By the end of the first decade of the seventeenth century, the official view of Spain's gypsies, of whether, as we might put it nowadays, they should be defined in behavioural rather than racial terms, had already begun to change. Others from what the social historian Antonio Domínguez Ortiz described as 'the oppressed classes of society – fugitive slaves, *moriscos*, Christians wanted by the law, criminals, adventurers and vagabonds' – had long been suspected, not without a touch of paranoia, of having joined up with gypsy groups.[36] He might have added runaway soldiers to the list. In 1643, the Council of Castile noted of two bandit gangs operating in La Rioja and led by the gypsies

Matías and Chaparro, respectively, that they were particularly dangerous 'because they offer refuge and asylum to fugitive soldiers from the Aragonese army'.[37] An interesting later example from 1680 is that of Francisco de la Puente Montecillo Miranda, a deserter who had escaped when the ship transporting him to prison in North Africa was forced by a storm to return to Cartagena. Subsequently gaoled in Valladolid because, the accusation went, 'he had gone around with gypsies and other undesirables, carrying pistols and other arms, and robbing and mistreating the travellers they encountered', he was ordered to be returned to Madrid and thence to Oran, the destination originally intended for him.[38] As far as *moriscos* were concerned, while they had long been involved in banditry in the south and south-east,[39] there were now reports that both they and gypsies were active as bandits in central and western Castile, too. In 1596, the abbot of the Cistercian monastery of Valparaíso in the province of Zamora, had written to the Count of Gondomar, at that time responsible for the military command of the Portuguese frontier and Galician coastline, that action was in hand to control the bands of *moriscos* and gypsies who were at that time engaged in such activities between Salamanca and Ciudad Rodrigo.[40] Such sporadic action did little to control the problem, however. An unsigned document, probably written in 1612, later lamented the depredations of gypsy bandits in villages near Sepúlveda, urging the king to command 'that they leave the kingdom, just as the *moriscos* are leaving', and adding for good measure that some thought that many of those going about as gypsies were in fact *moriscos*.[41] Certainly, some Granadine *moriscos*, forcibly resettled across western Spain after the second rebellion of the Alpujarras, had now chosen to abandon communities where, having endured great hardship during the dispersal itself, they had then found on arrival that they were anything but welcome.[42] Culturally and even linguistically unassimilated to the Old Christian majority, proud of their own traditions, lacking work or other means of sustenance, and hardly well placed to elicit much sympathy as mendicant vagrants, banditry must have seemed to some virtually the only option left.[43] Fiction served further to embed such claims in the popular consciousness, as in his widely read pseudo-autobiographical novel, *Vida del escudero Marcos de Obregón* (1618), Vicente Espinel's hero recalled 'the murders committed on the roads in those days by gypsies and *moriscos*'.[44]

As to whether gypsies and *moriscos* did in fact co-operate in these activities, that remains a tantalizingly open question. It is perfectly possible that a motley collection of non-gypsy deserters, slaves, and vagabonds sometimes saw the advantages of allying themselves temporarily with gypsy groups here and there, as Domínguez Ortiz suggested. But it remains to be proven that among the gypsies' occasional criminal confederates were to be found *moriscos*. It would not be at all surprising, however, if future research in local or family archives were to indicate that various forms of co-operation between gypsies and *moriscos* did in fact occur here and there. It has already been suggested, for example, that some of those 'grecianos' (Greeks) who applied to the town of Lorca in 1567 for the right to reside there as blacksmiths may in fact have had *morisco* blood. One, for example, was Pedro Melchor de Hacis, who, allowing for the vagaries of sixteenth-century Spanish orthography, shared his surname with the *moriscos* Diego and Gaspar de Acis, at that time resident in Sorbas 50 km to the south.[45] As Julio Caro Baroja observed, gypsies commonly augment their numbers in this way, as do certain peoples of North Africa and the Sahara, in order to maintain the minimum population density necessary for subsistence.[46] More generally, though, relations between gypsies and *moriscos* were probably little different from those existing between gypsies and Old Christians. In 1533, for example, the Archbishop of Granada wrote to complain to Charles V that 'many gypsies visit the *moriscos* and show them things involving sorcery and soothsaying and superstition, and they steal clothing from their homes and animals from their fields, and the *moriscos* complain and are scandalized to see that such things are permitted among Christians'.[47]

From 1609 to 1614, the attentions of the authorities were focused primarily on the expulsions of the *moriscos*. The first phase, the removal of those of the Valencia region, had been agreed in January 1609 by the Council of State. The proposal was approved by Philip III on 9 April, a date almost certainly chosen as a populist, face-saving measure calculated to shift the short-term domestic focus away from the humiliating Truce of Antwerp, signed on the very same day, and instead towards what it was hoped would instead be regarded by many Spaniards as a symbolic 'victory'. For might not these expulsions be represented at home as a reassuring and timely vindication of the much-prized reputation that now saw itself challenged on the northern European stage? This was a nation that still looked to the medieval figure of the Christian knight as its ideal of manly perfection, while for some Castilians in particular the sense of what it was to be a 'true', Old Christian Spaniard had since the late 1540s begun increasingly to turn on notions of blood and lineage.[48] Many Spaniards were thus predisposed to regard this final purging of the Moor as the welcome culmination of a great historical project, a 'success' that had been even longer in the making than the failure represented by what was effectively capitulation to the Dutch rebels. Spanish foreign policy in Europe may now have moved definitively towards retrenchment, but, as John Lynch put it, 'in Spain at least they were still masters and here they could find moral compensation for their defeat abroad'.[49] Philip III's favourite or *valido*, the Duke of Lerma, offered a similar interpretation of events eight years later when he told the Council of State that the king had resolved to announce the expulsion of the *moriscos* on that day precisely in order to mitigate the effects of domestic opposition to Spain's accommodation with the Dutch.[50]

Yet Lerma had not forgotten the gypsies. Hoping, no doubt, to extract further propaganda value from the policy of expulsion as the removal of *moriscos* from other areas went ahead, he now ordered the Council of State in August 1610 to explore the possibility of expelling them, too. It was, it is true, suspected that their removal would require a rather greater effort than had thus far proved necessary with the *moriscos*, but the idea was that this task would be entrusted to the Count of Salazar, who had already been charged with overall responsibility for the expulsions already under way:

> Your Majesty has been given to understand that there are a great many gypsies in Spain, and especially here in Castile. And since these are people who live without faith or the sacraments and whose only business is theft, he is resolved that they should be expelled from Spain; and he orders the *Sala de gobierno* to discuss how this might be accomplished and advise him of the outcome and of whether this should be entrusted to the Count of Salazar, so that he might expel them as he is doing with the *moriscos*, although greater rigour will be required in the case of the gypsies because they are an incorrigible people and live out in the countryside.[51]

At the *Cortes* of Madrid of 24 December 1610, the gypsy question was raised yet again. Delegates accused them of both theft and murder, of stealing from the poor, of living in sin and of being Christians only in name. They recommended that those refusing to settle in towns of more than 1000 households should be expelled from Spain and forbidden to return on pain of death. Why larger villages and towns were regarded as suitable was not recorded, though the reasons must have been similar to those given in a *consulta* of 1749, which noted of a similar provision of 1746 that it was intended to ensure 'that the justices have sufficient force available to correct their ways and that they [the gypsies] are able to find work and earn a living'.[52] The 1610 *Cortes* also recommended that not only should the gypsies' dress, language, and way of life be prohibited, but even the very word *gitano*, adding by way of justification the telling phrase, 'for they are not so by birth' ('pues no lo son de nación'). Gypsies should now, they proposed, be prevented on pain of death from dealing in livestock at all, or in 'other similar things which they are accustomed to buy and sell', while severe penalties should be reserved for those justices who neglected to enforce the law.[53]

Finally, on 23 July 1611, The Council of State made a recommendation to the king that the expulsion of the gypsies should in principle go ahead, though only after the last *moriscos* had departed the region of Murcia.[54] It argued that just as had happened in the case of the *moriscos*, it alone should be charged with responsibility for the matter, since it was assumed that the involvement of other, local tribunals would merely be a recipe for failure: 'Experience suggests that it is advisable for the public good to expel them from these kingdoms, and that this be done through this Council, because otherwise it will not be put into effect.' A second letter dated 28 August reiterates the point: 'the Council puts it to your Majesty that the fact that the expulsion of the *moriscos* has been accomplished so effectively is due to it having been channelled through this Council, and not through other courts, and so it should be with the expulsion of the gypsies'.[55] While the Council noted that it was well aware of the problems caused by the gypsies, it nevertheless argued that the latter could at least be regarded as more Christian than the *moriscos*, 'especially those of Valencia and Hornachos',[56] and should therefore 'be conducted to Christian lands, and not permitted to go to those of infidels'.[57] Where exactly those who might be charged with carrying out the expulsions were to deposit their charges was, unsurprisingly, not specified.

Nor was it altogether clear that Spain could afford further depletion of its population, even if those to be expelled were gypsies. Concerns had already been expressed about the likely impact of the removal of *morisco* populations from a number of areas where their labour was essential to agricultural production. Pedro de Valencia, for example, who like many others opposed expulsion, had noted in 1606 that 'to deprive the King and Kingdom of so many vassal households at a time when Spain is so short of people is no small matter', though he was careful also to rehearse the opposing, characteristically pathological argument, noting that such losses could nevertheless 'even be of benefit, as when a gangrenous foot, hand or other limb is amputated for the health of the whole body'.[58] In a Castile that was struggling to feed its own population, the loss of *morisco* agricultural labourers would inevitably have economic repercussions, albeit not perhaps on the scale of those that followed the flight of capital with the expulsion of the Jews in 1492; but their loss would still be felt, and not only in the areas most seriously affected, like Valencia and Aragon, but also by the royal exchequer, which would surely see tax revenues reduced. Nor would replacing this lost workforce be easy, especially during a period when Castile's population, always low in density at fewer than 20 per square kilometre compared to France, Italy, and the coastal regions of the peninsula, was anyway in decline, experiencing a 25 per cent fall between 1580 and 1646. Indeed, shortage of manpower had by now come to be regarded as a fundamental structural problem.[59] In a *consulta* dated 30 January 1610 the Council of State discussed the available options for bringing in foreigners to replace the expelled *moriscos*. Among them was a rather fanciful suggestion advanced by the Count of Castro that Greeks from the Morea or other areas under Turkish occupation, might be invited to fill the breach. Others disagreed, however, observing that the recognized agricultural skills and industry of the inhabitants of Lombardy, Bavaria or Mallorca would be more useful. The *comendador mayor* of León, Don Juan de Idiáquez, noted 'that in all these kingdoms there is a great need of people, and of those who are here, many are idlers', and he added once again that the principal need was for people to work the land. He thought, however, that what was required first, before any decision could be taken, was full consultation with landowners about precisely what their needs were likely to be. The Council was persuaded by this argument and the king duly replied that he would look into the matter.[60] His reaction now to the proposed expulsion of the gypsies must be read against this background. In a brief response to the Council, dated 23 July 1611, the same day it had written to him, Philip III asked how many gypsies would be involved and whether it might not be possible to 'extract some benefit from them and correct their despicable ways' by putting them to work as agricultural labourers.[61] The Council's reply has not survived, though any estimate by it of gypsy numbers would inevitably have been a speculative affair, not least because the very term *gitano* was now increasingly being used in court circles to denote a behaviourally rather than racially defined group. It was anyway not until 1695 that the first attempt to compile an official census of Spain's gypsies was made, though even this seems to have been lost, if, that is, it was ever completed.[62] The eventual outcome of these exchanges between Philip and his Council of State was a decree of 5 October 1611 which now specified the precise nature of the 'recognized occupations' that gypsies must take up. Henceforth, the phrase was to be understood to refer to 'work on the land, and nothing else'.[63] It was not without local precedent. Two years earlier, on 13 August 1609, the Council of Castile had responded to a request the previous day from the *Sala de alcaldes de casa y corte* and ordered all gypsies, male and female, to leave Madrid, take up fixed residence elsewhere, and devote themselves only to agricultural labour.[64] As far as demands for their complete removal from Spain were concerned, however, by the time of the last expulsions of the *moriscos* in 1614, the argument made by some that Spain could ill afford such population losses could no longer be ignored, and would in due course be invoked to help shape new anti-gypsy legislation. For the moment, however, the potential internal propaganda value of another announcement of expulsion represented too attractive a prospect to abandon, especially given the continuing chorus of calls for definitive action against the gypsies. Those charged with responsibility for responding to such calls would in due course adopt as an expedient an idea that had already been voiced in the *Cortes*. But almost a decade was to pass, amid continuing complaints from the *Cortes* and others, before the legislative spotlight really turned once again to what it was hoped would be a satisfactory solution to the gypsy question.

5

Representations

The 1619 *consulta*, the *arbitristas*, and the gypsies

On 4 October 1618, Philip III's favourite, Francisco Gómez de Sandoval y Rojas, Duke of Lerma, a man widely regarded as responsible for the corruption, nepotism and venality of the preceding years, was finally forced from power, though not before he had procured for himself a cardinal's hat.[1] He was removed in the end by a king who, unwilling to devote himself, and anyway unsuited to affairs of state, had for years depended instead on Lerma, having in 1612 effectively delegated to him wholesale the authority to govern Spain. Now, though, the monarch had become disillusioned with his *valido*.[2] The palace coup, engineered by an opposing faction that included the king's confessor, Fray Luis de Aliaga, and even Lerma's own son and immediate successor, the Duke of Uceda, did little to improve things in the short term. But the mere fact that things had finally changed at least allowed for some freshening of the political climate. As Lerma's grip on power loosened, and in a renewed and increasingly febrile atmosphere of political and economic crisis and growing recognition of the need for further, radical change, political debate in all quarters intensified. In 1616, in his first *consulta* for Philip III, the newly appointed President of the Council of Castile, Don Fernando de Acevedo y González Muñoz, a man of considerable rectitude, reported to the king on the depressing state of the realm as it appeared to him:

> I find, Sir, the Kingdom needful of justice and finance; your Majesty poor while many are made rich by their property; virtue, oppressed; nobility, forgotten; vileness, exalted; foolishness, esteemed; letters, neglected; the colleges unrewarding of virtue and letters, purity of

lineage and blood; our public offices occupied by those whose trade is bribery, some of whom are married to ladies from the households of *validos*, others to the daughters of physicians. The judge who dispenses justice and is honest and of pure blood I find to be downtrodden and poor; cupidity is prized; the churches are given over to worldliness; those of us who look to the common good are hated...[3]

Before his departure, Lerma, under intense pressure to act, had on 6 June 1618 finally created a special *junta de reformación* and instructed the Council of Castile to produce for the king a *consulta* indicating how best the dire problems confronting the nation might be remedied. For three decades Castile had seen serious crises affect both its population and its productivity, as well as a significant decline in silver remittances to the crown from the Indies – from 2 million ducats a year at the end of the sixteenth century to half that by 1619.[4] The report was duly prepared by a member of the Council, Don Diego de Corral y Arellano, and submitted on 1 February the following year. Awkwardly reiterative in structure, and disappointingly unoriginal for the most part, it nevertheless signalled a welcome official acknowledgement that reform was overdue, identifying seven areas that must be addressed if things were to improve. Of paramount importance was the fiscal system, which, it suggested, bore down far too heavily on Castile's rural poor, and which had led to serious depopulation of large tracts of potentially productive countryside. Instead, it argued, incentives should be provided to encourage a much-needed return to the land.[5] Part of the solution might be found by spreading the fiscal burden beyond a downtrodden and exhausted Castile to include 'the other Kingdoms and Provinces subject to your Majesty which do not participate in these taxes', but which 'are very populous, very rich, and where life is undemanding, even where the soil is poor and unable to provide as ours can'.[6] The *consulta* also took aim at the presence in the capital of so many foreign merchants, especially the Genoese, whose business activities it deemed prejudicial to the national interest. There was rather more to this than economic protectionism. Indeed, a prickly national pride bordering at times on xenophobia informed much Castilian political and economic writing of the day. Sancho de Moncada, for example, observed in that same year that 'it is an affront to Spain that its king should need foreigners, just as it would be to an honourable son to see his father reduced to begging'.[7] The *consulta* went on to cite excessive expenditure on luxury foreign imports, and proposed the introduction of sumptuary legislation, a measure designed in effect sharply to curtail increasingly lavish spending at court (the royal households' staff numbers had been allowed to double since Philip III's accession to the throne).[8] Finally, further growth of the religious orders, their ranks allegedly swollen by those joining them solely in order to escape grinding poverty, should be halted, and the 100 receivers appointed in Madrid in 1613 to compound the misery of those lapsing into bankruptcy should now be paid off.

Most of what the *consulta* contained had already been proposed by others. Indeed, in the later decades of the sixteenth and throughout most of the seventeenth century, Castile saw a veritable flood of pamphlets and treatises offering unsolicited and for the most part unoriginal advice to the king, his advisers, or occasionally the *Cortes*. The latter complained about the practice twice, in 1588 and again on 1 February 1618, when Don Luis de Castilla reminded his fellow *procuradores* that the *Cortes* had expressed its concern two decades earlier about the excessive attention paid by some to such suggested remedies.[9] It is in some of these tracts, unlike the 1619 *consulta*, that one finds references to Spain's gypsies, and, indeed, to the expulsions of the *moriscos*, both topics on which the *consulta* itself is deafeningly silent. Their authors, men of widely differing backgrounds, some of them intent primarily on self-promotion,[10] were drawn from the ranks of churchmen, scholars, soldiers, and officials of every stripe. They were known collectively as *arbitristas*, a term approximately equivalent in its distinctly pejorative contemporary connotations, to the 'projectors' of late seventeenth-century England. The *arbitrios* (projects or expedients) they proposed ranged from the frankly eccentric to others which, on the whole, were eminently sensible and reasonably well-informed. But contributions of the latter type failed to prevent the *arbitristas* in general quickly becoming the target of mockery by writers like Quevedo – hardly a shrinking violet himself when it came to venturing a political opinion – and Luis Vélez de Guevara, who called them 'the most pernicious madmen in the republic'.[11] Cervantes, too, took aim at them, despite his protest in the *Viaje del Parnaso* that 'my humble pen never flew through the satiric region, the reward for whose vileness is infamy and disgrace'.[12] As Part II of *Don Quixote* opens, his now apparently sane hero, quizzed by the barber as to what *arbitrio* he would offer the king, immediately takes leave of his senses again as he asserts that half a dozen knights errant would suffice to see off the threatening hordes of the Turk.[13] The *arbitristas*, like other writers of their day, were accustomed to cite classical and biblical sources to lend their work authority, but also relied heavily, and often uncritically, on borrowings from others, as well, sometimes, as on mere hearsay. Among those who promoted Spain's gypsies to the dimensions of a national problem was Francisco Fernández Navarrete. Adding his own concerns about gypsies, he glossed the 1619 *consulta* in his influential *Conservación de monarquías y discursos políticos* (1626), and he certainly knew the anti-gypsy diatribe of the Franciscan Melchor de Huélamo, citing it with evident approval in his seventh discourse.[14] So, too, did Juan de Quiñones in his rather later (1631) *Discurso contra los gitanos*. Sancho de Moncada, one of the more eminent of the *arbitristas* as professor of theology at the university of Toledo, drew extensively in his *Restauración política de España* (1619) on the work of his fellow churchman of that city, Pedro Salazar de Mendoza, who a year earlier had published his *Memorial de el hecho de los gitanos*, a work also mentioned by Navarrete.[15] And Salazar de Mendoza had himself drawn much of his material from a wide range of writings on gypsies from elsewhere in Europe, including two influential works from the first half of the sixteenth century, Albert Krantz's *Saxonia* and Sebastian Münster's *Cosmographia universalis*,[16] as well as others by Spanish authors. These included Francisco Fernández de Córdoba's *Didascalia multiplex* and Martín del Río's *Disquisitionum magicarum libri sex*.[17] The resulting eclectic but indiscriminate mix was sufficient to ensure that the *arbitristas'* views nourished, reinforced, and served further to disseminate a largely unexamined and, for the most part, utterly stereotypical view of the gypsies, as well as lending a spurious respectability to certain myths already in circulation. If one takes just one of their sources, in his *Libro primero de la vida y milagros del glorioso Confessor Sant Ginés de la Xara* (*Book One of the Life and Miracles of the Glorious Confessor Saint Ginés de la Jara*), the aforementioned Fray Melchor de Huélamo reported that there was nothing to be gained from whipping people like gypsies, since they already 'have calluses on their backs and a sense of shame three inches thick with mould'. Naturally, therefore, they regarded such punishments with contempt.[18] Still less were they deterred by sentences of internal exile (a sanction frequently invoked by the Inquisition in cases involving gypsies, if only in order to distance them temporarily from those gullible enough to have fallen for their spells, love potions, and other deceptions). Huélamo had also 'heard it said' that gypsy men exchanged their women on a whim, or even for money; and, ever keen to associate them with the Muslim threat, he added that in his opinion they must for that purpose possess 'some letter from the Great Turk, or from the Caliph of Baghdad', payment, he felt sure, for some dangerous display of aerial acrobatics or, even worse, a dance. His diatribe is headed 'the detestable and infamous *zarabanda*', a notoriously salacious dance often performed by gypsy girls and frequently condemned by seventeenth-century Spanish moralists.[19]

But it was to the question of expulsion that Salazar de Mendoza, Sancho de Moncada, and Fernández Navarrete turned their attentions. Navarrete considered the main cause of Spain's depopulation to have been the 'many and numerous expulsions of Moors and Jews, enemies of our holy Catholic faith'. But he nevertheless argued, drawing on contemporary discourses of racial purity and contagion, that Spain's rulers had always preferred to forego the advantages of a large population 'rather than consent to the presence in the mystical body of their monarchy of bad humours which, contagious as they are, could corrupt its good blood'. To be fair to Navarrete, he does go on to suggest that had it been possible to admit these people to honours like others 'before they reached a state of despair', it might also have been possible to rehabilitate them. Nonetheless, even allowing for the element of polemicist exaggeration that typifies much *arbitrista* writing, the wildly inaccurate figures he offers of three million Jews and two million Moors suggest just how large these demonized races could loom – or be made to loom – in the minds of Spaniards of the day. After lauding Spain's monarchs for their 'extirpation of false sects and heresies' and for 'cleansing [. . .] their kingdoms of these evil humours', he now turned to the question of what should be done about the gypsies 'who deceive not only ignorant and simple people, but also those who fancy themselves intelligent' and 'whose principal occupation it is to be common thieves, tricksters, and enchanters'. Their expulsion, he noted, had often been desired but never successfully put into effect.[20]

Pedro Salazar de Mendoza, genealogist and Canon-confessor at Toledo cathedral, was the only one of the three to devote his *arbitrio* exclusively to 'the gypsy question' of his title. He immediately announces his intention, which is 'to inform the King our lord of how necessary it is both for the service of God and the good of these Kingdoms to expel them from Spain'. Given his influence on Sancho de Moncada and others, it is worth devoting some attention to this work. An early passage will serve to give the reader some flavour of the exotic mix of fact, hearsay, exaggeration and myth that constitutes Salazar's treatise:

They [the gypsies] have become much worse, and have been encouraged to commit even more atrocious crimes as a result of the leniency and mercy with which they have been treated. This year they have been going around in troops of more than eight hundred between Castile and Aragon, stealing from those lands and committing other wicked offences which the Council has tried to punish. Just now, not long before your Majesty arrived at San Lorenzo, some of them were active in highway robbery around Valdemorillo [a village not far from San Lorenzo del Escorial], where they kept their womenfolk to conceal their activities. They killed a man and cut off his head between Galapagar and La Torre. Having inflicted many wounds on him, they stripped a hermit [the keeper of a shrine] naked on his way from Navalgamella to Valdemorillo.[21]

This, needless to say, smacks of the bogey-man, and is reminiscent of other, even more obviously demonizing claims circulating at around that time as the scapegoating of gypsies gathered pace. One such appeared in an anonymous verse of 1617 whose grisly title claimed that gypsies in the Sierra Morena had killed a member of a religious order before roasting and eating him, one of their women devouring his cooked head.[22] Once again, the profession of the alleged victim is designed to lend an even more acute sense of desecration to the violent breaking of taboos invoked (and doubtless invented) here to dramatize and impress upon the reader the author's spluttering moral indignation at the actual practices – lip-service to the faith, sorcery, banditry, theft of livestock, and so on – of which the gypsies had routinely been accused down the years. Nor should it be thought that this was a particularly eccentric or macabre example of megaphone anti-gypsy prejudice. Juan de Quiñones, as an *alcalde de casa y corte* one of the men responsible to the Council of Castile for the maintenance of law and order in and around the capital, had also read his Huélamo, Salazar de Mendoza, and Moncada. Some years later, almost as if determined to outdo his literary mentors, he recounted various examples of gypsy anthropophagy which, he claimed, had been reported to him. Once again, a selection from his *Discurso contra los gitanos* (1631) will suffice to illustrate the ill-disguised relish with which he took up the task:

And in 1629, while Don Martín Fajardo, a judge then prosecuting gypsies in Jaraicejo, was torturing four of them, they confessed to having killed and eaten a Franciscan monk on the Monte de las Gamas in the jurisdiction of Trujillo. And they had done the same thing to a gypsy woman and a female pilgrim. The mayor of Montijo told the said Martín Fajardo that as one of the inhabitants of the town was searching the countryside for a lost mare, he entered a ruined house in the village of Arroyo del Puerco to look for her and saw there some gypsies who were roasting part of a human being. He also says that a shepherd from Guadix, lost in the Sierra de Gadol, saw a light, and, assuming it to be shepherds, went towards it only to find a troop of gypsies roasting half a man while the other half hung on a cork oak. And when they saw him they told him to come and sit in the light of the fire and dine with them, and commented among themselves, 'this one's a plump one'. Feigning a wish to sleep, he raced down the mountainside and escaped from their clutches.[23]

Not yet content that his list of atrocities was sufficiently gruesome and shocking, Quiñones went on to claim finally that gypsies had killed and eaten a boy in the Sierra Nevada. That they counted young children among their victims was another commonplace of such diatribes. After a matter-of-fact claim that 'there is hardly a village in Spain, however small, where they have not perpetrated some great injury', Salazar de Mendoza had, for example, lamented the 'innumerable little children they have carried off to Barbary to sell', an accusation duly echoed a year later by Sancho de Moncada.[24] Both authors must have been aware that such horrific stories would send an especially cold shudder through Spanish readers mindful of the frightening scale of abductions of their countrymen and women by Barbary corsairs in the south, estimated by one historian to have exceeded 15,000 in the seventeenth century alone.[25]

The remainder of Salazar de Mendoza's text consists largely of second-hand observations or accusations directed against the gypsies: they are governed by a count or duke, who is always better dressed than the rest and who sends the men out to steal by night and the women by day, dividing up the spoils thereafter (this according to Sebastian Münster); it is to him that they go to resolve their differences, even when they are in villages where there are justices; they sell horses at knock-down prices, travelling to fairs to sell or exchange their stolen goods; the men travel on foot, while the women and children ride on donkeys along with their possessions; they go from province to province, rarely returning to the same place for many years; they speak many languages (an old notion in this instance probably derived from Martín del Río's *Disquisitionum magicarum*);[26] they are without religion, merely feigning acceptance of the beliefs of those in whose territories they happen to be; and the women are even worse than the men, because they go from door to door telling fortunes and entering people's homes; they teach their children the arts of theft and how, if caught red-handed, they should lay the blame on someone who cannot legally be sent to the galleys; gypsy men sometimes purchase women from their husbands; they live in caves or old, ruinous dwellings on the outskirts of inhabited places, and so on. Without directly acknowledging his source, in this case Francisco

Fernández de Córdoba's *Didascalia multiplex*,[27] he also re-cycles, as did Moncada and Quiñones in turn, the startling claim made in that work that gypsies had stormed the town of Logroño during the plague year of 1599, though no reliable evidence of such an event has ever come to light subsequently.[28]

Interestingly, Salazar refers to performances by gypsies designed to keep the attention of local people while their confederates set about burgling their homes:

> They always find ways to commit their crimes, especially through the use of dances on religious holidays, when people are more devout and their guard is lowered. There they pretend to be Apostles, here the Magi, and elsewhere the Seven Princes of Lara,[29] all of it to divert attention and entertain while they carry out their robberies.[30]

A little later, he cites one unnamed village where, by packing the residents into the church from which they had removed all the pews so that more people might enter in order to witness a promised Holy Thursday procession of penitents, the gypsies instead robbed them. He also claimed that gypsies pretended on another occasion to be arranging to put on a play (*una comedia*) in a village square, collecting money for that purpose in advance. After an announcement that a notable male dancer (*danzarín*) had been delayed and would instead arrive the following day, the performance was duly 'postponed', only to see the gypsies decamp with the money at midnight.[31]

It is impossible to know how much truth there was to such colourful claims. Certainly, it would not be surprising to discover in a polemical text of this nature that they were based on little more than rumour, probably much spiced in transmission; or they may simply have been invented in order to lend a spurious credibility to Salazar's generic complaints about gypsies; such 'editorial' meddling was not uncommon in the period, and Salazar is, after all, silent on when or where these incidents were supposed to have taken place. On the other hand, it is known that from the second half of the sixteenth-century plays were performed not just by professional actors in the urban public theatres, but also in rural villages, where *comedias*, including 'lewd and salacious plays' ('farsas desonestas y livianas'), which were not written down, were performed by motley groups of travelling players, with the villagers themselves sometimes taking roles.[32] It seems perfectly reasonable to suppose that gypsies, too, given their tradition of performance and their much-lauded skills as musicians and acrobats, may have involved themselves in such activities, though further evidence will have to emerge before it can be confirmed that this was indeed the case. Certainly, Cervantes wrote in *La gitanilla* that 'there was not a town, village or hamlet where they [the gypsies] would not be called to enliven local religious festivals or other private celebrations' and later has a soldier speak of them 'dancing from village to village'.[33] Whilst literary sources must of course be treated with due wariness and circumspection, as must the claims of the *arbitristas*, it seems highly unlikely here that Cervantes would have incorporated such a detail in his tale if it had no basis whatsoever in his extensive first-hand experience of rural Spain south of the Tagus. And it is known that gypsies regularly danced, sang and tumbled in Corpus Christi processions across Spain, as in Guadalajara in 1488, Córdoba in 1604 (when *morisco* and Portuguese dances were also performed), Alcalá la Real in 1531, Granada in 1531, 1607, and 1618, Cádiz in 1664, the dance involving 'nine persons [gypsy women] each with a tambour', Rute (Andalusia) in 1669 'to adorn' the festivities, and, not least, Jaén.[34] There the gypsies were a regular feature of the feast of the Corpus, contracted to dance year after year throughout the seventeenth century and probably long before that. The procedure was similar every year. A contract would be drawn up between the city authorities and one or two gypsy impresarios, typically *vecinos* of the San Ildefonso or San Lorenzo quarters. Prominent among these was one Pascual Mediano, himself a dancer, who performed on repeated occasions not only in the Corpus processions, but even in Jaén Cathedral before the high altar. The contract would stipulate the exact number of gypsy dancers, male and female, required, as well as tumblers and accompanying singers and musicians, whose instruments included tambourines and, just occasionally, guitars. The women were to appear suitably decked out for the occasion, dressed 'gypsy style with our farthingales' ('a lo gitano con nuestros guardainfantes'), as the contract for eight female dancers and one male agreed on 17 May 1645 by the gypsies Sebastián Gutiérrez and his wife María de Vargas put it. On that occasion, their payment consisted of 27 ducats, a sheep, an *arroba* (16.4 litres) of wine, and one and a half bushels of wheat. An agreement of 6 May 1604 noted that the gypsies were to provide an advance demonstration of their skills to the authorities on Trinity Sunday, 'as is the custom'. That such contracts were agreed even in years when the municipal authorities were acutely short of funds is surely an indication of the popularity of these events among ordinary people.[35] On one occasion, on 7 May 1617, the Corpus even provided the gypsies Diego Quiñones and Joan Maldonado with an excuse to write to the

Jaén city aldermen Don Alonso de Godoy, Don Alonso de Guzmán and Don Hernando de Vera to request the release from gaol of Joan del Pozo and one other gypsy, who, they said, were needed to dance in the procession. They undertook to ensure that the two would not leave the city, adding that were they anyway to do so, they would undertake to find replacement dancers at their own expense.[36]

Corpus Christi was not the only Church festival at which gypsies could play a role. From 1589 in Almería, they performed every year at the celebrations of the feast of Saint Stephen on 26 December, until in 1595 they were eventually forbidden to take part. Certain 'indecent things' sung by them in church were cited as the reason.[37] Finally, if the *Encyclopedia española jurídica* published in Barcelona in 1910 is to be believed, gypsy dances even formed part of the public festivities after the marriage of Philip II and Elizabeth Valois on 31 January 1560, the very same year in which Philip reiterated his father's 1539 legislation against gypsies.[38] In 1543, Princess María of Portugal, the future Philip II's cousin and first wife, was reportedly received in Medina del Campo with a spectacular performance which included a curious battle between Moors, gypsies, and Christians, though the 'gypsies' on that occasion seem in fact to have been artisans from the town. A similar battle was staged in Toledo, though in this case the costumed 'gypsies' were children of eight or nine years of age, who were reported to have fired their arquebuses 'with astonishing skill'.[39]

To return to Salazar de Mendoza, perhaps his most intriguing, if unoriginal, claim once again concerned the question of who exactly the gypsies were:

> The Gypsies have taken with them many idlers and vagabonds to live their life of freedom. For it is well known that many of those going around with Gypsies, both men and women, are Spaniards, and the same thing happens in other provinces.[40]

One source of this notion was the Jesuit Lelio Bisciola, whose *Horarum subsecuiarum* Salazar cites,[41] noting that its author had dismissed as pointless attempts to investigate the origin of the gypsies, since, as Salazar puts it, they were merely 'the scum, dross, and filth of each nation'. In the early period, before the 1600s, except for the occasional official assertion that others were joining the gypsies, as in Charles V's 1539 ordinance, the historical evidence for such claims is patchy, to say the least of it, though one encounters the odd, tantalizingly inconclusive detail. On 14 October 1562, for example, the elderly Andalusian gypsy

Catalina, questioned by the Toledo Inquisition about her family, replied with understandable caginess that her father Francisco 'knew of nothing other than wandering the world' and that her mother Juana 'had gone around in the company of gypsies'. Of course, any implication that Juana was not of gypsy birth, if intended, could equally be interpreted as an attempt by the daughter to distance herself as best she could from this despised pariah group and the almost automatic assumption of guilt that went with that status.[42] Later, however, and more compellingly, on 4 March 1633, a *consulta* of the Council of Castile noted that hunger and poverty were inducing some people to join up with the gypsies.[43] And on 10 April 1639, the Count of Salvatierra, future viceroy of New Spain and a man who had had some personal dealings with gypsies, wrote from Granada to the colonels' *junta* that it should 'be aware that even though they are called gypsies, there are many who are not, and who seek protection among them in order to live in freedom'.[44] In 1674, Manuel Montillo, writing from northern Andalusia, complained that 'through fear and in order to safeguard their lives, your Majesty's subjects befriend them, and other wicked men join up with the gypsy rabble, and women even marry them', support for this last claim being found in census figures gathered just over a century later.[45]

Similar generalizing claims were made subsequently by Sancho de Moncada in the eighth discourse of his *Restauración política de España* (1619). 'Those going around Spain', he wrote, 'are not gypsies, but rather swarms of layabouts and atheists, people with neither law nor religion of any kind, Spaniards who have taken up this gypsy way of life or sect and who every day accept into it more of the nation's idlers and ne'er-do-wells'.[46] The term 'sect', with all that word's damning implications in seventeenth-century Spain of secret heresy, was used in relation to Spain's gypsies not only by Melchor de Huélamo and, 20 years later, Juan de Quiñones, but also by the Council of State. It observed in a note to Philip III probably dating to 1612 that 'they are a bad example, they teach bad ways, and there are enough reasons to suspect that they have their own sect, given that they do not live as Christians'.[47] Like Salazar de Mendoza, Moncada pressed for expulsion, offering a litany of reasons why gypsies should no longer be tolerated in Spain. They should go, he argued, because they are foreigners who most people believe came with the Moors; they are everywhere held to be spies and traitors; they are idle, useless vagabonds who live as parasites on the poor and who are 'much more useless than the *moriscos*', who through their labour at least provided something to the royal exchequer; gypsy women are 'common whores' and do 'great damage to your Majesty's subjects' with their 'dances, gestures, and obscene words and songs'; gypsies are all thieves (he repeats Salazar's claims that they sell children to the Moors and confer among themselves in 'gobbledygook' in order not be understood by outsiders, a notion borrowed in this case from Salazar de Mendoza, who in turn borrowed it from Angelo Rocca's *Bibliotheca apostolica Vaticana*);[48] they are enchanters, magicians, fortune-tellers and chiromancers, given to palmistry and superstitious practices; and they are thought by 'very important men' to be heretics, idolaters or atheists. But Moncada's arguments in respect of expulsion are such that he risks being caught in a contradiction. On the one hand, after congratulating Philip III for having demanded the departure of the *moriscos*, 'even though there were many of them, and our population, commerce and royal revenues, trades and agriculture were inevitably left wanting', Moncada argued that 'since the gypsies are few in number [by comparison], and totally useless for anything, it seems necessary to expel them, given the great damage they cause'.[49] Here he is, attempting to counter two anticipated objections to this proposed policy:

The first is that the laws of Spain and the aforementioned resolution in the *Cortes* [originally of 30 July 1618, though Moncada gives 1619] allow the gypsies to choose to live in large villages [rather than leave Spain]. This, it seems, would be better than to expel them. But experience, acknowledged by important men, has demonstrated that it is not good to admit these people, because their homes are thieves' dens from which they go out stealing across the land.

The second is that it seems a pity to banish the women and children. But here we can adduce your Majesty's blessed action in expelling the *moriscos*, and their children along with them, via your royal edict [. . .].[50] And the most heinous crimes are those committed by gypsy women, it being generally known that gypsy men eat from what their women steal; and there is no law that obliges us to raise wolf cubs in the certain knowledge of the damage they will do to our flock in the future.[51]

On the other hand, he was equally adamant that the gypsies were actually just the criminal dregs of Spanish society and that it should therefore be possible through enforced sedentarization to rehabilitate them. 'These people are not from Egypt', he wrote, 'but rather they are Spaniards who take up the gypsy way of life (*gitanismo*), which consists of wandering around in troops and stealing, etc.' His true position is best explained by what follows:

> And by forcing them to support themselves and live a settled life with trades or masters, they will simply be Spaniards, and we shall rid them of their gypsy ways, and what we should do is expel them in so far as they are gypsies, which is the intention of my discourse.[52]

Having already quoted it among his opening remarks, Moncada now again cites the phrase first used at the *Cortes* of 1610, and revived at those held in Madrid between 1617 and 1620: 'And they should not be permitted to use the dress, language, or name gypsies, for they are not so by birth, and this word [*gitano*] and way of life should be shown to be false and consigned to perpetual oblivion.'[53]

The gypsies in Spanish literature

Early modern Spanish literature's representations of gypsies, like the diatribes directed against them by the *arbitristas*, owed at least as much to myth as to reality. To the extent, therefore, that they served further to nourish, reinforce and disseminate the largely prejudiced view of gypsies already in circulation, a brief, selective survey of such representations must inevitably form part of the historical narrative. It must do so because such misrepresentations have throughout the gypsies' history been used both to drive and justify the repression and exploitation to which they have long been subjected. I shall therefore confine most of my comments to the prejudiced misrepresentation of gypsies in the works selected. However, I shall also cite certain others that seem to me of particular interest in terms of the light they seem to cast on authorial attitudes towards gypsies. It is not my purpose here to engage in a more general, literary reading of the larger concerns identifiable in the different works cited, though the move from history into literature will be marked by some temporary departure from the chronological progression that has for the most part structured the narrative to this point.

Gypsies made their first, fleeting appearance in Spanish literature in 1499 in the *converso* Fernando de Rojas's hybrid novel in dialogue form, the *Comedia*, or, as later editions have it, *Tragicomedia de Calisto y Melibea*, popularly known from about middle of the sixteenth century as *La Celestina* after the aged bawd and sorceress who features in the work. The brief reference in Act XI by Calisto's servant Pármeno to the trick employed by 'those from Egypt' of distracting the attention of people they intended to rob by reading their palms while regaling them with a combination of sweet words and fast talking is fairly representative of the stereotype re-cycled in most subsequent literary references to gypsies.[54] In 1521, the Portuguese Gil Vicente's brief but vivid *Farsa das ciganas* offered a similarly stereotypical portrait.[55] Despite its title, it was written in the lisping Castilian associated in literature throughout the early modern period with gypsy speech. Its four gypsy women and three men address the audience, begging for alms, cajoling them with exaggerated and florid compliments, and offering to read their palms.[56] The gypsy Auricio offers a filly for exchange – though he will naturally require 100 *reales* to sweeten the deal. And playing simultaneously to the audience's presumed anti-gypsy prejudice and anti-Semitism, Claudio offers to exchange a horse obtained, he says, from a Jew. The animal's provenance, that is to say, is offered in conscience-salving mitigation of the act of receiving what the spectator is thus implicitly invited to assume are stolen goods. The gypsies also play on exotic myths of origin as Giralda refers to the banks of the Nile, while Martina seizes the opportunity to mention their noble 'Grecian' blood. Song and dance, spells guaranteed to ensnare the will and affections of otherwise reluctant males, glimpses of the future, especially the identities of future husbands, all are offered in the brief compass of just over 120 lines. The depiction is credible enough taken on its own terms. This, after all, is theatre – albeit no more than a sketch – in which actors perform gypsies performing gypsies. And there is no reason to suppose that it does other than reflect equally performative gypsy behaviours observed at first hand by Vicente in the real world around him, even if, then as now, they reveal little or nothing of substance about the actors hidden behind the mask.

Gypsy women also make a number of appearances in the work of the sixteenth-century Sevillian goldbeater turned playwright and actor-manager, Lope de Rueda, specifically in his *Comedia llamada Medora*, *Comedia llamada Eufemia*, and the *paso*, or single-scene comic sketch derived from the *Medora*, *La gitana ladrona* (*The Thieving Gypsy Woman*). In an early version of one of the most enduring of demonizing gypsy myths, a gypsy woman is reported in the prologue to the *Medora* to have stolen a boy child, replacing it with her own, ailing son, who subsequently dies.[57] The lisping speech (*ceceo*) associated with gypsies is used in the *Eufemia*, but only intermittently in the *Medora* and the *paso*. Even then it is used only for effect as the *gitana*, having neglected previously to do so, 'remembers' to lisp as she enjoins her non-gypsy interlocutor, the lackey Gargullo, not to touch a bag of diamonds and rubies she has previously stolen while she absconds in order to evade the authorities. Her plan, once the immediate danger has passed, is to return, collect the bag and decamp to Andalusia.[58] In both the *Medora* and the *paso*, the *gitanas* briefly employ the playwright's comic simulations of the Spanish gypsies' mongrel Romaní. The *gitana*'s phrase 'chuchuli, mechulachen' captures admirably the ring of the vestigial remnants of that tongue nowadays known as *caló*, a cryptological varietal of Castilian Spanish distinguished by its Romaní loan-words.[59] One should add that the accusation routinely levelled at gypsies by Salazar de Mendoza, Moncada and Quiñones, among others, that they spoke their hermetic 'gobbledygook' when they wished not to be understood by non-gypsies was doubtless as true then as it is now.[60] Perhaps they did so, however, somewhat more fluently than their present-day descendants, who typically only replace certain individual Spanish words with their own *caló* vocabulary on such occasions.[61]

Rueda certainly influenced Cervantes, who, in the prologue to his *Comedias y entremeses*, recalled having seen the playwright-manager's work as a youth in Seville, reserving high praise for him.[62] Cervantes, of course, incorporated gypsies in a number of his own works. They appear or are referred to in *Don Quijote*, in the Exemplary Novels *La gitanilla*, *La ilustre fregona*, *El licenciado vidriera*, and *Coloquio de los perros*, in his play *Pedro de Urdemalas* and in the *entremés* or interlude *La elección de los alcaldes de Daganzo*. Like Rueda's *Medora*, both *La gitanilla* and *Pedro de Urdemalas* play on the myth of gypsies as baby-snatchers, and in *La gitanilla* the narrator observes, perhaps with Rueda's *gitana* in mind, that the gypsy lisp is in fact the work of artifice rather than nature.[63] In *Pedro de Urdemalas*, in a manner again reminiscent of the *Medora*, the gypsy Inés's theatrical use of the lisp is intermittent, informing her speech when, for example, she is extolling the dubious pleasures of gypsy life or begging for alms, but not otherwise.[64] In *La ilustre fregona*, a gypsy attempts to sell a donkey 'which kept moving more on account of the quicksilver he had put in its ears than any agility of its own'.[65] The same trick is picked up from the gypsies by the hero of Jerónimo de Alcalá Yáñez's picaresque novel *Alonso de muchos amos* (1624–6), who also learns to 'file their teeth, removing some as necessary' in order to reduce what is in this case a horse's eight years of age to the appearance of a much more saleable three or four.[66] In Vicente Espinel's *Vida del escudero Marcos de Obregón* (1618), on the other hand, the gypsies' technique for selling back to its rightful owner a mule so skittish as to be 'worse than a devil' involves transforming it into a model of docility by feeding it two litres of wine.[67] As to Cervantes, of all his works it is of course *La gitanilla* which features gypsies most prominently. Yet neither the work's heroine Preciosa, stolen as a baby, nor her suitor Andrés are in fact genuine gypsies, both having been born into noble families, though Preciosa only discovers her true origins as the tale ends. The device of the false gypsy is also employed elsewhere by Cervantes, and doubtless played to the increasingly common belief, referred to previously, that outsiders were indeed joining forces with gypsies in Castile. In the play *Pedro de Urdemalas*, the eponymous hero, who in a late soliloquy describes himself as 'a Proteus',[68] 'becomes' a gypsy (temporarily) as well as undergoing various other transformations, before embracing a life of performance as an actor as the play ends. And in *Don Quijote*, the almost equally protean Ginés de Pasamonte – alias Ginesillo de Parapilla, alias Maese Pedro the itinerant puppeteer – seems on the whole to inhabit a liminal realm at the indeterminate edges of the gypsy world, putting in an appearance at one point astride a donkey and 'dressed as a gypsy, whose language and many others he knew as if they were his own'.[69] The reference to language is not fortuitous: belief in the polyglot skills of the gypsies was, as already noted, a common-place re-cycled by Martín del Río, Salazar de Mendoza, and others. That said, Cervantes's use of the false gypsy is driven by primarily literary considerations. In *La gitanilla* in particular, the device is of fundamental importance, essentially as an enabling vehicle for the transgressive voice of what I have argued elsewhere to be the work's quietly insistent satire on the ruling élite of Cervantes's day by a 'gypsy' heroine who is revealed in the end to be nothing less than the daughter of a *corregidor*.[70]

On the other hand, Cervantes's 'real' gypsies, by which I mean those who are not in fact of 'Old Christian' blood, derive on the whole from the common negative stereotype peddled by writers like Melchor de Huélamo and others like him. Thus Cervantes's gypsies are reported to enjoy remarkable powers of physical endurance, honed by long exposure to the elements; they are reputedly able to resist physical punishment or even torture; they are scandalously irreligious; they use unconsecrated ground to bury their dead; their men casually replace older for younger women; they practice incest (because they marry within the Church's prohibited degrees); and, as dedicated practitioners of the arts of theft, they use their traditional blacksmithing skills mainly in order to forge tools designed to be used for break-ins – these claims are variously to be found in the eulogy of gypsy life by the gypsy patriarch in *La gitanilla*, the account by the *pícaro* dog Berganza of his time with the gypsies in *Coloquio de los perros*, and the gypsy Maldonado's invitation to Pedro to take up their way of life in *Pedro de Urdemalas*.[71] In each case, the claims echo similar ones made by Fray Melchor de Huélamo, although, as already suggested, such beliefs were common currency in seventeenth-century Spain.[72] Cervantes's treatment of the gypsies is characteristically much subtler than that of the Franciscan, however. If one takes Maldonado's speech in Act I of *Pedro de Urdemalas*, for instance, recourse to Sebastián de Covarrubias's contemporary dictionary, the *Tesoro de la lengua* (1611), suggests that most of the terms 'naively' adduced by Maldonado to extol the virtues of gypsy life tended in fact to be negatively rather than positively inflected. So, terms like 'zuelta' (actually a lisped *suelta* meaning free and easy), 'libre' (free), 'ancha' (relaxed), especially when applied to the noun 'vida' (life), as they are here, also signified 'loose-tongued' and 'lacking respect' ('suelta' and 'libre') and 'impious' or 'ruled by the passions' ('ancha'). As to 'holgazana' (indolent), for its equivalent noun 'holgazán' Covarrubias gives 'he who does not wish to work and wanders around as an idle vagabond', a definition freighted with all the condemnation reserved for such individuals by crown, *Cortes*, and *arbitristas* alike. Both here and in the speech of the patriarch in *La gitanilla*, the gypsies are, that is to say, made to condemn themselves out of their own mouths. It is not quite a blanket moral condemnation, however. Preciosa, the false gypsy heroine of *La gitanilla*, complains that 'we are not all bad', the narrator later observing that 'even among devils, some are worse than others, and among many bad men, there is usually a good one to be found'.[73]

More often than not, however, early modern Spanish literature's typically very brief references to gypsies simply condemn them as thieves, fortune-tellers, or weavers of spells. In Fray Gregorio de Alfaro's *Vida ejemplar de don Francisco de Reinoso* (1617), they are contemptuously dubbed 'the pestilence of the Republic', and the author adds, no doubt with the expulsions of the *moriscos* in mind, that unlike other, greater and even more intractable problems, it has not yet been possible to find a remedy for this one.[74] Three years later, Fray Alonso Remón published his *Guía y avisos de forasteros que vienen a la Corte* under the pseudonym Antonio de Liñán y Verdugo. Focusing in picaresque style on the vast legion of idlers and confidence tricksters to be found in the capital, he at one point refers to those who dupe 'people who are simple and easy to persuade, like women', offering to read their palms and 'selling them cat for hare, very much in the gypsy fashion'.[75] In Mateo Alemán's *Guzmán de Alfarache*, a work Cervantes certainly knew, gypsies are dismissed as thieves and fortune-tellers, in this case by an author who had witnessed at first hand the sufferings endured by their brethren condemned to the mercury mines of Almadén, where many were sent (he was in 1593 appointed 'visiting judge' there).[76] Elsewhere, in the *Segunda parte del Lazarillo*, the bitterly anti-clerical Juan de Luna enlists the gypsies, described as 'a lure and refuge for rogues, church of apostates, and school of wickedness', as suitably fiendish company for a motley collection of 'clerics, friars, nuns or thieves who had escaped from gaol or their religious communities'. After adding for good measure that 'among them, the most villainous were those who had abandoned their monasteries, exchanging the contemplative life for an active one', he goes on to offer a sardonic vignette of two 'gypsies', a thick-set man and a round-cheeked woman, who, behind the wall of an orchard, sing a verse of the psalms of David to each other. They are, the hero is piously informed, a monk and a nun who have joined the gypsies 'desirous of professing a more austere life'.[77]

The theatre, as we have seen, tended on the whole to exploit the gypsies' potential as exotic or comic figures, and gypsy dancers certainly put in appearances here and there. Lope de Vega's *El robo de Dina*, for example, has such a dance in Act II, while in Tirso de Molina's *La fingida Arcadia* the Countess Lucrecia refers to gypsies reading palms and dismisses them all as thieves.[78] Gypsies also figure among the low-life characters of the short Spanish *entremés* or comic interlude – even after a 1633 decree prohibiting their representation in any form whatsoever. Jerónimo Cáncer y Velasco's *Entremés de los galeotes* (*Galley Slaves Sketch*) of 1659 features a gypsy dance,[79] and even in the court playwright Calderón's *Las visiones de la muerte*, gypsies feature as the thieves and dancers of stereotype. A gypsy woman also appears in his 1661 *Mojiganga de la negra, que se hizo en fiesta de sus Magestades*, declaring her intention to tell the fortune of the new prince, the future Charles II, born in Madrid on 6 November that year.[80] In the same author's *entremés La franchota*, published in 1672, the *franchotes* of the piece are not specifically identified as gypsies, but it is hard to believe that an urban seventeenth-century audience was not being invited by the playwright to associate them with the gypsy way of life, especially since the notary of the piece suspects they intend to go around the village singing and begging for alms. The word *franchotes* (Frenchies) was used as a catch-all term for unidentified foreigners, 'Frenchies' by default, who in this case speak a comic gibberish which is in fact peppered with Italian rather than French words.[81] As Calderón's long-winded notary reports the arrival of 'a troop of men and women' (*tropa* was the word routinely employed to describe bands of gypsies in legal documents of the day) to the mayor, his ignorance of who these strangers actually

are is underlined as he resorts to a garrulous listing of everything they
are not:

> There are many who are of the opinion
> that these people are the greatest thieves;
> because they are neither English,
> nor German, nor Turkish, nor Irish,
> nor Swiss, nor Medes, nor Romans
> nor from the cantons, nor Persians, nor Italians,
> nor does anyone know their homeland, state or name.[82]

There are just a handful of literary references to gypsies that suggest
a degree of authorial sympathy for them quite out of kilter with official
attitudes of the day. Lope de Vega's play *El arenal de Sevilla* is a case in
point. It, too, employs the device of the false gypsy, in this case one of
the play's two heroines, Lucinda, who, in order to preserve the decorum
required of her noble status, disguises herself in order to search for her
lover Don Lope. After wounding a noble rival in Valladolid, he has fled
south from the authorities and is now seeking to arrange passage from
Seville to the Indies. The opening stage direction of Act II accordingly
has Lucinda 'dressed as a gypsy and very dashing', while Florelo offers
her the wholly conventional advice that she will not need to know
the gypsy tongue, since merely speaking Castilian Spanish oddly and
lisping after their fashion will ensure that she is taken for one of them.[83]
Shortly thereafter, however, two sea captains, Fajardo and Castellanos,
conduct the following, very unconventional exchanges. First, Castellanos observes of gypsy women that they are 'very scornful' – of non-
gypsy men like himself – and 'notably chaste'. And he adds that 'they are
singularly faithful to their husbands', the use of the word (*ley*) 'law' or
'fidelity' in the original ('tienen extraña ley/con sus maridos') suggesting
a recognition of the internally 'policed' strength of the social conven-
tions of endogamy, chastity, and fidelity referred to here and which
are even today characteristic of Spanish gypsy society.[84] Fajardo then
addresses the 'gypsy' Lucinda:

Fajardo: Where is your husband?
Lucinda: Close by, may God protect him.
Fajardo [*to Castellanos*]: He must be in the galleys,
imprisoned without ever having committed an offence.
These women are alone,
and how loyally they go down to the port

when it is known for certain
that the galleys of Spain are about to arrive.
There they take them money,
gifts, clothing, shoes,
so much so that I would be a *forzado*
just to experience true love.[85]

A certain authority and insistency is lent to this simultaneous expression
of disapproval of the practice of condemning gypsies to the galleys
merely for being gypsies and admiration for the stoicism and loyalty
of their womenfolk by the fact that Fajardo is himself revealed to be a
galley captain.[86] The exchange continues:

Castellanos: Become a gypsy, then.
Fajardo: Yes, I shall.
Castellanos: There's no more certain road
to the galleys.

One passage from Jerónimo de Alcalá's somewhat later *Alonso de
muchos amos* also suggests a cautiously sympathetic attitude to the plight
of gypsies condemned to the oar:

But if our gypsies, who never see the sea except when sent to the
galleys, manage to complete their sentences without dying (which
is what usually happens), they return in such a state as to be
more suitable for a hospital for the incurable than a night under
the stars.[87]

Less well-known is the sometime royal scribe to Philip II, and close friend
of Lope de Vega, Juan de Piña, author of the novel *Casos prodigiosos y
cueva encantada* (1628). In this work Piña begins one episode by enumer-
ating all the usual clichés about gypsies found elsewhere, culminating
in the claim that they are 'killers and gaol-breakers' and that 'they think
nothing of being whipped, and little of being sent to the galleys'. The
author goes on, however, to recount a brief tale involving an 'almost
Ethiopian' gypsy prisoner, Pedro de Malla, whose release from custody
is arranged by the adventurous hero, Don Juan Bernardo, impressed by
the gypsy's 'graceful bearing'. Malla repays his benefactor by refusing to
sell him an injured mule which, when sold to an unwitting dupe, is soon
discovered to have been stolen and returned to its owner, leaving the
purchaser 100 ducats out of pocket. Don Juan's reaction seems designed

to mitigate somewhat the earlier, dutiful condemnations of the narrator: 'it seemed to Don Juan that these were genteel, yes, genteel thieves, and that all the proof that was needed to send them to the galleys for life was their use of gypsy dress and that language of theirs, recognized not in Egypt, but rather in Castile'.[88]

But such sentiments, to the extent that they suggest something other than routine moral condemnation of gypsies, represented the exception rather than the rule. As the ethnologist Julio Caro Baroja observed, Cervantes is perfectly prepared to concede that gypsy girls are of necessity precociously acute and quick-witted,[89] though one should add that the cliché of the astute gypsy is also found in works ranging from Fernando de Rojas's *Celestina* to Baltasar Gracián's 1642 treatise on literary aesthetics, *Agudeza y arte de ingenio*.[90] But when in *Coloquio de los perros* he refers to the gypsies' practice of endogamy, he has the dog Berganza add cynically that they marry among themselves merely in order to prevent outsiders learning their evil ways.[91] More tellingly, in *La gitanilla* the old gypsy patriarch's boast that in his community 'there is no adultery' is not only preceded by the 'throwaway' concession, 'although there is a lot of incest', but is followed by a contradictory 'and when there is [adultery], [. . .] we kill them [the women] and bury them in the mountains as if they were noxious animals'. The claim that the chastity and fidelity of gypsy women, lauded in the old gypsy's inadvertently self-condemning speech, are for Cervantes the product of the threat of masculine violence rather than any freedom of choice is finally reinforced as the old patriarch casually adds of gypsy women that 'with this fear and apprehension they endeavour to remain chaste'.[92] Paloma Gay y Blasco has observed even of present-day Spanish gypsies that 'men and women alike stress that women are more evil and have less capacity for *conocimiento* (understanding), and hence deserve less respect from others than men – characteristics that make it right that women should be "below" or under the authority of men'.[93]

6
Purging the Body Politic

By 1615, with the expulsions of the last of Spain's *moriscos* having supposedly been completed the previous year, the *Cortes* were ready to turn once again to the gypsy question. Now they picked up the threads of that earlier debate (see Chapter 4, pp. 61–2) which, while the expulsions were in progress, had for more than four years been held largely in abeyance.

The royal ordinances of 1619 and 1633

At the *Cortes* held in Madrid in 1615, the gypsy question was raised on three separate occasions. On 3 and 9 April that year, the *procuradores* discussed the question of expulsion and agreed to submit a proposal to Philip III, noting on 9 April that 'since no remedy has yet been provided and because it is so fitting and necessary, it should be carried out without further delay'. On both occasions, they stressed their desire to see 'the word [*gitano*] completely eradicated'.[1] On 10 June, the *Cortes* debated a number of items relating to reform of the *Mesta* submitted by the latter's own Council. The first of these was a request that the gypsies, long a thorn in the side of sheep-owners, be expelled from Spain and that its own *alcaldes entregadores* (peripatetic judicial officers) be empowered to punish those gypsies they apprehended in the course of their duties.[2] Since the need for root-and-branch reform of the *Mesta* had arisen largely out of complaints about the arrogant abuse of power in the countryside by these same *alcaldes entregadores*,[3] the *procuradores* unsurprisingly refused to entertain the second request. They did, though, agree to submit to the king the request for expulsion, which, after all, was consistent with their own recommendation of four years earlier.

On 30 July 1618 the *Cortes* returned to the issue once again, specifically in the form of a resolution based verbatim on clause 35 of the *Cortes's* proposal of 24 December 1610. This, it will be recalled (see p. 61–2) had suggested that the gypsies should be required either to accept sedentarization in towns and cities of more than 1000 households, or leave Spain. Any indicators of gypsy identity were to be eradicated, including the very name. By far the most draconian aspect of the resolution, however, was its recommendation that the death penalty be applied for any breach of these provisions, even where gypsies had done no more than to continue to deal in livestock or other prohibited items. Some *procuradores* were clearly uncomfortable with this aspect of the proposal, though it was approved in the event by a majority vote. Fifteen voted in favour of the resolution as it stood, including Don Lorenzo Ramírez, the only one present who had been in attendance at the *Cortes* of 10 June 1615. Eight either voted against it, or suggested amendments, mainly involving replacement of the death penalty by flogging and the galleys for gypsy men and flogging and banishment for the women. Don Francisco de las Infantas said he would approve it provided the gypsies forced to settle in the towns were permitted to engage in trade. Three, however, Don Juan Trillo, Don Pedro de Céspedes, and Don Baltasar de Góngora, found they could not support it at all, the last two arguing that the king should instead demand that laws already in place be properly enforced.[4]

Against this background, it is clear that the royal decree issued subsequently by Philip III on 28 June 1619 represented more than just another expulsion order. It was rather the culmination of years of debate in the *Cortes* and, of course, followed in the wake of the great reforming *consulta* of earlier that year. In the light of previous failures, physical expulsion of those refusing to settle must have seemed a somewhat unrealistic aim even to those framing the order, though they clearly considered the threat worthy of reiteration. But they were also concerned to expel an idea. The order represented an attempt officially to deracialize Spain's gypsies and consign the very word *gitano* to oblivion once and for all. In so doing, the decree sought in one sense to insure itself against failure. If this latest attempt to rid the nation of its wandering gypsies via forced sedentarization and assimilation were once again to come to little or nothing, then what could not be achieved in reality would be achieved, in one sense at least, via language. It would be achieved, that is to say, via the symbolic erasure of notions of *gitano* identity conceived in terms of racial difference. With the expulsions of the *moriscos* still relatively fresh in Spaniards' minds, the political expediency of removing at the stroke of a pen another 'foreign' contagion threatening the body of the state would hardly have gone unappreciated. The order's tacit appeal to the linguistic equivalence of *gitano* and *egipciano*, terms used almost interchangeably until late in the seventeenth century, allowed it quite reasonably to revive the phrase used of the gypsies in the *Cortes* of 1610 and repeated at those of Madrid on 30 July 1618, 'for they are not so by birth' ('pues no lo son de nación'). The word 'nación', of course, combines the notions not just of common descent, but also, etymologically, of birth. Had not these people been in Spain now for over two hundred years? Born and bred there, how could they be considered anything other than Spaniards, albeit of the worst sort? Attitudes like those of the Jesuit Martín del Río, who could hardly bring himself to believe without attributing the skill to magic that a gypsy 'count' he had met in León in 1589 'spoke Castilian Spanish as perfectly as if he were from Toledo', were by now simply anachronistic – even if they found echoes in the writings of Sebastián de Covarrubias, Salazar de Mendoza, Sancho de Moncada and, for that matter, Cervantes.[5] Racial difference in so far as it might be said to apply to gypsies would henceforth be officially denied, just as it had been downplayed in the past in the interests of the policy of exploitative assimilation long pursued by the authorities. These wayward Spaniards were now forbidden to speak, dress, or describe themselves as gypsies. Needless to say, none of this implied that they were to be regarded as any better now than they had always been thought to be in the past. Accusing them of murder and theft, especially the theft of livestock belonging to the poor, the decree duly ordered all those failing to take up settled residence in towns of at least 1000 households to leave Spain within six months. Any who returned thereafter, or, as the *Cortes* had requested, infringed any other provision of the decree – based almost verbatim on clause 35 of the *Cortes*'s resolution of 24 December 1610 – would, it announced, incur the death penalty.[6]

However, there may also have been another, more politically sensitive motivation behind the new decree, perhaps again inspired by memories of the propaganda exercise led by the announcement of the expulsion of the *moriscos* a decade earlier. The 1619 decree was issued at Belém in Portugal, where, against the advice of the Council of Castile and most of his ministers, Philip III had taken his 14-year-old son, heir to the Portuguese crown, to receive the oath of allegiance, and where he intended to convene a *Cortes*.[7] He had left Madrid on 22 April, arriving in Belém in mid-June, accompanied among other notables by his confessor, the Inquisitor General Fray Luis de Aliaga, Melchor de Molina, of the Council and Chamber of Castile, and the Count of

Olivares. Both location and timing suggest circumstantially that the new anti-gypsy decree, as a post-*morisco*, post-Lerma restatement of the credentials of Philip III's government as self-appointed guardians of Spain's Old Christian identity, may have been intended to divert attention from other, deeply unpopular initiatives which now risked undermining that very same reputation.[8] These concerned the Portuguese crypto-Jewish or *marrano* financiers who, some hoped, might with their wide network of Jewish contacts in northern Europe and elsewhere be enlisted to replace the now widely despised Genoese in support of the Spanish crown.[9] Its grave financial difficulties had been newly exacerbated by Spain's military intervention following the revolt in Bohemia in 1618 and the looming prospect of further conflict with the Dutch with the expiry in 1621 of the Truce of Antwerp. Lerma had some years earlier made several attempts to bring Portugal's financial administration into the orbit of Spain, despite the fact that Castile's western neighbour was both entitled and determined under the union to enjoy fiscal independence; and he had also tried to raise revenue by selling privileges to Portuguese crypto-Jews.[10] In 1618 the *Cortes* had discussed the issue and several *arbitristas* including González de Cellorigo in his 1619 *Alegación en que se funda la justicia* (*Argument for Justice*), a work later placed on the Inquisition's index, had argued against the exclusion of *conversos* from honours and office.[11] In the event, a combination of royal piety and the re-emergent martial Castilian nationalism of the previous few years ensured that the by then ailing Philip III would refuse to embark on such a politically risky course of action.[12] Instead, it would be taken forward by the powerful figure of Olivares as part of a wide programme of reform early in the reign of Philip IV; and this amid and despite a resurgence of popular anti-Semitism fuelled by the growing influence of Portuguese *marranos* in Castile since its annexation of Portugal in 1580.[13] J. H. Elliott put it thus:

> The sudden prominence at the court of crypto-Jewish Portuguese bankers and businessmen symbolized the inner contradictions of a programme of reform which had depicted purification as essential to survival, and now had recourse to those very elements which the popular mind most associated with the contamination of Castile.[14]

While the 1619 decree doubtless encouraged further sedentarization of gypsies, royal fiat alone did nothing to banish them from the consciousness of other Spaniards. Even those who had little or no personal contact with real gypsies were perfectly likely to have been exposed to their exotic and always transgressive homologues in literature or the theatre. Cervantes's popular tale *La gitanilla*, which had of course been in circulation since 1613, was just one of a number of works, including plays and short theatrical interludes, which featured gypsies; and in 1632, just one year before the government turned once again to legislation, the playwright and future secretary to Philip IV, Antonio de Solís y Rivadeneira, wrote a play, *La gitanilla de Madrid*, roundly based on that earlier tale.[15]

Yet it was actually the *Mesta*, incomparably weaker now than it had been in the time of the Catholic Monarchs, though still not wholly without influence, that seems to have provided the initial *casus belli* for the next, even more comprehensive attempt symbolically to expel Spain's gypsies via legislation. In a *consulta* of 10 February 1633 addressed to Philip IV, the Council recorded that 'one of the greatest calamities suffered by stockbreeders is the gypsies, who, divided up in troops, take their animals, consuming what they need and selling those that are left with the same freedom as if they were their own'.[16] It noted that even though the *Mesta*'s own officials had been mandated by the crown to take action against the gypsies, the situation in the countryside had not improved. Rather things had become much worse, and it added – surrendering more or less unconditionally to hyperbole – that what had once been merely a little local difficulty now threatened 'the peace and security of these realms'. The following month, another *consulta* discussed the measures that would be needed to boost the breeding of livestock, citing the gypsies as the principal cause of what had, it insisted, become a national problem. The Council did, though, make a point of rejecting expulsion as a possible solution, explicitly giving the need to arrest further depopulation and the gypsies' now officially deracialized status as its reasons:

> And having discussed the options at length, it has not seemed to us necessary now, as it must have done in the past, to order the gypsies to leave, because the depopulated state in which these kingdoms find themselves since the expulsion of the *moriscos*, and as a result of present necessities, does not permit of any further loss, no matter how light, especially of these people, who are not *gitanos* either by nature or origin, but rather through contrivance and roguery, and who, once reformed, will adopt the ordered habits and way of life of everyone else.[17]

Taking the provisions of the 1619 ordinance as its starting point, it went on to make a number of specific recommendations, all of which duly found their way into a rather poorly drafted royal ordinance issued in Madrid by Philip IV on 8 May 1633. This once again sought 'to rid the language once and for all of the word *gitanos*'. Henceforth, no one might refer to these people as gypsies. The ordinance asserted that those calling themselves *gitanos* 'are not so, either by origin or by nature' and demanded, quite unrealistically, that they abandon once and for all occupations forbidden to them, cease travelling to fairs, and dress, speak, and take up the same kinds of work as other Spaniards. This, of course, was for many tantamount to a recipe for starvation. The penalties to be applied to gypsies who failed to obey would be 200 lashes and six years in the galleys for men, and exile for women. Henceforth, the ordinance continued, 'neither in dance nor any other kind of event is the representation, dress, or name of the gypsies to be permitted'. Transgressors in respect of this last prohibition – presumably non-gypsies complicit in such activities were envisaged – were to be exiled for two years and fined 50,000 *maravedís*, this to be doubled for a second offence.[18] There is no evidence, however, that the threat had much effect, especially outside the capital. In Jaén, for example, the civic authorities continued to contract gypsy dancers and acrobats for the city's Corpus Christi celebrations of 1634, 1636, 1642, and 1645, just as they had done previously.[19]

The 1633 ordinance also granted permission for all justices, royal, noble, and ecclesiastical, to continue the pursuit of marauding bands of gypsies across neighbouring jurisdictions, and pointedly extended the same privilege even to the popularly resented *alcaldes entregadores* of the *Mesta*. Wherever possible, prisoners once apprehended were to be transported immediately to the nearest district under royal jurisdiction, or, failing that, to the nearest *alcalde mayor*. Once under lock and key, justice was to be administered swiftly, and the penalties stipulated by the law were to be applied to those convicted 'with the utmost rigour', including for those caught with firearms – no fewer than eight years in the galleys. And yet, in a manner rather clumsier even than that of Sancho de Moncada's argument in the *Restauración política de España*, the 1633 ordinance eventually collapses into self-contradiction. For while it begins by dismissing the notion that gypsies enjoyed any separate racial identity, it nevertheless implicitly acknowledged them as at least in some sense ethnically different, undermining its opening proposition by insisting that the ordinance also applied to those who had merely adopted or affected the gypsy way of life:

> And gypsy men or women who for just reasons do not merit either the death penalty or the galleys are to be sold as slaves, including those

who are effectively gypsies by virtue of their language or conduct, and the price obtained for them and all the goods found with them should be used to defray the expenses incurred during their capture.[20]

It is easy to sense the crown's frustration as it yet again feels obliged to add, 'and we command the members of our Council, *Audiencias* and *Chancillerías* to punish severely those justices and judges who neglect their duty in this matter and who fail to pursue and imprison the aforesaid criminals'. This 'sweeping decree', as Klein described it, was in his view 'the last and most reactionary confirmation of the antiquated claims of the *Mesta*'. In Klein's view, the ordinance represented an attempt by the Council – a court of law as well as an administrative body[21] – to roll back what it regarded as unacceptable encroachment by the *Chancillerías* on its traditional jurisdiction in respect of the granting of pasturage leases. In the early years of the seventeenth century in particular, the *Chancillerías* had exhibited a marked tendency to find in favour of local people in their innumerable Cain and Abel disputes with the *Mesta*'s itinerant magistrates, the *alcaldes entregadores*, whose activities were popularly regarded as an unwarranted, not to say cavalier, interference in local affairs.[22] Although the *Mesta* managed in the 1620s and 1630s to win a number of such cases on appeal, the courts still seemed bent on clipping the *entregadores*' wings. In 1629, for example, they had found in favour of the town of Belalcázar (Córdoba) against an *entregador*, overturning what for as long as anyone could remember had been the traditional right of such officials to try cases involving gypsies and others accused of the theft of livestock.[23] In 1633, the crown reacted by attempting to bolster the *Mesta*, as in the 8 May ordinance on gypsies, and to restore some of the privileges traditionally enjoyed by Spain's transhumant herdsmen. Unsurprisingly, the policy had only very limited success, since it was diametrically opposed both to the popular mood and to market pressure for ever more pasture land to be turned over to arable use.[24]

Sedentarization and strategies for survival

The ultimate aim of the flawed 1633 ordinance was to rid Spain of its gypsies. It sought to achieve this by denying their existence whilst simultaneously, if self-contradictorily, insisting on their exploitative assimilation to a majority culture within which, largely isolated from their fellows, they would safely diminish over time. They would do so, moreover, or so it was hoped, while providing cheap labour as and when needed on the land. This seems an appropriate juncture, then, at which to ask just how effective in more general terms were attempts over the early modern period to integrate Spain's gypsies into the larger community. Both the 1633 ordinance and the *consulta* that preceded it had revealed that such sedentarization as had already occurred had in fact merely led to the formation of *gitanerías*, gypsy *barrios* in the towns and cities to which those gypsies able or willing to do so had gravitated. Legislation had thus not only failed to achieve the desired effect of diluting their strong, contradistinctive sense of group identity, but had also ensured that their strength in numbers in such areas had done nothing to curb the criminal activities of which they continued to be accused. While the natural habit of birds of a feather doubtless had a part to play, the process of ghetto formation was further encouraged by hostility from elements of the non-gypsy population, which, taken together with economic factors, conspired to ensure that these struggling incomers tended to be confined to the social and physical margins of the local communities into which they were moving. Now, with little thought for local Old Christian reactions or the practicalities involved, let alone any concern for what would inevitably be further disruption of the lives of gypsies who had already complied with the letter of the law, the 1633 ordinance attempted belatedly to undo the damage: 'within two months the aforementioned are to leave the *barrios* where they live as gypsies, split up, and mix with other householders, and they are not to meet, either publicly or in secret'.[25] One is reminded of the scheme put forward in the *Cortes* in 1594 by Jerónimo de Salamanca and Martín de Porras.[26] No doubt it was now hoped that the inevitable genetic attenuation that would ensue if the terms of the new ordinance could be implemented would, over the course of time, see the gypsies effectively disappear altogether.

Many continued to resist sedentarization, however, fearing with good reason that registration and a fixed abode would make them much more vulnerable to persecution by the authorities. As demonstrated even by the new demands made in the 1633 ordinance, those who did comply with the requirement that they settle in towns could easily find that they were merely exchanging one set of problems for another. Yet if there were places where their reputation ensured that were never likely to be welcomed as neighbours, there were others, especially in the south, where, despite their marginal status, they had long been regarded as making a useful, indeed essential contribution to the local economy in their traditional roles as blacksmiths, livestock traders, shearers, muleteers, basket-weavers, and slaughtermen or butchers, a profession which by the eighteenth century had become something of a gypsy monopoly in Andalusia.[27] Just as with other forms of *convivencia*, that is to say, the state of gypsy – non-gypsy relations at any given point varied not just as a function of fluctuating levels of distrust or prejudice, but also pragmatically according to local circumstances and needs. The later decades of the sixteenth century, for example, saw gypsy families contribute to the repopulation of the Kingdom of Granada after the forced dispersal of the *moriscos* across Castile in 1570. There were, in all likelihood, gypsy populations already living in the frontier towns where, it has been suggested, they may originally have served as blacksmiths and farriers to Christian forces engaged in the Reconquest.[28] Some evidence for this hypothesis is found in the census of gypsies ordered in 1783 by Charles III for the town of Álora (Málaga), which records a 'José Román, by trade a blacksmith, a native of this town whose first ancestor came here at the time of the Reconquest plying the same trade'. Another gypsy, Carlos Cortés, applying for the right to reside in Játiva in 1746, noted that his family had until 1708 lived in Illora (Granada), 'since the days when the said town was won by the Catholic Monarchs and was populated by gypsies'.[29] Now, moving to Lorca, Vera, La Zubia, and other towns, they were able to provide a range of ancillary services and skills lost to those areas with the removal of the *moriscos*. When in 1567 Juan Medrano and six other 'grecianos' asked the town council of Lorca if they might take up residence there as blacksmiths, their petition was rejected. Four decades later, the same town council actively requested the gypsy blacksmith Sebastián Maldonado to move from Totana to Lorca, where his skills were by that time sorely needed.[30] In the eighteenth century, which saw a new intensification of repressive measures against gypsies, both Aguilar de la Frontera and Benamejí in Andalusia attempted in 1746 to have their gypsies exempted from the demand that all gypsies move to one of the 75 large towns in which Ferdinand VI had ordered them to take up residence. They did so on the grounds that their supporting role as blacksmiths was of fundamental importance to local agriculture.[31] The request from Benamejí nevertheless suggests just how marginal and precarious a niche existence they were managing to eke out:

They are in a way useful to local people, because they are needed [...] for their skills as blacksmiths, since farm-workers take their ploughshares and other tools needed for working the land to them for repair, especially because since the death of Rafael Navarro de Alcántara, master blacksmith and locksmith, who lived in this town and who was not himself a gypsy, no other non-gypsy [*castellano*] has been able to establish himself here, finding it impossible to make a living from such a small population.[32]

Vélez-Málaga, too, argued that its gypsies practised,

> mean and humble trades, blacksmithing, weaving baskets, and clipping draught animals, horses and mules, serving the common good and the commercial activities of the inhabitants of the town, muleteers, people passing through, and farm labourers . . .[33]

And, its argument continued, these trades had long been considered their more or less exclusive preserve, 'rooted and constituted in the class and nature of the said gypsies', despite the existence of an occasional non-gypsy blacksmith here and there. Antonio Domínguez Ortiz noted that in Seville in 1698 the *Asistente* (Chief Officer of Justice) of that city made a representation on behalf of gypsies who served as drummers and fife players in companies of militia, asking that they be exempted from laws compelling them to work on the land,

> since these people are needed for this purpose, there being no one else to perform the role, and since they receive no wage or other emoluments whatsoever, and live by working as blacksmiths and are settled with their families in that city . . .

The request was duly granted, though this merely amounted to a recognition that in Seville, as elsewhere in the south, gypsies had continued for the most part to pursue their traditional occupations.[34] Their circumstances were, however, complicated by the fact that they were frequently excluded from occupations requiring guild membership. In Málaga, where gypsy blacksmiths formed their own *cofradía* (guild) of Saint Sebastian, an attempt by them in 1784 to disband this *cofradía* and join that of the city's locksmiths met with violent protests from the latter, despite the fact that a royal ordinance of the previous year had prohibited such exclusionary practices.[35] Indeed, Domínguez Ortiz went on to suggest that one of the reasons so many gypsies worked as blacksmiths in Seville was that this profession was not governed in that racial melting-pot of a city by guild exclusions such as a need to demonstrate 'purity of blood' before a candidate might take up a particular profession.[36] As it was, the gypsies' service as drummers for the militias was not always quite so voluntary – on 23 May 1643, for example, the *corregidor* of Jerez sentenced a number of them to fulfil that role, specifically ordering that this should be without pay.[37] However, once enlisted, willingly or otherwise, some even managed to reach the New World, notwithstanding the fact that they were specifically prohibited from travelling there by the Laws of the Indies. Such was the case of the drummer Mateo Navarro, a native of El Puerto de Santa María and son of a gypsy of the same name, whose death was reported in Veracruz in 1701.[38]

In other places, 'settled' gypsies were regarded as a disturbing, even disruptive presence by their neighbours, who, watching the comings and goings of other gypsies whose names had not been officially recorded in municipal registers and tax-lists as the law required, suspected both them and their hosts of complicity in all manner of crimes committed in the surrounding countryside. In 1629 in the town of Hinojosa del Duque, some 90 km north-west of Córdoba, the *corregidor* and chief justice of neighbouring Belalcázar, Don Miguel Naharro del Aguilar, investigated just such a complaint. He was informed that the non-registered 'vagrant' gypsies Agustina de Malla and Gracia de Heredia, both from Jerez de los Caballeros, were living there 'under the protection' of gypsies officially sedentarized in the town, who had thus ignored earlier warnings that they would be severely punished for admitting other, unauthorized individuals in this way. Questioned about her relationship with the sedentarized gypsies Juan and Juan Manuel Tejedor, the 35-year-old Agustina, who described her profession as 'spinning and sewing, like other women', said she had arrived in Hinojosa a week earlier at the behest of a female cousin who lived there. She denied under oath any impropriety, claiming that the scandalous rumours circulating were merely a result of her regular 'communications' with the gypsies in question. The replies given by the 25-year-old Gracia, now like Agustina languishing in the local gaol, were almost identical, except that she added that the cousin in question was 'a crippled gypsy woman'. She, too, denied that she was living in sin with either of her gypsy hosts.[39] But rumours of sexual scandal were in some ways the least of it. Their hosts also stood accused of sheltering other gypsy outlaws, vagrants with whom, it was claimed, they would venture out at night to steal livestock and provisions from shepherds grazing their herds on neighbouring pasture rented from the Duke of Béjar.[40] It seems in this particular case that the gypsies were living among the Old Christian inhabitants of the Calle de Alonso Caballero; and if those called to give evidence are to be believed, they left a good deal to be desired as neighbours. One witness, a 68-year-old man, complained that 'every night there are quarrels between the said gypsies, with disputes and fights involving knives which disturb the neighbours'. He added that the trouble would not stop until well after midnight and that the neighbours dared not leave their homes to earn a living for fear of ill-treatment at the hands of these interlopers. His evidence was supported by another householder, Juan López, who added that the town had known no peace since the gypsies had arrived there.[41] What is most revealing, however, about such documents, at least in terms of the gypsies' social organization, is that they offer a glimpse of the extremely fluid social and spatial strategies typically adopted by them to allow more effective exploitation of marginal economic opportunities, including the kinds of illicit activities referred to here. As Teresa de San Román has pointed out, such strategies rely crucially on extreme flexibility both in respect of the opposition mobility-settlement and the size at any given juncture of gypsy groupings, which, depending on local conditions and the possibilities offered for subsistence, might vary from a mere handful to well over a hundred individuals.[42] Needless to say, the strength of kinship bonds within the extended gypsy patrigroup was (and is) of fundamental importance in the maintenance of these support networks, though one should add that this would not of itself have precluded co-operation between different patrigroups.

Not all gypsies were poor, however. According to eighteenth-century documents requesting the Council of Castile to acknowledge them as 'Old Castilians' and thus exempt them, at least in theory, from the many restrictions placed on gypsies, the Montoya family, residents of Villanueva de los Infantes, were comparatively prosperous, owning their own home, arable land, 20 saddle-horses and mules, and other assets. They had, it was claimed, lived as *vecinos* in Villanueva from time 'immemorial' and their status as good citizens was attested to by the fact that they had been ignored by the *Santa Hermandad* of Ciudad Real, which nevertheless continued to pursue gypsy criminals in the area 'as it has always done'.[43] But if gypsies occasionally enjoyed relative wealth, this could also provoke the spite and envy of their neighbours. The Montoya family complained bitterly about the malevolence of the mayor of Villanueva, alleging that he continually obstructed their efforts whenever they sought permission to leave the town for any reason, and that he had suborned local witnesses, some of whom he had gaoled, forcing them to give false testimony against them. He had then, they alleged, seized all their property, agricultural implements and animals, selling the latter off at half their true value.

If sedentarized gypsies were often regarded as an economic asset in small communities in Andalusia, the same cannot be said for Valencia, where the authorities endeavoured for years to exclude them from the kingdom. The vicissitudes of gypsy life there, as experienced by another Montoya family – the name is common among gypsies – in the late seventeenth century, provide a case in point, and illustrate well the struggles for jurisdiction and authority which so often characterized relations between centre and periphery, between the crown and the kingdoms. On 13 November 1679 in Madrid, the Council of State heard a petition from the gypsy María de Montoya 'which requests your Majesty to command the *Hermandad* not to molest her, her husband, or her gypsy relatives, in view of the fact that they live decently and without causing scandal in the town of Junquera'.[44] Despite its qualms about gypsies in general, which it made a point of noting, the Council nevertheless recommended in this instance that Charles II accede to the request. The following year, he did so, personally authorizing María de Montoya, her husband, seven children, and two brothers to settle in the town. Ten years later, the viceroy of Valencia, the Count of Altamira summarily withdrew the Montoya family's right to reside there in response to continuing complaints from the Estates of the Valencian *Corts* that the royal order was invalid and in contravention of the provisions of the *furs*, the kingdom's jealously guarded regional laws and privileges. When the right of residence was restored to them two years later on appeal, the then viceroy, the Marquis of Castel Rodrigo, protested the decision vigorously, initially without success. In 1695, however, in an ominous indication of how the times were changing, a royal order of 25 January finally authorized Castel Rodrigo to act against Valencia's gypsies, rescinding in the process the privileges granted to the Montoya family 15 years earlier.[45]

As the 1633 *consulta* noted, sedentarization had failed to achieve its objective of reining in gypsy criminality. It therefore recommended the dispersal of gypsies living in the *gitanerías* among the Old Christian populations of the towns where they had settled, partly in order to remove them from the ringleaders who, it was assumed, were responsible for organizing their criminal activities. The *consulta* added,

if your Majesty is served to promulgate this law, it may be that many of the gypsies who are currently settled in towns will, in order not to incur its penalties, leave and join up with those who go about stealing, so that it would be advisable to order that none of them be permitted to leave their town of residence for six months, on pain of becoming the slaves of anyone who apprehends them.[46]

The recommendation was duly incorporated in the royal ordinance. What is telling about it, however, is the Council's confident expectation that the wholly unrealistic nature of the demands made by the law on the one hand, and the severity of the penalties it provided on the other, would, unless this further restriction were introduced, encourage precisely the opposite of the outcome intended. Certainly, the scandal of gypsy banditry in the countryside showed as few signs of abating after the 1633 ordinance as it had done before that date. In 1674, writing from Andalusia, Manuel Montillo complained that marauding bands of gypsies had plagued the region for 40 years and that neither on the open road nor in populated areas were people safe from them.[47] Banditry was an endemic problem in the south, in the kingdom of Valencia, and, to a slightly lesser degree by this time, in Catalonia. While most bandits were of peasant stock, in Jaén, Écija, and a number of other Andalusian towns, certain members of the nobility were either actively complicit themselves in such activities, or were rumoured to protect those who were, including gypsies and *moriscos*. In Jaén, for example, Don Juan de Frías and Don Pedro de Escobedo, the latter a knight of the Military Order of Calatrava, were in the 1680s jointly responsible for wine smuggling and the violent extortion of money from ordinary people living in the area. In Valencia, members of the clergy often lent support to bandits, whose violent solution to grinding poverty was frequently admired in the communities from which they had sprung, a pattern repeated in Andalusia and New Castile.[48] Some, like the Franciscan friar Francisco Sánchez, were even bandits themselves, responsible for both theft and murder.[49] Further north, banditry, whilst somewhat less prevalent, remained a significant problem. In 1633, the *Juez de Comisión* or special commissioner for gypsies, Juan Hurtado, reported that he had arrived at the town of Hinojoso de la Orden (today Los Hinojosos) in La Mancha to investigate not just the activities of the gypsy bandits who had reportedly been plaguing the area for two years, but also those of non-gypsies who had sheltered them or received stolen goods from them. He soon found his progress obstructed, however, as the town's magistrate and others, including 'Doctor Don Fernando de Salazar, a judge who says he is from the Council', repeatedly challenged his jurisdictional competency as an agent of the crown in territory owned by the Military Order of Santiago.[50] In 1638, gypsy bandits were reported to be active around Coruña del Conde, north of the Guadarrama mountain range.[51] And in 1639, Pedro Marcos, *alcalde mayor* of Palenzuela, was instructed to pursue and apprehend 'troops of gypsies' who had used two nearby villages as bases from which to carry out robberies in the surrounding area. In particular, it noted, they had ransacked a coach on the road from Burgos to Valladolid, stripped and robbed the *alcalde mayor* of Noreña (Asturias), waylaid many students on their way to Salamanca, and raped 'many women', before making good their escape by crossing into a neighbouring jurisdiction. The letter duly authorized Marcos to pursue the malefactors across other jurisdictions, setting a time limit of 30 days after which such politically controversial operations must be terminated.[52] On 16 February that same year, Don Enrique de Salimar, *alcalde del crimen* of the Valladolid *Chancillería*, received a royal commission instructing him to proceed against the 'many gypsies and bandits' who, 'together or on their own account', had been responsible for 'many deaths, thefts, burglaries and robberies on the open road' which, it noted, had been committed across the length and breadth of Old Castile.[53]

However, the urgent tone of the letter and its demand, identical to the one made in the letter previously cited, that all appeals be referred directly to the Council (presumably of Castile) and no other tribunal, also suggests a darker purpose; for by 1639 the need for oarsmen for Spain's Mediterranean galley squadrons had once again become acute.

Philip IV and the manning of Spain's galleys

The difficulties earlier encountered by Philip II finding men for the rowing benches continued through his son's reign and beyond. Anxious like his father before him to exploit to the maximum the manpower potentially available to the galleys in Spain's gaols, Philip III had decreed in 1611 that prisoners sentenced to the oar were no longer to be freed on appeal or have their sentences commuted to prison terms. The order was intended to apply not just to the appeal courts, the *Chancillerías* and *Audiencias*, but even to the Council of Castile itself.[54] Similar policies were pursued by subsequent monarchs, though not without significant opposition from the *Chancillerías*. Indeed, throughout the seventeenth century the crown continued with very limited success to exhort law officers across the country to prioritize and expedite cases pending in the courts which might help to maintain the flow of prisoners condemned to the oar. By the time of Philip IV's accession to the throne in 1621, the problem had become more intractable than ever. Throughout his reign, the squadron of Spain was normally hundreds of oarsmen short of its required complement, the figure soaring in 1647 to 1387, with the result that almost half of the squadron's 11 galleys could not be deployed.[55] As the supply of convicts continued to dwindle, those already serving in the galleys as *forzados* were frequently refused release even after their sentences had expired. This could involve them being retained illegally as *buenas boyas forzados* – the title is oxymoronic, *buenas boyas* historically being the term used for volunteer oarsmen – a status that should theoretically have triggered better treatment and rations than those received by other *forzados* in the notoriously under-provided galleys.[56] But prisoners could just as easily find themselves forced to continue to serve with no improvement whatsoever in their wretched conditions, perhaps condemned to remain at the oar because of some failure to pay an earlier fine or a misdemeanour committed while they were still serving their original sentence.[57] This prospect encouraged some with access to the necessary funds to buy slaves, usually Muslims, to replace them on the rowing benches, a practice acknowledged and approved in a royal decree of 1642, which merely stipulated that the slaves in question must first be deemed physically fit for the task by the galley's officers.[58] On 13 November 1653, Philip IV ordered *forzados* to be retained in the galleys after their sentences were complete but paid as volunteers, and on 22 May 1657, imposed on gaolers who allowed *forzados* to escape a 100 ducat fine, to be used to purchase a slave to replace the escapee.[59]

By the mid-1630s, just as in the time of Philip II, a combination of exceedingly dilatory appeals procedures, jurisdictional disputes, escapes from gaol, corruption, and a lack of the funds needed to ensure that those convicted were subsequently delivered to the ports had conspired to make it virtually impossible to maintain the supply of *forzados* to the galleys. This was despite the fact that the Mediterranean galley squadrons had been run down under Olivares in favour of Spain's Atlantic fleet, from around 75 hulls in 1619 to 42 in 1634, the squadron of Spain having been slashed in 1621 from 21 galleys to just 12.[60] The perennial problem of finding crews was reflected in the change in policy recommended on 15 December 1638 by the *Junta de Galeras* (Galleys Board), which argued that *forzados* already in service should no longer be used for building projects or agricultural labour during the winter months, but should rather be rested, enabling them to recover their strength so that they might at least perform adequately during the next sailing season.[61] Given the coercive and sometimes violent recruiting methods routinely employed during Philip IV's reign to enlist ordinary seamen for Spanish naval vessels, not just in Galicia and Andalusia, where such tactics were the norm, but even in Vizcaya and Guipúzcoa,[62] it was but a small step to the policy he was to adopt in 1639 in respect of the gypsies. They, it was hoped, would now be used to boost the numbers recruited to the *chusma*, as those on the rowing benches of the galleys were collectively known. A royal ordinance four years earlier had ordered, yet again to little effect, that all able-bodied gypsy males of between 20 and 50 years of age and without a trade or a master to serve be apprehended and sent to the galleys.[63] Now, on 20 May 1638, Philip IV once again ordered justices across Spain to apprehend gypsies in their areas, and noted in particular that because of the lack of oarsmen, part of the squadron of Spain was unable to put to sea.[64] But it soon became clear that this order, too, had failed, almost certainly, as the *Junta de galeotes, esclavos, y gitanos* complained the following year, because information had leaked out in advance about what had been intended to be a co-ordinated and synchronized action involving the authorities of Castile, Aragon, and Valencia – a tactic designed to inhibit the gypsies' ability to frustrate their pursuers simply by crossing into another jurisdiction.[65] On 9 February 1639, building on the precedent set by his grandfather, Philip IV sent a new instruction to the *Chancillerías* and all of Spain's justices, royal and seigneurial. First, mandatory sentences to the galleys were not to be annulled, changed, or reduced in any way, a practice seen far too often in the *Chancillerías* for the crown's liking; and secondly, other sentences, including the death sentence, should be commuted wherever possible to service at the oar. When the number of prisoners so sentenced reached 20 – or in distant Galicia, 12 – the men were immediately to be transported to the centres from which they would be taken directly to the galley ports on the south and south-eastern coasts.[66]

Yet even when a man was condemned to galley service, it was by no means certain that his sentence would be carried out as intended. In March 1639 in Madrid, 11 gypsies were sentenced, along with two slaves, to four years at the oar. A letter signed by Juan de Quiñones and two other judges instructed the alguacil Martín de Cuellar to escort them from the capital to Toledo. From there, having been handed over to the *alcalde* of that city's gaol, they were to be escorted to the galley ports. But the letter also insisted that the group be accompanied by the royal notary Mateo de Vitoria. It was to be his job not just to certify that the prisoners' heads, whiskers and beards were shaved clean, but also to ensure that the one *real* per day issued for the sustenance of each prisoner was actually spent by their guards on the food for which it was intended.[67] More worrying for the authorities, however, was the fact that it was difficult to guarantee that such prisoners would ever even reach the southern and south-eastern ports to begin their sentences. Indeed, the crown special commissioner Pedro de Amezqueta, charged with ensuring that appeals pending in cases of men sentenced to the oar should be expedited as a matter of urgency wherever possible, was ordered by Philip IV in a letter of 23 March 1639 to investigate the escapes over the winter of 'many men condemned to the galleys' from gaols in Córdoba, Málaga, Jaca, and the towns of Vilches and Mengíbar in the province of Jaén.[68] And there were clearly suspicions in Madrid, to put it no more strongly than that, that these cases were not unique, since the letter also asks Amezqueta to report back not just on these escapes, but also on 'any others you find to have occurred in the areas through which you travel'. Nine years earlier, on 15 September 1630, Philip IV had noted that the corruption of gaolers and others involved in the transportation of *forzados* to the galleys and other prisoners to Spain's North African penal colonies meant that 'although large numbers of criminals are given these sentences, they are rarely carried out'.[69] Certainly, the open road could present its opportunities. José de Pellicer, for example, reported that on 15 September 1643, a string of convicts being transported to the galleys from the gaol at Toledo had managed to escape, murdering their escorts in the process.[70]

It is nevertheless an indication of the tensions existing by this time between the Council and the *Chancillerías*, which were inevitably reluctant to bow to this latest attempt to usurp what they regarded as their proper function as courts of appeal, that the king's instruction of 9 February was, by and large, ignored. So, too, was a second attempt to introduce similar measures the following year.[71] On 13 April 1639, the king ordered justices in Aragon to hunt down gypsies reported to be in their areas, informing other justices both there and in Castile and requesting their assistance as necessary.[72] Finally, on 19 November, the *Junta de galeotes, esclavos, y gitanos* recommended to the king a proposal brought forward by the Protonotary of Aragon, Don Jerónimo de Villanueva, the Count-Duke of Olivares's right-hand man, which insisted once again on the real urgency of the need to man and arm the galleys, pointing out that these were the first line of defence for the nation's eastern and south-eastern coasts. The gypsies were once again to be the principal target:

And since the *Junta* judges that condemnation to the oar is nowhere more justly employed than in the case of these people, it is of the opinion that by expediting the necessary decrees through the Secretariat of State in order to ensure greater secrecy, and if your Majesty sets a fixed date for implementation across the whole of Spain, he should be able to order *corregidores* and other justices in all the kingdoms, on the date indicated, to apprehend and imprison all gypsies found in their areas of jurisdiction. And your Majesty should order that the dispatch is not to be opened until the day it is to be implemented, and even then in conditions of great secrecy and caution, so that none may manage to escape...[73]

The proposal noted the obstructiveness of the *Chancillerías* the year before, reported to it by Amezqueta. Now, it insisted, the *Chancillerías* and other justices should be instructed 'not to meddle in this or any related matter', either under the pretext of lengthy appeals procedures or, indeed, by dint of simply pardoning prisoners so condemned, as they had too often been wont to do. The *Sala de Alcaldes, Chancillerías* and *Audiencias* should further be required by the Council to submit a report to it every 15 days detailing the prisoners held and the stage their cases had reached, all of which should in any case be resolved within 60 days. This should all be done 'with great speed, because last year these orders were not executed as they should have been'. Philip IV professed himself well satisfied with the proposal, though he reduced the reporting period to eight days and added that the *Junta* should meet once a week to monitor progress.[74] The result was an order issued in conditions of great secrecy a month later which required all able-bodied gypsies and slaves to be sent to the galleys.[75] 'It was issued on the same day in all the kingdoms of Castile', reported the chronicler José de Pellicer in his entry for 27 December 1639.[76] Only later were sedentarized gypsies exempted.[77] As to its success, the very sparse quantitative data available suggest that inability or failure to enforce the law, successful evasion thereof, or subsequent escapes continued even then to be widespread. Surviving records at Cartagena, where many of those convicted were sent for embarkation, show that 141 men, about 13 per cent of those who arrived there between 1639 and 1641, were registered as gypsies.[78] While this doubtless represented an increase on those apprehended previously, it was still clearly a very long way from the clean sweep that had been demanded by the legislators in Madrid. No figures, however, are available for El Puerto de Santa María, the other main point of embarkation for men sentenced to the oar, so it remains possible that this figure may under-represent the numbers apprehended.

7
The Spanish Church and the Gypsies

The relationship between the Spanish Catholic Church and the gypsies was played out over the early modern period on two main and in some ways overlapping fronts. There were, of course, the strident condemnations of the gypsies' way of life by clerics such as Melchor de Huélamo, Salazar de Mendoza, Sancho de Moncada, and others. These reflected, and not infrequently amplified the Church authorities' serious concerns about the gypsies' irreligion or notoriously tenuous or, as many thought, wholly feigned attachment to the faith. In 1601, even the Archbishop of Toledo and Primate of all Spain, Bernardo de Sandoval y Rojas, Lerma's uncle, echoing demands progressively enshrined in legislation from the time of the Catholic Monarchs, instructed both ecclesiastical judges and ordinary clergy to see to it that gypsies in their areas were baptized.[1] They should also ensure, he added, that efforts were made to assimilate these wayward people to the manners and morals of mainstream society. In September the following year, in the Synodal Constitutions of his diocese of Cuenca, the bishop and future Inquisitor-General Andrés Pacheco expressed similar concerns about the spiritual welfare of both the area's re-settled Granadine *moriscos* and its gypsies. The clergy must in future ensure, he insisted, that these people received the Sacraments of Baptism, Confirmation, Matrimony, Extreme Unction, and Confession, reporting progress and seeking approval from the bishop's vicar-general before finally administering the Holy Eucharist to suitably prepared individuals. Once again, the emphasis was firmly on assimilation, pastoral care and, above all, careful monitoring and control by local clergy.

Issues relating to gypsies were raised periodically by the Church, in 1580 in Tarr___a, where the archbishop labelled them 'liars, thieves, and wicke_____',[2] in 1660 and 1682 in Toledo, and in 1626 in Cuenca, where con____ __ __at the prohibited degrees were being ignored led to the introduction of a rule stipulating that all gypsy marriages must be approved by the bishop or vicar-general unless the couple involved had been resident for ten years in the diocese.[3] For the most part, however, the ecclesiastical authorities seem to have been content to leave matters relating to gypsies in the hands of parish priests. Where they did express concerns, these almost invariably reflected worries about the impossibility of exercising proper pastoral control over non-sedentarized groups. The Inquisition, of course, also investigated gypsies, just as it did others from Spain's dispossessed underclasses – and, one should add, for similar offences. These included sorcery and superstition, which could involve little more than adding a few words to a prayer or, in one case in Granada in 1635, that of 'Ángela, daughter of a gypsy', simply placing such a 'superstitious prayer' under an altar, an act which earned her an inquisitorial warning.[4] But it certainly would not be accurate to describe the Inquisition as having actively, let alone zealously pursued gypsies. It is true that the inquisitors did examine dutifully the cases reported to them, usually, but not always, by non-gypsies nursing this or that grudge; but one sometimes senses behind their bureaucratic meticulousness a less than firm conviction that some of the activities brought to their attention really deserved to fall within the purview of an organization supposedly devoted to the eradication of heresy. In fact, despite the punishments periodically inflicted on them by the Inquisition, Spain's gypsies often had good reason to be thankful to the Church. Throughout the sixteenth and seventeenth centuries it proved time and again to be one of their more reliable and effective protectors, frequently sheltering them from the none-too-gentle attentions of the increasingly frustrated civil authorities, beside whom their treatment at the hands of the inquisitors could sometimes seem almost benign. A long-running polemic centred on such regular 'abuses' of ecclesiastical sanctuary naturally ensued, and was finally resolved only in the middle of the eighteenth century, when the Spanish authorities reached an accommodation, a political fudge, actually, with the Vatican.

Inquisition

The Inquisition, or New Inquisition introduced in Castile in the 1480s by the Catholic Monarchs and always closely reliant on the crown, was modelled faithfully on its medieval forerunner in Aragon. However, it soon came to form a central element of the Church-state apparatus of power in a Castile which now found itself at the centre of empire.[5] It even had one of the administrative councils of government devoted to it. Established in 1488, the Council of the Inquisition, also known as the *Suprema*, was presided over by the Inquisitor-General, the only member of the council appointed by Rome rather than the king, who could nevertheless nominate suitable candidates.[6] The Inquisition had originally been re-introduced with the specific aim of investigating reports of heretical beliefs and practices among New Christians, especially religious backsliding by *conversos*. But it also investigated *moriscos*, many of whom had received virtually no instruction in the faith. One should add that this was not particularly unusual, since ignorance of the Church's teachings was also widespread among their Old Christian neighbours, especially in the sixteenth century, as the inquisitors were all too aware.[7] By the time the latter turned their attention to gypsies nearly six decades later, they had widened their net considerably, investigating cases of bigamy, fornication, and usury among Spain's Old Christian as well as its convert populations.[8] Unfortunately, there are significant gaps in the Inquisition's records, especially for the early years in Castile, though later documents also frequently failed to record crucial details such as the sentences passed. But those that have survived show that over the next two and a half centuries it investigated at least 170 gypsies, most of them in the seventeenth and eighteenth centuries.[9] The number seems surprisingly low, especially when one considers the virulent nature of the diatribes periodically directed against them by figures of authority within the Church. It has sometimes been suggested that the gypsies' poverty may have acted as a deterrent to the inquisitors, since the property of those accused was normally sold off as necessary and used to pay for the upkeep of prisoners as they languished in the Inquisition's gaols awaiting trial. Indeed, Melchor de Huélamo claimed that even the civil authorities were failing to prosecute gypsies precisely because the latter owned nothing worthy of confiscation to offset the expenses incurred in their arrest.[10] Such seizures had frequently been demanded by the legislators in Madrid,[11] and, despite Huélamo's protest, the fact was that the gypsies' possessions, especially their animals, were quite often confiscated. This is what happened, for example, in the case of the gypsies of Hinojosa del Duque, their seven donkeys eventually being seized and sold at public auction on the orders of the Duke of Béjar.[12] Of gypsies processed by the Inquisition, approximately half (83) appeared before the tribunals of Granada (48), Seville (19), and Córdoba (16). This does not mean, however, that Andalusia's inquisitors were more zealous than others in their pursuit of gypsies. Rather the figure for the south is almost certainly roughly proportional to the significant numbers of gypsies who had taken up settled residence there, numbers later confirmed by the census undertaken at Charles III's behest in 1783. The fact that they were sedentarized in towns and villages meant that the Church authorities were less inclined to fret about their spiritual welfare than that of their itinerant counterparts. But that same sedentarized – or semi-sedentarized – status also rendered those denounced to the tribunals by their neighbours much more liable to be apprehended and incarcerated. Of other gypsies processed, most were brought before the tribunals of Valencia (23), Toledo (17 or 18), and Cuenca (13). The remaining tribunals of Barcelona, Las Palmas, Llerena, Logroño, Madrid, Mallorca, Valladolid, and Zaragoza all saw fewer than six individuals, or, in the case of Santiago, none at all.

As to the charges, about 65 per cent of those brought before the tribunals had been accused of sorcery. Yet the Inquisition's standard terminology here, *hechicería* (sorcery or witchcraft) failed in any sense adequately to represent the nature of the offences of which gypsies, usually women, stood accused.[13] These typically involved spells, curses, incantations and potions designed, as the inquisitors were very well aware, to exploit the gullibility or wishful thinking of those sufficiently naive or desperate to allow themselves to be duped. Whether designed to cure an ailment or induce one, engender love or dispel it, enchant or disenchant, the gypsies' remedies naturally came at a price. This was, of course, an age that believed in witchcraft, but as an eighteenth-century instruction to inquisitors pointed out, the activities of gypsy women were normally to be regarded as fraudulent rather than heretical, designed as they were to obtain money by deceiving 'ignorant persons'.[14] Prejudice and sheer malice often drove the denunciations anyway, and few believed that activities such as these constituted serious heresy, much though they may have disapproved of them. In practice, the sentences applied in such cases, which varied according to the perceived seriousness of the offence and, to some extent, from tribunal to tribunal, were if anything less severe than those handed down for blasphemy, a charge which accounted for around 20 per cent of those summoned before the Inquisition. Just under 10 per cent were charged with other verbal offences of various kinds – potentially heretical *proposiciones* in the jargon of the inquisitors. The remaining charges, which were obviously very few in number, included bigamy (four cases, one of whom escaped from gaol), sacrilege, sexual offences, allegedly Lutheran, or Judaizing practices, and even, in the case of the gypsy Gabriel de Chaves, having attempted in 1608 to cross from Marbella to 'Barbary'. This last case was investigated by the Granada tribunal, which suspected Chaves of intending to renounce the faith in favour of Islam, a chameleon stratagem not infrequently employed by those who fled to North Africa to escape justice for crimes committed in Spain. Chaves was tortured twice, but denied the accusations. The inquisitors did not believe him, however, sentencing him to 100 lashes and six years in the galleys.[15]

One man brought before the Granada tribunal in 1577 accused of an heretical proposition was named as Fulano ('what's-his-name'), 'whom they call "the Gypsy" ', but who was subsequently described as a *morisco* from Baza, perhaps because he was reported to have said that 'the worst *morisco* is better than the best Christian'. María de N., charged with superstition in Valencia in 1747, was described as 'a woman married to a gypsy', though she may have been of non-gypsy birth herself, as may Ana de Alarcón, described in the same way and accused in Granada of bigamy in 1645. In 1733, the gypsy Isabel Franco, known as 'the Flea', appeared accused of sorcery before the Murcia tribunal, where she was described as the wife of Francisco Montoya, by profession a barber. In several cases, the gypsies involved are described as 'wandering' or of no fixed abode. The gypsy María de Torres, who came before the Murcia tribunal in 1638 charged with sorcery, was described as a 'passerby' from Seville, the widow of one Diego Hernández, who had died while serving in the galleys. In 1625, the gypsy María Bustamante appeared before the Valladolid tribunal accused of burying her husband in accordance with certain Jewish rites, while María Hernández was accused in Granada of sorcery with a group of persons suspected of Jewish sympathies.[16] A few sexual offences were also investigated. One 18-year-old gypsy blacksmith from Écija, named simply as Montoya Mellado and accused of sodomy, usually referred to as the *pecado nefando* ('abominable sin' or 'sin that must not be spoken of'), saw his case suspended in Valencia in 1597 because of the flimsy nature of the evidence against him – although such suspensions still left the accused facing the permanent threat of a renewed investigation.[17] His alleged partner had been tortured on two occasions, but had consistently denied the charge. Had he not done so, both he and Montoya Mellado could have expected severe punishment. By that date, such cases were investigated by the Inquisition only in the Crown of Aragon, jurisdiction over such cases in Castile having passed in 1509 exclusively to the civil courts.[18] Another gypsy, Joan Mario, accused of a similar offence 14 years earlier, was condemned in Zaragoza to be whipped and serve four years in the galleys. Even this sentence was not particularly representative, however, since the Zaragoza tribunal enjoyed a reputation for great severity in such cases, and quite frequently condemned such offenders sentenced to death in the later sixteenth and early seventeenth centuries.[19] In Castile, another gypsy, Juan Escudero, a native of Barcelona resident in Dos Hermanas near Seville, was in 1580 given an even lengthier sentence for 'simple fornication'. This phrase normally referred to heterosexual intercourse between consenting but unmarried adults, but in this case seems merely to have related to Escudero's claim that his crudely expressed intention to 'mount' both a female prisoner and her daughter was, in his opinion, not sinful.[20] His case, not to mention his theology, was not helped by a series of blasphemous outbursts in which he was reported to have said 'better the devil than God', and, according to one witness, that he intended, when released, to go around burning all the crucifixes he could find. Escudero's case was investigated by the Granada Inquisition, which required him, somewhat contradictorily, to abjure his sins *de levi*, the form of words usually reserved for lesser offences, but then serve a hefty six years at the oar. No doubt their decision owed something to the tribunal's awareness that Chaves had previously served ten years in the galleys, having been convicted of killing a boy at whom he had thrown a rock.[21]

Even seemingly very minor charges were sometimes pored over for possible heresy. In Barcelona in 1608, Gratiniana Bustamante was brought before the inquisitors merely for reading palms, though one should add that this was not the first time her activities had been brought to their attention. They duly sentenced her to 50 lashes and banishment. That said, fortune-telling was more often than not regarded as a minor offence by the Inquisition,[22] despite Pedro Ciruelo's warning in the 1530s that 'it is a superstition and diabolical divination; and those who practise it have a secret pact with the devil, who very cunningly stirs their imagination to make them say things without knowing why they are doing so'.[23] Occasionally, the inquisitors found themselves dealing with cases in which the combined gullibility and cupidity of the alleged victim must have seemed to outweigh the alleged offence of the accused. One such was that of María de Heredia, a Galician gypsy married to a Cádiz blacksmith, who was accused in Seville in 1637 of telling fortunes and 'discovering treasures'.[24] With the expulsion of the *moriscos* almost three decades earlier, rumours had begun to circulate about buried money and other possessions left behind by *moriscos* who, it was imagined, planned one day to return to recover them,[25] this despite that fact that most of those expelled were actually poor labourers or artisans.[26] But such rumours played to a curiously persistent popular conviction among Old Christians that the *moriscos*' notorious parsimony must mean that they were hoarding money somewhere, and were thus easily exploited by gypsies claiming to be able through occult means to identify where this hidden wealth might be unearthed.[27] At any event, the tribunal seems to have considered María's offence a fairly minor one. It instructed her to abjure her sins *de levi*, reprimanded her, and put some distance between her and her suggestible clients by sentencing her to four years internal exile.

The sentences handed down to gypsies by the Inquisition often, though by no means always, combined corporal punishment with various forms of spiritual penance. With some notable exceptions, they tended on the whole to be lighter than those they could expect to receive from civil tribunals.[28] But they did not differ in type or severity from those imposed on the numerous non-gypsies sentenced for similar offences. The decision as to which penalties to impose depended essentially on two considerations, first, the degree to which the activities described or the words used by the offender were deemed truly to smack of heresy or to have caused profound offence, and, second, the previous behaviour of the individual called to account. Occasionally, exemplary punishments were ordained, as in Mallorca, where in 1606 the gypsy Isabel Graciana was found guilty of superstitious practices and sentenced to 100 lashes, a public shaming, and 'perpetual' internal exile, her inquisitors recording that her punishment was specifically intended to be an example to others.[29] In the case of two gypsy women, María and Magdalena, charged with sorcery before the Toledo tribunal in 1623, the transcripts do not record the sentences they received; but they do observe that, whilst there were certainly grounds for regarding them as guilty of sorcery, due recognition should also be given to the fact that the case had involved 'a good deal of fraud and trickery through which they sought to obtain money'.[30] Sentences for both sorcery and blasphemy could accordingly range from the mere warning issued to the gypsy María de Montoya, accused of sorcery in Granada in 1697, to the draconian sentence handed down for a technically similar offence in Córdoba in 1745 to the 57-year-old gypsy, Isabel de Escobedo. She was ordered to be paraded at one of the Inquisition's elaborately choreographed public rituals known as an *auto de fe* ('act of faith') wearing insignia declaring her a cheat and a liar. She was also to be given 200 lashes, the maximum number normally allowed, these to be administered as she was driven through the streets, and was then to be expelled from Córdoba and its environs for six years. In 1606, the gypsy Sebastiana de Vargas from Jerez was processed by the Seville tribunal, again charged with sorcery. One of the two female witnesses, anxious for news of a son who had travelled to the Indies, claimed to have been told by Sebastiana – it is not clear who approached whom – that she could, for a price, bring him home 'in two weeks'. She had then proceeded to invoke the aid of executed criminals, as well as 'Barrabas, and Satan and all the devils', conjuring the woman's son to return. Sebastiana quickly confessed, saying that she had only done it for the money and for no other reason. She was required to abjure her sins *de levi* and sentenced to be shamed publicly and whipped through the streets of Seville.[31]

As to blasphemy, the range of sentences passed suggests that the inquisitors were occasionally sympathetic to the fact that temperament and circumstance could sometimes conspire to provoke an outburst that might later be regretted. A concordat of 1512, later confirmed in a papal bull, had early established that only cases of blasphemy involving heretical questioning of God's omnipotence should properly be brought before the Inquisition, though it had little effect either in Aragon or Castile. In Castile, a royal ordinance of 1515, which alluded to a memorandum requesting inquisitors not to investigate comments made by individuals who were playing cards or under the influence of alcohol, was similarly ignored.[32] In 1605, Luis de Montoya, a gypsy from Jerez, was denounced to the Inquisition in Seville by two women who reported events which, they claimed, had taken place three years earlier. The long delay between offence and denunciation inevitably suggests that it may have been malice or a grudge rather than some sudden pricking of conscience that provoked their action. The younger of the two told the inquisitors that Montoya, who had just lost his money at the card-table, had returned home, seized a crucifix, and shouted 'you don't want to help me, God, even though I have you in my home'. Then, clasping the figure's left leg between his teeth, he had broken it before using a lighted candle to destroy various images of saints and a picture of the child Jesus. The witnesses claimed that when asked why he had done it, Montoya had replied 'because they don't help me when I'm gambling'. However, he subsequently declared himself utterly contrite and explained that he was at the time 'consumed with rage at having lost and altogether beside myself'; and he added that he well understood that such images should be venerated, before throwing himself on the mercy of the inquisitors. They instructed him to abjure his sins *de levi*, attend just one mass as a penitent, and warned him not to re-offend.[33]

Not all blasphemers escaped quite so lightly. In 1559, the Toledo tribunal investigated the 22-year-old gypsy Francisco de Gales. It had been claimed that 'in conversation with certain persons, the aforementioned Franciso de Gales had said that God was not for everyone, and that he was as just as God, which caused a great scandal'.[34] Gales had already been languishing in one of the Inquisition's cells for some time and was anxious to encourage the tribunal, given, as he put it, 'the hardships I have already endured in its prisons', to inform him as soon as possible of his sentence:

> I am a young Christian, and the things I said are things men say (*palabras de hombre*), and I was not in my right mind, and as soon as I came to this Holy Office I made a statement and confessed the truth at the first hearing, and I am not even twenty-five...[35]

He attempted a plea in mitigation, arguing that the second of his remarks in fact demonstrated his keen appreciation of divine justice. But he also admitted that he had said these things 'not being myself or possessed of my natural judgement, on account of having drunk a good deal'. The inquisitors were not impressed on this occasion. It had originally been demanded that he be condemned for perjury, heresy, and apostasy. In the end, he was sentenced to 100 lashes. Others, like the gypsies sentenced for blasphemy in Valencia in 1690, Juan and Diego Montoya, were even less fortunate. They were ordered not only to be paraded at an *auto de fe*, gagged and dressed as penitents, but also to receive 100 lashes, and, having been exiled from Valencia, to serve three years in the galleys followed by three more in prison.[36]

Women were sometimes also treated harshly. When the Andalusian gypsy Catalina appeared before the Toledo tribunal in October 1562 accused of blasphemy, she explained that, when on the previous Thursday or Friday she had arrived 'worn out from the rain and cold' in a village whose name she could not remember, its 'hospital' or shelter had refused to take her in and a group of youths throwing stones had pursued her into the surrounding countryside. This continued 'until they drove her out of her mind, and, angry and freezing cold, she had said that she cursed God and would break into pieces the first cross she saw'. She claimed immediately to have repented this outburst, which, she insisted, had happened only once. She also denied having made certain other, scatologically blasphemous remarks attributed to her by her accusers, who, she said, had held her prisoner for three days before bringing her before the tribunal. The inquisitors questioned her about her family, which included 17 brothers and sisters and an uncle, Francisco, who, she told them, 'led a troop of gypsies who killed him in La Mancha over a small matter'. As usual in such cases, they also attempted to assess her knowledge of the faith, which proved to be virtually nonexistent. They sentenced her to be gagged and given 100 lashes through the streets of Toledo. She had, it is true, been whipped once before, for theft in Jaén; but the sentence was unusually harsh, imposed on a woman who, claiming ignorance of her own age, was estimated to have been about 60.[37] Nonetheless, of the 19 cases of blasphemy and 24 cases of sorcery involving gypsies that have come down to us via the Inquisition's records and where the sentence is stipulated, 10 and 13, respectively, did not involve the corporal punishments of flogging or, for men, condemnation to the galleys at all. Sometimes, they elicited no more than a warning or a requirement that those accused attend a mass. More often, they would be penanced, required to abjure their sins *de levi*, and perhaps be paraded and publicly shamed at an *auto de fe*, in which case they would be kept waiting to hear their sentence until the actual ceremony.[38] In over half of these cases, the gypsies were also sent into internal exile for periods varying from one to eight years, with all the disruption to lives, livelihoods – and, of course, the crown's sedentarization project – that this inevitably entailed.

There were occasions, too, when the inquisitors showed themselves willing to take account of age and infirmity when deciding a sentence. When the 14-year-old gypsy Manuel Montoya was convicted of blasphemy in Valencia in 1618, he was instructed to hear just one mass, though he was still sent into internal exile for one year. In another case, the gypsy Matías Montoya was excused the galley service to which he had earlier been condemned, after managing to satisfy the tribunal from his gaol cell that he was suffering from consumption.[39] And in one early case examined in Toledo in 1549, Jorge Santarem, accused of sacrilege, was merely penanced, the inquisitors accepting that he suffered from epilepsy. The tribunals had to be convinced, though, since exaggerated histrionics by gypsies involving feigned madness and a variety of other ills, including selective amnesia when it came to providing autobiographical details, including even the names of close relatives, were a wearily familiar feature of such proceedings.[40]

Such tactics, and the gypsies' liberal use of aliases, meant that the civil and ecclesiastical authorities often found it difficult to establish the precise identity of those involved in cases they wished to investigate. In 1626, for example, a gypsy named as Lucero Malla was denounced to the Inquisition in Toledo as a bigamist. The informer, unusually, was another gypsy, Miguel Garcés.[41] His motives are not recorded, but they must have been powerful to make him break what for many gypsies was an unwritten law. Garcés himself told the tribunal that such was the gypsies' 'style and reason of state' that it would be difficult to obtain witness statements from them, even though many knew about the affair. He added, 'if they even discover that this witness has informed on the aforementioned individuals, they will all of them turn against him and kill him, even if it is necessary to travel fifty leagues to do so, of that you may be certain'.[42] The accused, Malla, who was said at that time to be in gaol elsewhere for another offence, was described as 'a young dancer of medium stature with a freckled face', and was alleged four months earlier in Ocaña (Old Castile) to have married 'the daughter of the horse-breaker, who is another gypsy and householder of the town' while already married to another gypsy girl in Llerena (Extremadura). The tribunal's investigations in Ocaña revealed that four or five months earlier a gypsy announcing himself as Diego de Alvarado and a gypsy girl named María de Torres had indeed presented themselves to a priest there named Pantoja and asked him to marry them on the spot. Pantoja initially tried to persuade the couple to wait until the following day. But after an intervention by another priest, Pedro de Buendía, who encouraged him to accede to their request precisely on the grounds that it was so very unusual, not least because the couple were gypsies, he agreed. After the documents presented by Alvarado had been scrutinized and his bride-to-be had been examined – successfully, it would seem – to verify her knowledge of the faith, Pantoja duly married them. The ceremony took place in the presence of the notary, Luis Casarrubias, and other Old Christian residents of the town, one of whom later observed, anecdotally, that this was the first time he had ever seen or heard of married gypsies. Afterwards, Alvarado asked the village carpenter Cristóbal Pérez to go home and fetch his guitar and a celebration ensued at which the groom lived up to his considerable reputation – several witnesses reported having seen him perform in different villages – as 'a very fine dancer'. The solemn blessing or 'veiling' four days later was attended by a large number of people, gypsy and non-gypsy alike. However, the case, fraught with difficulties as it was, could not be brought to a conclusion. The priest, Pantoja, could only recall that Diego de Alvarado was dark-haired and a dancer. Whether he was also the dancer Lucero de Malla, as the informant claimed, is impossible to know, as is the reason for the urgency of the gypsies' seemingly unprecedented desire to embrace Christian matrimony. The inquisitorial record of this case does, however, offer a glimpse, as María Helena Sánchez Ortega noted, of the apparently cordial relations between Old Christian and gypsy communities in Ocaña, even if the latter were still regarded after two hundred years already spent in Spain as 'a strange, different, and picturesque group'.[43]

Finally, I turn to a curious case that was brought to the attention of the Toledo tribunal in August 1624. It concerned events which had taken place that summer in Madrid and involved not only a number of women, gypsy and non-gypsy, but also, allegedly, certain unnamed individuals from the very highest levels of Spanish society. The main witness in the case was a 54-year-old Irish gentleman named as Don Juan de Falbeo, possibly a corruption of John Falbe or Falbee, who lived in the calle del Olmo in the parish of San Sebastián. He had been a resident of Madrid for 20 years and declared himself to be 'in the service of his Majesty' and of the Catholic Church. At that time, this seems to have amounted to him spying, rather ineptly it must be said, on the 'many heretics' he and others believed to be associating in certain less reputable areas of the capital.[44] He was acting, he claimed, 'on the orders of an important churchman', who was not only his confessor, but who also confessed ministers of the king. While Falbeo went about his business in the seamier quarters south of the Plaza Mayor, intense political speculation at court that summer had given way to a growing conviction that the Count of Olivares, concerned about the family succession, was now intending to marry his 14-year-old daughter Doña María de Guzmán y Zuñiga to the young Ramiro Núñez de Guzmán, Marquis of Toral, who had been brought to the court from León. There is no doubt that there were those who opposed the match as preparations went ahead. Many had assumed that the Count of Niebla, son of the Duke of Medina Sidonia would be the obvious choice, though there were also other possibilities. Nonetheless, the marriage contract was eventually signed on 10 October that same year.[45] It was in this somewhat unlikely connection that Juan de Falbeo claimed to have been informed in July by an *alcalde de la corte*, Alonso de Baldenebro, that certain persons were desirous of seeing the 12-year-old Ramiro rendered impotent. Baldenebro had been told this by a member of the Marchioness of Toral's household, Juan Pinedo, who said that he in turn had been told by 'a gentleman from Vizcaya'.

Falbeo told the tribunal that his necessarily clandestine activities had already led him to Puerta Cerrada, close by the Plaza Mayor, and to a 'secret' tavern there. It was run by a 27-year-old woman from Valladolid called Agueda, along with her husband, Alonso de Arellano. It was, he said, a place 'where many people from every nation go'. He had spoken to Agueda on a number of occasions, 'striking up a friendship with her in order to avoid suspicion'. A few days before his encounter with Baldenebro, Falbeo had seen 'a gypsy woman wearing a cloak in the Spanish style' enter Agueda's home and converse with her in secret.

Agueda had later told him that 'this was a woman who knew a great deal and whose house was visited by many illustrious and important people to whom she would give advice and show many strange things'. The gypsy was, Agueda assured him, 'a witch and sorceress' and knew both how to make a man fall in or out of love – Agueda, it appeared, had engaged her for both purposes – and how to make him impotent or, indeed, to reverse the effect as required. His appetite whetted, Falbeo reported back to his confessor, and was instructed to investigate further. Agueda duly accompanied him to a house in the calle de Arganzuela not far from the Plaza de la Cebada and the Rastro. Agueda went in, and while Falbeo listened at a window, spoke to a gypsy woman inside. The latter, he reported, had showered Agueda with flattery and had asked how she might be of service. She had said that she wished to help in order to please Agueda, not out of self-interest, since she had already been offered all she could possibly desire if she would 'make the one marrying the Olivares girl impotent'. Hearing this, Falbeo told the tribunal that he had 'muttered to himself, "if only I had Baldenebro and four good men here", and wondered whether it would be better to apprehend them immediately or report the matter to the Inquisition'.

While he debated whether what would presumably have amounted to overwhelming force was actually necessary under the circumstances, a much younger gypsy named as Catalina came out of the house and noticed what he was doing. Caught in the act, he went straight in and attempted to reassure the women inside that he could be trusted and that he was not a law officer. An older gypsy, María or Mariana, the dark-skinned (*tostada* or 'toasted') wife of a brick-maker – there is considerable uncertainty about names in the witness statements – was not remotely disposed to believe him; and, when he claimed merely to be accompanying Agueda, accused him of intending to denounce them to the Inquisition, adding, 'if you want to know anything, it's in order to do us harm'. Undeterred, Falbeo proceeded to confirm her suspicions by asking her directly about the matter of Olivares's daughter, to which 'she replied with great anger that he should mind his own business, and that many illustrious and noble persons of great importance at court were in contact with her'. A little later, Falbeo added that Agueda had claimed to have overheard the gypsies saying that the person who had paid the gypsy to make Ramiro de Guzmán impotent was 'a gentleman of the habit [a member of one of the military orders] at court'.

Agueda's testimony followed a labyrinthine and even more colourful course, one involving cures and spells, much description of the crossing of palms with silver, and tales of gypsy women moulding waxen effigies and conjuring up, among others, 'the devil Bullaque and Calderón and all those in hell and the Queen Sardine and la Jacarandina and Martha Martha who art in hell'. Although she admitted to having paid the older gypsy woman to put a spell on a man 'who had tricked and dishonoured her' so that she might in the future do with him as she wished, she was much less forthcoming when it came to questions about the future husband of Olivares's daughter. She claimed not to remember what had been said as Falbeo listened at the window, though she did recall having heard some such tale from another woman. The Inquisition naturally took a certain interest in the case, given the quality and rank of the intended victim, but the evidence, which might more fittingly have provided the plot of a *comedia*, was pitifully unconvincing. The gullible and hapless Don Juan de Falbeo, persuaded by his own zealotry and the malicious rumour mill of the court, had obviously been determined from the outset to see fire behind the smoke; and this, together with the simple Agueda's easily exploited suggestibility, was enough to set the machinery of the tribunal in motion. It is unclear how many gypsies were in fact involved, or, indeed, who they actually were. Names cited by witnesses included María or Mariana, Ana or Adriana, who had a withered arm and was later said to have fled to Valladolid after her involvement in a serious robbery, the young Catalina, and the much older María Hernández. In the end, as if to underline the point, the person eventually apprehended in relation to the case in December of that year was named as Isabel Cortés, a 20-year-old gypsy who had reportedly come to Madrid to seek the release on appeal of her husband, who had been condemned to the galleys. Her sentence, if there was one, was not recorded. The marriage of Don Ramiro and Doña María went ahead as planned on 9 January 1625. Tragically, Doña María died at the end of July the following year, having given birth two days earlier to a stillborn daughter. Don Ramiro went on, as the Duke of Medina de las Torres, eventually to become viceroy of Naples in 1636.[46]

As I have suggested, if certain of the gypsies' activities could occasionally invoke the wrath of the Inquisition, their relationship with the Church at a local level was on the whole characterized by the considerable protection extended to them by ordinary members of the clergy across Spain. It is thus to the matter of ecclesiastical sanctuary that I now turn.

Sanctuary

The question of jurisdiction was a recurring cause of friction between civil and ecclesiastical authorities in Spain throughout most of the early modern period. In 1476, Ferdinand and Isabella had found it necessary to warn ecclesiastical judges not to overstep their jurisdiction in the kingdom of Aragon;[47] and in 1493, another royal ordinance issued in Barcelona, which reiterated the monarchs' commitment to defend the Church and its privileges, insisted nevertheless that such defence should henceforth be the province of the civil rather than the ecclesiastical authorities:

> Ecclesiastical judges must not and should not use or avail themselves of temporal weapons in the execution of ecclesiastical justice, nor should they recruit bands of people or be the cause of any public disturbance, because they have no need of such things, since, if the help of our temporal authority is needed, we have instructed that, where a just request is made, anything necessary for the defence of the Church and its property and areas of jurisdiction should be provided.[48]

The Catholic Monarchs, and Ferdinand in particular, did manage to exert sufficient pressure to ensure a significant rolling-back of Rome's influence in what they regarded as properly internal matters, as well as contriving to gain access to some of the Spanish Church's vast wealth. However, the continuing limitations on the power of the monarch in early modern Spain, especially where the Church's traditional prerogatives were concerned, were not to be underestimated. All appointments to the Spanish episcopate and archiepiscopate still had to be approved by Rome, except in the kingdom of Granada after 1492 and, later, the New World, when Julius II's bull of 1508 conceded the universal *Patronato* there to the Spanish crown.[49] Rome also appointed the Inquisitor-General, who presided over the *Suprema*. And without the agreement of the pope, the crown could neither alienate church lands nor remove or modify the clergy's extensive privileges, which included exemption from taxation; nor could it make changes to the jurisdiction of the Inquisition, or, at least in theory, the temporal jurisdiction exercised by ecclesiastical authorities over the extensive territories owned by them.[50] The use or, depending on point of view, abuse of sanctuary in churches, monasteries, or even cemeteries by gypsies and others in need of a safe haven, including bankrupts in flight from their creditors, also had a long history in late medieval and early modern Spain.[51] For over two centuries, the Spanish Church fought tenaciously to preserve the right to offer sanctuary to those who sought it. Given that this effectively represented yet another limitation on royal jurisdiction, it faced repeated challenges by a crown which, at least from the time of Philip II, gave every sign of being rather less concerned with law enforcement *per se* than with political and economic expediency, specifically in respect of the need to find *forzados* for the galleys. Even before that, however, the issue of sanctuary had engendered a number of bitter disputes. At the *Cortes* of Valladolid in 1542 the *procuradores* requested Charles V to instruct justices across Spain to respect ecclesiastical sanctuary and cease the practice of forcible removal of suspects from churches and monasteries where they had taken refuge, except where the crimes were of sufficient gravity as to merit such action.[52] Their request was repeated at the *Cortes* celebrated in Madrid in 1551:

> justices and judges have little respect or reverence for churches and holy places, and, contrary to what is provided by the laws of these kingdoms, disregard the sanctuary of the churches and, without proper legal sanction, remove people from them by force, breaking their way in through doors and roofs...[53]

The cost of repairs should, they argued, be borne by those who caused the damage, which might help prevent such abuses in the future. Charles agreed and issued appropriate instructions. By 1566, however, Philip II, faced with the growing problem of manpower shortages on the rowing benches, issued an ordinance instructing the clergy to deny ecclesiastical sanctuary to those, including gypsies, who had been sentenced to the galleys. Where they refused to do so, the justices should remove the fugitives anyway, which, the ordinance added, they were entitled under the law to do.[54] The principle, he argued, had been enshrined in law as early as the thirteenth century, in Alfonso X's *fuero real*, which insisted that it was not the Church's role to protect known thieves, arsonists or other serious criminals from temporal justice.[55] The Church continued to put up fierce resistance, however, and even when fugitives were forcibly removed from a church and tried by the civil authorities, it would usually insist that they be restored to its protection thereafter. Indeed, ecclesiastical law asserted that such individuals continued to enjoy what came to be known as 'cold immunity' (*iglesias frías*, literally 'cold churches') until they were so restored. In some cases, those responsible for the forcible extraction of gypsy men and women from churches where they had sought sanctuary were even excommunicated, like the *corregidor* of Plasencia in 1695.[56]

The frustration felt by the civil authorities as a result of these wrangles could sometimes take an ugly turn. An undated document, probably written in 1631 or 1632, since it refers to Juan de Quiñones's 'very recent' discourse on gypsies, took issue with the *alcaldes* of the Valladolid *Chancillería* for their brutal treatment of 'some gypsies' – the number is not specified – whom they had been ordered to restore to Church sanctuary. Their reaction had been to use a branding iron to burn the words 'thief, ecclesiastical sanctuary' into the men's faces, an act they sought to justify by appealing to the authority of Aristotle and the philosopher's views on slavery. The document rejected their argument, insisting that the *alcaldes* had greatly exceeded their authority, first, because their jurisdiction was effectively suspended while a legal decision on the men's claim to ecclesiastical sanctuary was still pending, and, secondly, because 'to have branded them was worse than condemning them to the galleys, since that penalty would have been temporary and could have been revoked, whereas branding on the face cannot, and lasts for life'.[57] It was not the first time such questions had arisen. The *Cortes* of Valladolid had as early as 1548 petitioned Charles V to permit the faces of thieves, 'of whom there are so many that people cannot cope', to be marked in this way, adding that if such men re-offended, they should be hanged or sent to the galleys.[58]

From about the middle of the seventeenth century, the issue of ecclesiastical sanctuary gave rise to a number of polemical tracts written by churchmen and law officers alike. The role of the Church as protector of gypsies and others accused of serious crimes had been condemned in 1639 by the *Junta de galeotes, esclavos, y gitanos*. It expressed particular concern about the increasing tendency of ecclesiastical judges to grant sanctuary even to prisoners who had originally been arrested in places that were not under their jurisdiction:

There are many criminals held for serious offences in gaols in Madrid and throughout the kingdoms who, in order to avoid punishment by using deception, concocted evidence, and false witnesses, claim the sanctuary of the Church [. . .] because ecclesiastical judges commonly accept the evidence presented by the prisoners, and whilst it is necessary and just to preserve the Church's right to grant sanctuary to offenders who take refuge there, the shelter and protection contrary to truth and justice of criminals who are not in reality entitled to sanctuary, and who were not in fact removed from churches, also represents an offence to that same Church.[59]

In 1644, the argument was taken up by Doctor Pedro de Villalobos, Dean of the Law Faculty at the University of Salamanca. The Church, he argued, must no longer extend its sanctuary to the gypsy bandits who were plaguing the area, 'perfidious enemies within', as he put it, of a Spain 'surrounded by foes and whose frontiers are under assault', words indicative of the deep sense of crisis in Castile inspired by the rebellions in Portugal and Catalonia four years earlier, as well as the decisive defeat of Spanish troops by the French at Rocroi in 1643.[60] He had produced his tract at the behest of the city's *corregidor*, Don García de Cotes Morejón y Vega. Don García had been asked to restore the gypsy Santiago Maldonado, at that time languishing in the royal gaol in Salamanca accused of being a bandit leader, to the sanctuary of the parish church where he had originally been apprehended in the village of Topas. Maldonado and his heavily armed band of 'thirty to forty' confederates had allegedly been active over a wide area, especially in El Cubo de la Tierra del Vino, Valdelosa, Santiz, Mayalde, San Cristóbal del Monte, and other villages just north of Salamanca. Further south, they were reported in Escurial de la Sierra to have routed a company of soldiers on their way to Ciudad Rodrigo, who, moved by the complaints of the inhabitants, had attempted to eject the gypsies from the village. Maldonado, a 'captain of bandits', as Villalobos put it, reportedly affected a distinctly military style, sporting a coloured sash worn right to left from shoulder to waist, 'which is the military insignia of that office', and even availing himself of a bugle 'with which he went around as if at war, plaguing the countryside, villages, and roads'. According to testimony given on 23 July by Antonio Madrigal, a resident of Topas, to Don García's lieutenant Francisco Colloto, the gypsies were based in a ruined house outside Calzada de la Fuente. From there, he said, they would go out to steal grain, horses, mules and donkeys, which they would then sell or exchange in other villages in the area. He also accused them of preying on travellers, 'and in particular innkeepers transporting wine to and fro'. Maldonado himself was said to have murdered a woman in the cemetery of El Cubo de la Tierra del Vino 'merely because she reproached him for his wicked way of life', while he and his son Cazano, who was eventually shot dead by one of Maldonado's own band, were reported to have killed another gypsy, Sebastián de Malla, in the village of Ventalbo near Zamora, 'as is well known'. Part of the evidence had come from another of Maldonado's band, his brother Francisco, known as 'el Zurdo' ('Lefty'), who, having initially managed to escape 'by the skin of his teeth', was finally captured by Don García after a two-day pursuit across the country between Zamora and Toro. Don García duly handed the gypsy over to the *corregidor* of Toro, who, after extracting a confession which implicated Santiago Maldonado in all manner of crimes, hanged him.

The Public Prosecutor was not, however, persuaded of Santiago Maldonado's guilt, and had therefore demanded that the gypsy be returned to the church at Topas, though he did accept in principle that ecclesiastical sanctuary should not be extended to anyone who could be shown with due rigour to have been responsible for crimes of such gravity. Villalobos, who also believed the gypsy to have been implicated in the murder of a priest in Avedillo, took the opposite view, arguing that Francisco Maldonado's confession alone was sufficient proof of his brother's guilt, 'however much the Public Prosecutor seeks to discredit and disparage it in his writings'. What strikes the reader more than anything else, however, is the vehemence with which Villalobos reacts to the thought of these people taking up residence in the house of God,

> lodging in the churches of Carrascal and El Cubo as if they were country inns, with all their clan of young children and women (they call them wives, though that is untrue), sleeping there with them and turning these into places of concubinage and lewdness instead of prayer and purity, and bringing in and feeding their horses, mules and donkeys, so that God's church is converted into a stable or barn, with manifest disrespect for Him and contempt for His sacred images, filling His sanctuary with abominations as horrible to recount as they are to hear.

Villalobos had declared at the outset his intention to discuss the crimes of the gypsies and the reasons why it had been found necessary the previous year to promulgate yet another royal ordinance against them. Interestingly, the ordinance in question, issued in Madrid on 15 June 1643, did not in fact mention gypsies, though it had indeed been introduced in an attempt to combat the growing problem of banditry in Castile. It referred to

> different troops of degenerate people, thieves and highwaymen, who carry out acts of revenge, playing out their private hatreds and enmities on the roads and inflicting suffering on small villages, where they oblige the inhabitants to provide for and help them, committing serious crimes and offences against the Lord God.[61]

How, then, is Villalobos's assertion that gypsies were the intended target of the legislation to be read? On the one hand, it could indicate that, following the line taken by Sancho de Moncada and enshrined in law in the 1619 and 1633 ordinances, he understood the word gypsy as a catch-all term for those who affected a particular style and involved themselves in criminal activities such as banditry. On the other hand, given that many Old Christians, including even members of the nobility, are also known to have been involved in banditry elsewhere in Spain,[62] it could also reflect the kind of unexamined prejudice that could make of the gypsy an easy scapegoat for the crimes of others. The fact that the 1643 ordinance exhorted the populace to take violent retributive justice into its own hands would in the event hardly have helped to discourage such abuses. Referring once again to the bandit gangs roaming Castile, it continued as follows:

> And we authorize any person, whatever his status or condition, to injure, kill, or capture them without incurring any penalty whatsoever, and to bring them dead or alive before the judges of the districts where they were captured or killed. And where it is possible to take them, they are to be hung, drawn and quartered and deposited on the roads or in the villages where they committed their crimes, and their belongings are to be confiscated for our exchequer.

Another contributor to the debate was Doctor Juan de Quiñones, author of the 1631 *Discurso contra los gitanos* and now promoted lieutenant to the *corregidor* of Madrid. In a pamphlet probably dating to 1654 and addressed to Philip IV, Quiñones noted that many of those responsible for what he deemed a growing epidemic of robberies were going unpunished:

> This vice of thieving is, Sir, very widespread in these Kingdoms. The gaols are full of thieves, and the scaffolds are (as they say) empty: many are apprehended, and just as many are released: many are the nights when there are robberies, and few the mornings that see floggings, except on rare occasions.[63]

In particular, he requested the king to seek a solution to the problem of the frequent abuse of ecclesiastical sanctuary by those accused of such offences:

> The impudence of the thieves has reached such a pitch that even if they are apprehended in a tavern or eating-house, or in the street, they call it a church and claim to have been removed from it. And

the worst of it is that they substantiate their claims using evidence supplied by other thieves. . .

Quiñones added that the gypsies were particularly accomplished in such evasive arts. But he recognized that the monarch's role as guardian of the Church's traditional prerogatives put him in a difficult position and acknowledged that the safest course might be for Philip to seek a papal brief instructing the Spanish clergy to refuse sanctuary in such cases.

The problem was further compounded for the civil authorities by that fact that if an individual accused of some minor offence was forcibly removed from a place under ecclesiastical jurisdiction and then released, rather than being formally restored to the Church, that same individual could continue to claim 'cold immunity' even if re-arrested later for a different, much more serious offence.[64] This is what happened in 1700 in the case of the gypsies Agustín de Montoya, Francisco de Heredia and Álvaro de Heredia, all of whom, sentenced by the *Real Chancillería* of Granada to ten years in the galleys (their offences are not specified), claimed immunity. They cited the fact that nine years earlier they had been extracted by royal justices from the shrine of the Magdalena outside Daimiel, and although later released, had not been restored to their remote place of sanctuary as required by ecclesiastical law.[65] The memorandum from a scandalized Council of Castile to Charles II recording these events noted that the ecclesiastical judge of Ciudad Real and the Campo de Calatrava had immediately intervened to prevent the removal of the men from gaol in Málaga to the galleys. It also noted that even when the civil authorities were able to prove that an individual had since his release entered churches on many occasions, the fact that there had been no formal restitution meant that he was still entitled to claim 'cold immunity'. 'Those who use this resource most frequently', it added, 'are gypsies, who with their sharp wits and those who customarily help them, find it easier to produce the evidence they require'. A short post-script then added that while it might safely be assumed that most gypsy claims to 'cold immunity' were false, 'they never lack people prepared to swear on oath on their behalf, motivated by misplaced charity or other unworthy concerns'.

A similar case occurred in Ocaña in 1705, when attempts to arrest two vagrant gypsies led to one taking refuge in a church while the other was gaoled and sentenced to six years in the galleys. However, the gaoled gypsy also claimed ecclesiastical sanctuary and, it was feared, was sufficiently wily to succeed in getting his way, the justices adding that the Council of Castile had in 1664 issued an instruction that suspects were no longer to be removed by force from church. They noted, too, that in their search for a troop of gypsies said to be engaged in 'extortion' in the area, they had met with 'little or no support' from either civil or ecclesiastical authorities in the villages through which they had passed.[66] This was not unusual. In 1722, a group of four, heavily armed bandits reported to have robbed travellers on the roads to Lora del Río (Andalusia) and in Extremadura were discovered by the authorities to be living, along with a number of gypsy women, in the monastery of San Francisco at La Campana in the marquisate of Villanueva del Río, where the Superior, Father Joseph, did all he could to resist their extraction. At least three of the four men were evidently gypsies. The other, a relatively well dressed, dark-skinned individual sporting a bonnet, tricorn hat and short white cloak, was interrogated by the *alcalde* and governor Juan Julián de Peñalbo y Salvatierra. He gave his name as Andrés Díaz de Palacios, lately a soldier in the service of the king. He had, he claimed, married a gypsy, much to the consternation of his family, who now wished to kill him. He had thus been forced to flee with his wife, two brothers-in-law and an old man in search of a place safely to settle. Father Joseph, meanwhile, sought to delay further action by insisting that he could not deliver his charges into the hands of the lay authorities without consulting a higher ecclesiastical authority. Nor could he hand over any livestock or arms. This last point was, of course, of crucial significance, since gypsies caught with weapons were automatically liable to the death penalty. Unfortunately for Díaz de Palacios, three recent arrivals in La Campana, an itinerant trader from Córdoba and two villagers from Hornachuelos, recounted a rather different version of events. The trader claimed to have seen Díaz de Palacios in Pozoblanco, where the latter had attempted to pass himself off as a constable (*alguacil*) of Ciudad Real. He had also heard not only that the group had been ejected from La Hinojosa, but that they had been involved in an armed skirmish in La Cardenchosa, in the Sierra Morena south of Fuente Ovejuna. This was confirmed by the two inhabitants of Hornachuelos, who told of how the authorities in Fuente Ovejuna, informed of the presence of bandits in La Cardenchosa, had travelled there to arrest them. In the ensuing fight, one gypsy had been killed and another, a woman, had suffered a broken leg. Of their pursuers, one had been shot and wounded in the chest, while another had made it known that Díaz de Palacios and one other gypsy had previously served in the galleys. Finally, on 28 November, Peñalbo de Salvatierra returned to the monastery with 12 armed men. Refused entry once again, he summoned a locksmith, who let them in. The gypsies were duly discovered in one of the monks' cells and, despite at least one shot being fired, an agreement was eventually negotiated whereby Father Joseph and his Franciscan deputy would enter the cell first to establish that the gypsies had no weapons before delivering the group, which included two children of two and ten years of age, into the hands of the governor. The latter accepted this obviously protective ruse under protest, and the gypsies, though gaoled, were not subsequently charged with the possession of weapons.[67]

Despite the Council's loud protests in 1700, jurisdictional disputes involving gypsies between the lay and religious authorities continued until well into the eighteenth century.[68] A commission eventually set up by Philip V in 1721 to investigate the matter concluded two years later that the abuse of sanctuary in general, and 'cold immunity' in particular, had been the principal reason for the failure of anti-gypsy legislation since the time of the Catholic Monarchs.[69] In the end, an agreement that saved face all round was finally reached with Rome in 1748. But it was only reached after Philip V had two years earlier decreed that justices should henceforth extract gypsies from the churches where they had claimed sanctuary, ignoring protests from the clergy, while in cases of 'cold immunity', the Church's efforts to have gypsies restored to it should be forcefully resisted.[70] Now, however, the 1748 concordat, announced by the Apostolic Nuncio on 20 June and which took up a suggestion originally advanced by the Council, allowed for gypsies legitimately to be removed from the churches where they had claimed sanctuary and transported to others located firmly within the perimeters of enclosed penal colonies.[71] The effect, discussed in Chapter 9, of this removal of ecclesiastical protection would be little short of catastrophic for the gypsies.

8
The Failure of the Laws and the Last Habsburg

The failures of anti-gypsy legislation

Philip V's commission took the view in 1723 that the Spanish Church had for two centuries, through its insistence on the inviolability of ecclesiastical sanctuary, acted as the principal protector of the gypsies. Lacking any specific religious or liturgical tradition of their own, some gypsies, especially those who had been granted *vecindades*, had nominally accepted the Church's teachings, even if only to the extent of baptizing their children. Spurred on by such small successes, the Church's attempts to shelter these wayward people from the civil authorities doubtless reflected a parallel urge, as infantilizing and sanguine as it was didactic, to save them from themselves, too. It is true that the Inquisition did summon gypsies before it on charges ranging from blasphemy and superstition to sorcery, and quite often as a result of denunciations by non-gypsy neighbours with whom the accused had been in dispute. But it tended for the most part to hand down sentences that were less – sometimes much less – draconian than those routinely imposed by the civil authorities, even for similar offences. On occasion, the inquisitors would merely require the accused to attend a mass or two to atone for what were more often than not misdemeanours fuelled by abuse by non-gypsies, alcohol, or simply the need to make enough money, albeit via deception, in order to subsist. Yet, despite the commission's findings, the sanctuary offered by the Church, vitally important though it was, was by no means the only reason for the failures of anti-gypsy legislation in pre-Bourbon Spain. That the laws had not been enforced as desired was acknowledged time and again by the crown, and of course accounts for their continual reiteration or reformulation over two centuries, usually with increased penalties. Indeed, had the crown ever even come close to achieving its stated objectives, by the middle of the seventeenth century there would hardly have remained in Spain an itinerant gypsy against whom to legislate. But remain they did, and complaints about their criminality, irreligion, and reputedly scandalous lives continued much as before, well into the eighteenth century and beyond. This is not to suggest for a moment that the gypsies were not persecuted. They were. The suffering of those sent off, for example, to serve in Spain's Mediterranean galley squadrons or the mercury mines at Almadén must have been terrible indeed.[1] But most were not sent, despite Philip IV's order of 1639 which had finally insisted that all able-bodied gypsy males be put to the oar.

In fact, it is clear that laws designed to control Spain's gypsies were not, indeed could not be enforced to anything like the extent desired by those who framed them. The difficulties encountered by the crown in its attempts to enforce its will, to translate its nominal authority into the effective exercise of power, have been the subject of a number of studies over recent years.[2] Seen in this wider context of the discontinuity between theory and practice, it becomes much easier to understand the reasons for what was recognized even by contemporaries as the inefficacy of anti-gypsy legislation over much of the early modern period. What emerges, as I have suggested, is a picture of early modern Spain in which, far though the royal writ was held imperiously to run, the reality at a local level was that demands from the centre were quite often resisted or, one way or another, frustrated. True, the notion that the king represented the embodiment and guarantee of law and justice was one to which most Spaniards readily, even fervently subscribed – at least in theory. In 1643, the political theorist Diego Saavedra Fajardo cited Alfonso the Wise and the great medieval law code the *Siete partidas* in order to make precisely this point: 'For just as the soul rests in a man's heart, and through it the body lives and is nourished, so in the king lies justice, which is the life and nourishment of the nation and its authority.'[3] Even Sancho Panza reminds Don Quijote in the *galeotes* episode that 'justice [. . .] is the king himself',[4] while in his picaresque novel *El viaje entretenido*, Agustín de Rojas Villandrando put it almost as succinctly, rhyming 'where there is no king, there is no law' ('donde no hay rey, no hay ley').[5] But while theory and practice continued locally to enjoy a hopeful *modus vivendi* of sorts, the match, unsurprisingly, was ever less than perfect. I. A. A. Thompson has observed of early modern Castile as a whole that 'local power, as a general rule, prevailed over central authority', so that the crown was obliged with weary regularity to acknowledge its 'inability to translate command into compliance' on the ground.[6] The plain fact was that various forms of reluctance, resistance, or simple inability to comply with the crown's wishes were common, a fact of life at every level of society, while wrangles over jurisdictional competence, endemic corruption, and interminable appeals procedures also continually bedevilled efforts to enforce the law. 'Curavimos Babylonem, et non est sanata', wrote Salazar de Mendoza, citing Jeremiah 51:9, a singularly appropriate choice as he embarked on his own lamentation, bewailing the manifest failures of Spain's laws against gypsies.[7]

As I suggested earlier, however, there was another issue which, almost from the outset, was to have fundamental implications for the way anti-gypsy legislation developed in Spain and elsewhere. Not only did the Habsburg regime repeatedly legislate to sedentarize, assimilate, and control Spain's gypsies; in the seventeenth century it also sought, in more than one sense, to legislate them away altogether. Central here is the question of precisely who or what the gypsies were understood to be. An increasing tendency to deny the gypsies a separate ethnic identity had by the second decade of the seventeenth century been fully incorporated into official government policy. In a Spain whose ruling elites still defined themselves via the discourses of lineage, religious zeal and martial prowess, a Spain which sought its identity in the crusader spirit of a largely idealized past, whose conquest of the New World represented what Sánchez-Albornoz called a 'projection of the Spanish Middle Ages in space and time',[8] a way had to be found to deal with the seemingly libidinal, recalcitrant, and irrepressible otherness of the gypsy. Henceforth, went the official line, gypsies were to be regarded as Spaniards, wayward, ruinous, and of the lowest sort, naturally, but Spaniards nonetheless. So it was that in 1631, in his vitriolic *Discurso contra los gitanos*, typically derivative and salted liberally with demonizing myth, as most anti-gypsy tracts were, Juan de Quiñones could paint this essentially deracialized picture of Spain's gypsies:

That they are known as gypsies has more to do with the fact that they copy the latter in their disgraceful way of life than with any idea that they are their descendants. And so it is that this vile rabble consists of nothing other than men and women on the run because of their crimes or debts, rebellious and criminal people who, because they cannot remain in villages where they are known, retreat to the mountains or to sparsely populated villages off the beaten track where they can hide. [. . .] there is no doubt that they were born and raised in these Kingdoms, even if some going around with them are from other nations; and this is how the gypsy-style sect is made up, and every day they admit into it useless idlers and dissolute ne'er-do-wells, to whom they easily teach their language.[9]

Several of Quiñones's phrases were repeated verbatim from Sancho de Moncada's 1619 *Restauración política de España*, which itself had borrowed heavily from Salazar de Mendoza's *Memorial de el hecho de los gitanos*, written a year or so earlier. By the time Quiñones wrote his diatribe, the idea that Spain's gypsies amounted to nothing more than a ragged agglomeration of the delinquent dregs of Spanish society was common currency in official circles. No doubt there were reasons why some Spaniards may have found it convenient or necessary to pass themselves off as gypsies. Such a stratagem may even have had a certain deterrent value for those with reason to fear the authorities. Throughout the seventeenth and early eighteenth centuries, numerous documents attest to the reluctance of local justices, who were invariably short of resources, to undertake the always difficult and frequently dangerous pursuit of gypsies. A note to Philip V written on 8 September 1705, referred, for example, to the royal ordinance concerning gypsies published earlier that year, and complained about the *Hermandad's* lack of financial resources, which made a concentrated effort to hunt down gypsies in the countryside impossible. Instead, it continued, the President of Castile had been requested to instruct that the villages through which the agents of the *Hermandad* passed in pursuit of their duty should make a contribution to help defray the cost of such sallies.[10] As it was, throughout the seventeenth century and well into the eighteenth, the dangers confronting those, principally the *Hermandad*, who attempted to hunt down gypsy bandits were not to be underestimated. The *Cortes* of Madrid of 8 November 1610 were, for example, presented with a report which noted that:

The roguish way of life of these people has come to such a pass that there are whole companies of men and women, all of them with arms and shotguns, who, when they come to a village, are given whatever they demand in the hope that they will not resort to violence. And when information about them is received and an attempt is made to do something to punish them, they are so cunning and wild in their ways that they can never be found, and when they are, they resist and have been responsible for many deaths, and then they leave their women and flee, because they are so swift that nobody can follow them.[11]

On 16 October 1638, one of the witnesses called before the *alcalde mayor* Juan García de Córdoba to give evidence relating to the theft by gypsies of livestock in the village of Retortillo near Soria reported that 'it is said that they come so well armed with shotguns and pistols that the justices of small towns are afraid to take them on, except in the company of other law officers'.[12] That same year, in Coruña del Conde, north-west of Aranda del Duero, an *alcalde* ordered by the king to apprehend a group of gypsies accused of a litany of crimes in the area, put the problem more succinctly: he just replied, 'Let the Lord Admiral of Castile come and catch them, because I don't dare.'[13]

Repeated attempts to legislate away Spain's gypsies via expulsion or assimilation had undoubtedly encouraged the gradual process of sedentarization that had been going on for over a century; but they evidently had little effect in terms of curbing the gypsies' illegal activities or their recalcitrant determination to continue, on the whole, to disaffiliate themselves culturally from mainstream Spanish society, preserving some sense of group identity in the process. As suggested earlier, most of the central provisions of the 1633 pragmatic closely reflected the recommendations of a *consulta* of March that year on the continuing depredations suffered by the *Mesta* at the hands of gypsies. This had claimed that sedentarization had actually encouraged precisely the opposite of the effect intended:

> rather, having been allowed to take up residence in towns, they have kept up their wicked way of life and, congregating as gypsies, travel around different parts of these kingdoms invading small villages with such superiority of numbers and sowing such fear among the inhabitants that some abandon their homes, while others are obliged to accommodate and feed them, in the hope of being left enough to sustain themselves. And as want is greatly on the increase, it is thought certain that many criminal elements are joining up with the gypsies, so that if a remedy is not found, it may eventually prove impossible to find one that does not involve a great deal of bloodshed and expenditure.[14]

Similar claims are made in a fascinating letter of 23 May 1674 addressed to the Queen Regent Mariana and written from Porcuna, Jaén, by Manuel Montillo, a priest and lawyer. Its contents relate to the period of 40 years that Montillo had already spent in Andalusia. In it he complained that there had been 'little or no observance of the laws against gypsies promulgated in these kingdoms from the time of the Catholic Monarchs to Your Majesty's own day'. Accusing the gypsies of being thieves, highwaymen, and even paid assassins, he nevertheless observed ruefully that 'they are not short of protectors and supporters'. The letter merits quotation at length. It continues as follows:

> While the gypsies continue to commit so many serious crimes every day in these Kingdoms, over the last forty years I have seen not one of them hanged and few sent to the galleys, and this despite the fact that *all* of them are condemned to the oar by law and by virtue of the fact that they are gypsies. And this is why this race of people has become so strong today [. . .] and they are multiplying rapidly, because they breed one with another just as they please, whether married or not, and have therefore increased excessively in numbers. In fact, there is not a village or its surrounding land which is not populated by gypsies, who must have come from other parts. And many small villages fear them and are intimidated and held under subjection by bands of fifty or a hundred gypsies who help each other. And many of the older men have horses with bridles and spurs and are equipped like cavalrymen with double carbines and arquebuses, which they use both to carry out their robberies and to minimize the risk to themselves.[15]

Montillo's letter also suggested that the gypsies' normal practice of endogamy was not always adhered to in Andalusia. This doubtless explained some of the support, or at least acquiescence, enjoyed by gypsies in certain areas. He noted grimly that 'through fear and in order to safeguard their lives, your Majesty's subjects befriend them and other wicked men join up with the gypsy rabble and women even marry them'. It is not possible at this remove to quantify mixed marriages between gypsies and non-gypsies at the time Montillo was writing, given that no census figures are available for the seventeenth century. But there is no question that there were exceptions to the general endogamy of gypsy lineages. When some figures do become available, in the 1783 census of gypsies ordered by Charles III, it is interesting to note that, while endogamy continued to be the normal practice, one in eight gypsy families in Utrera, admittedly an exceptional case, was of mixed blood and there were a significant number of mixed marriages elsewhere.[16] The picture, as one would expect, varied from one locality to another. María Helena Sánchez Ortega has noted that the Inquisition's own records make it abundantly clear that gypsy–non-gypsy relations, while deeply hostile in some villages, were nonetheless excellent in others.[17] There were frequent claims, too, that there was no shortage of ordinary people prepared to receive stolen goods from the gypsies or, indeed, to offer them protection. For example, several villagers called as witnesses in the case of the stolen horses and mules of Retortillo, cited earlier, claimed that the animals would be taken to other, distant villages where the gypsies would take advantage of their 'many receivers of stolen goods and other protectors' in order to trade their ill-gotten gains.[18]

That the gypsies enjoyed a degree of sympathy and/or support in certain quarters is further evidenced in the letter to Philip IV of 19 November 1639 from the *Junta de galeotes, esclavos, y gitanos*.[19] The gypsies had, of course, long been regarded as obvious candidates to man the oars as *forzados*. Referring to a previous ordinance, presumably the one promulgated in 1635, which had ordered all gypsy males between 20 and 50 years old be sent to the galleys,[20] it argued that 'either because of the lack of secrecy, or the slackness or negligence of the Justices, that initiative came to nothing and only served to ensure that many gypsies crossed into France or took to the mountains'. The tactic of retreat to nearby mountainous areas, alluded to by Cervantes,[21] is mentioned in a royal ordinance of 1705, which noted of the gypsies that 'they camp on the plains close to the mountains, to which they withdraw when any attempt is made to apprehend them, travelling from there to other places where they commit the same crimes'.[22] But leaks, laxity, or dereliction of duty on the part of the authorities at a local level, the gypsies' long practised mobility, and their use of and familiarity with difficult terrain were not the only obstacles to be overcome. The letter goes on frustratedly to lament the gypsies' habitual abuse of Church sanctuary, the unconscionable delays in the hearing of appeals at a time when the government was desperate to see convicted gypsies (and others) sent as quickly as possible to the galleys, and, not least, the corruption of galley captains, gaolers, and justices alike. Against this background, the crown had earlier that year recalled and strengthened legislation first passed under Philip II which had demanded that the sentences of those condemned for serious crimes be commuted wherever possible to galley service.[23] This included even the death sentence. And the Council had demanded in February that appeals by convicted gypsies and bandits still outstanding in the *Chancillerías* be remitted to it for urgent resolution. The commission issued to Enrique de Salimar, the *alcalde del crimen* of the Valladolid *Chancillería*, to apprehend gypsy bandits in Old Castile went on to insist that any appeals that might legitimately be lodged by those sentenced as a result of his activities should indeed be heard, but only 'before our Council and not elsewhere or in any other tribunal'.[24]

But resistance continued, even at the highest levels. The *Junta de Galeotes, esclavos, y gitanos'* letter goes on, for example, to note that 'in some villages under seigneurial jurisdiction many gypsies are protected and defended by the nobles themselves and by their servants'. A little later, it describes the experience of Pedro de Amezqueta, an *alcalde de casa y corte* and the crown's special commissioner in Andalusia and Murcia with special responsibility for ensuring that eligible convicts were sent to the galleys. The letter notes that Amezqueta had one year earlier sent 400 men to the galleys, though the fact that vagabonds, healthy beggars, bigamists, perjurers, blasphemers, procurers, homosexual men, donated slaves and any man resisting arrest could also be sent to the galleys makes it unlikely that more than a small proportion of this number were gypsies. Asked to investigate and expedite suitable cases pending in the courts, he had travelled to Andalusia, where, the letter notes, he spent three days going from place to place, 'in the face of great resistance from some members of the nobility and even from the Justices themselves'.[25] Elsewhere, too, gypsies seem to have enjoyed seigneurial protection, as the special commissioner Juan Hurtado, charged with ensuring that the laws against gypsies were enforced, discovered when he travelled in 1633 through lands owned by the Military Order of Santiago and the Marquis of Villena.[26]

There were a variety of reasons, not always particularly edifying, why people from such a wide cross-section of Spanish society should have chosen to protect, assist, or simply turn a blind eye to the gypsies and their activities. The role of the Church has already been discussed. But another factor was certainly the jealous reassertion by elements of the nobility of their seigneurial jurisdictions and privileges. Even in 1710, the French ambassador in Spain reported that royal jurisdiction extended to only 200 of the 700 towns in Castile,[27] this, of course, against a background in which power was still effectively a matter of consent, of continuing negotiation between the king, his ministers, the aristocracy, and even, *de facto*, lesser officials.[28] Henry Kamen summarized the pre-Bourbon situation thus:

Spain under Charles II continued to be governed as it had been under Philip II, by a kind of consensus between various local interests of which the nobles, the Church, the urban oligarchies and the local tax-farmers were the most important. Habsburg Spain was stable because it was largely self-governing, not because it was governed by an absolute monarchy.[29]

It is clear, too, that a low-level 'black economy' based on the sale or barter of stolen goods operated sporadically in certain areas in ways that tended to favour the gypsies. It was widely believed, too, that ostensibly sedentarized gypsies were in some places as thick as thieves with local officials, bribing them as the situation warranted with a share of their ill-gotten goods. In Ciudad Real, the *Hermandad*, thwarted in its attempts to have a group of gypsies expelled from the city, even accused the *corregidor* of protecting them.[30] Then again, fear of revenge, imagined or otherwise, and encouraged by a lack of any real confidence in the authorities' ability to uphold the law, also played its part. In 1757, the Governor of the Council of Castile and Bishop of Cartagena, wrote to the Secretary of the Navy that he was deeply suspicious of the many appeals presented by gypsies incarcerated there, because support for these had invariably been drummed up among those, including fellow gypsies, who had a vested interest in seeing them released, and because of 'the fear in which they are held by magistrates'.[31] And in a report on the gypsy problem in October 1763, the then Public Prosecutor José Rodríguez de Campomanes noted that it was difficult to prove their crimes, not just because of those who protected them, but also because of the fear they inspired in those who might otherwise have denounced them.[32] Meanwhile, in more remote areas, sheer ignorance of the law almost certainly allowed gypsies to continue living more or less as they had always done.[33] Finally, laws which typically vilified all gypsies, which sought to carry off their menfolk or deprive them of their traditional occupations without providing any viable alternative, and which too often signally failed to distinguish between criminal elements and those who lived quiet, scandal-free lives, must inevitably have elicited a certain sympathy for the latter among at least some of their non-gypsy neighbours.

In Andalusia, meanwhile, some gypsies adopted another stratagem in an attempt to insulate themselves against the worsening civil climate. In a letter of the 8th of April 1639, Gaspar de Bracamonte, a member of the Council, informed the *Junta de Execución* of an offer he had received from one Sebastián Maldonado, a gypsy from Cazorla, a man 'very well known in that area and of good character'. Maldonado had offered to raise 200 men 'of his nation' to serve the king as soldiers.[34] What the letter does *not* say is that in that capacity they would be likely to benefit from the not insignificant measure of protection afforded by the *fuero militar*, the source of regular jurisdictional disputes between civil and military authorities in which the latter could usually be guaranteed to prevail.[35] Two days later, in another letter of 10 April that same year, the Count of Salvatierra relayed to the Colonels' Junta a virtually identical offer made to him by a gypsy from Triana, Sebastián de Soto.[36] Maldonado had claimed to be the grandson of a captain who had served in the war in the Alpujarras, while de Soto declared that he had served both in the army in Flanders and in the navy. Both Bracamonte and the count stressed the gypsies' physical endurance exposed to the elements in open country and their experience with firearms, and both observed, by way of further encouragement, that this proposal might, after all, be a way of ridding Spain of them. The gypsies' offers were not unconditional, however. De Soto demanded that he be made a captain, while Lázaro and Simón de Soto must be appointed ensign and sergeant, respectively. Maldonado insisted that if he recruited other gypsies, 'your Majesty must give his Royal word not to use them for any other purpose than the military exercise of warfare'. Forced service at the oar could not, of course, conceivably be represented in such honourable terms. Indeed, later that year, the *Junta de galeotes, esclavos, y gitanos* suggested that prisoners guilty of crimes not automatically meriting a term in the galleys might nevertheless be offered some remission of sentence in return for volunteering to serve for a fixed term; but it felt obliged to add that they would only do so 'with the wage and rations of volunteer oarsmen and with a declaration that this service should not offend their honour and reputation'.[37] As it was, the fate of Maldonado and de Soto's offers is summed up by a laconic marginal note in a different hand on the second of them. It simply reads, 'it is better not to accept this proposal'.

A similar tactic was employed as a desperate last resort by gypsies attempting to avoid arrest in Madrid in March 1639. One of crown's special commissioners for gypsies, the judge Juan García de Córdoba, mentioned earlier, had been pursuing a troop led by the gypsies 'Pitocho', 'El Valiente', Salazar, and Juan González. All four stood accused of stealing a valuable consignment of silk and other goods being transported from Madrid to Lisbon on behalf of a Portuguese merchant resident in the Spanish capital. The merchant's representative, Manuel Fernández, dispatched from Madrid to seek action by local justices in villages north east of the capital where it was suspected the gypsies had traded the stolen goods, reported that he had met with open hostility there. Indeed, he had even been threatened with imprisonment. García de Córdoba, too, faced various forms of obstruction by local people, some of whom had dealt in the stolen goods which the gypsies had sold in La Puebla de los Valles and other villages in September 1638 'at such low prices that many people went from there to buy them'. As the judge prepared to leave an inn in the village of Buitrago at six in the morning on 8 November, he found his way barred by the innkeeper, Alonso Rodríguez. Seizing his bridle, Rodríguez told him that he had been informed by the ecclesiastical judge for the area that he had already excommunicated García de Córdoba for failing to restore to Church sanctuary a gypsy imprisoned in the village. What was more, he would excommunicate the innkeeper, too, if he allowed the special commissioner, his men, or any of the horses and mules they had captured with the gypsy to leave. The latter, coincidentally named Francisco Rodríguez, had been detained that same September in open country beside a nearby river, so one assumes that his claim to sanctuary must have been one of 'cold immunity'. Despite the fact that he was the only (presumed) witness to the original crime in custody – his confederates had all managed to escape – he was later released without García de Córdoba's knowledge or consent. Meanwhile, amid much shouting which quickly attracted a number of other locals to the scene, García de Córdoba responded by threatening the innkeeper with 200 lashes and a 200 ducat fine. At this, Rodríguez quickly saw the merits of allowing the group to leave.

The special commissioner's pursuit of the gypsies later took him to Alcalá de Henares, where two of them had reportedly 'gone around at night with shotguns and on horseback and resisted the rector of the said university', only to be arrested in the end by the *corregidor*'s lieutenant for causing an affray. García de Córdoba subsequently arrested 11 other gypsy men and women in the town. To do so, he enlisted the help of students from the university, since the lieutenant, hearing that the judge was in pursuit of the same two gypsies he had imprisoned, had ordered them to be set free. García de Córdoba immediately intervened to prevent their release, arresting the gypsy woman who had requested it. The gypsies then claimed ecclesiastical sanctuary, citing as witnesses to their right to do so the town's drummer and a groom. García de Córdoba, needless to say, did not believe a word of it, but the gypsies were immediately supported by the ecclesiastical judge, who swiftly produced the requisite papers. García's only remaining option was to complain to the Council of Castile. He was, he said, particularly anxious to prosecute one of the gypsies, a sorcerer in whose dwelling had been found 'a linen purse with some pieces of human tongue and a slip of paper signed by Juan Díaz, a clergyman from Meco, containing superstitious words invoking the Saints and the Lone Soul for lascivious, lewd and lustful purposes'.

Díaz was duly summoned to explain his behaviour to the Inquisition, which promptly demanded that García de Córdoba hand over all the papers pertaining to the case. He refused, presenting them instead to the Council. Unable to punish the gypsies who had claimed ecclesiastical sanctuary – these included the 'sorcerer' – the special commissioner vented his frustration on those who remained. Seven gypsy women were to have their heads shaved and ears notched before being banished from Castile never to return on pain of death. One man, whom he accused of using a false name on a document recording his betrothal to a gypsy girl, was sentenced to an extraordinary ten years in the galleys to be followed by ten further years in the mines at Almadén, 'which', the judge added, 'amounts to a death penalty' (the death rate among gypsies at Almadén was anyway high). Another, described as 'a gypsy novice, a 14-year-old lad from Vizcaya', he sentenced to six years in a penal colony. When, in the end, he caught up with 'Pitocho', 'El Valiente', Salazar, and Juan González in Madrid, he found they had already enlisted, noting, 'I have seen them here in Madrid dressed as soldiers'.[38] They had done so in the nick of time, for by then such abuses had already come to the attention of the king and moves were afoot by March effectively to suspend the *fuero militar* in the capital, though the royal order to that effect was not issued until 16 August that year.[39]

Tightening the noose: the late seventeenth century

Resistance to the crown's policies towards Spain's gypsies continued throughout the seventeenth century and was acknowledged in royal decrees issued in 1673 and 1693 and in two ordinances promulgated in 1692, and 1695, respectively.[40] The decree issued on 27 July 1673 observed of the gypsies in general that 'these people were accorded shelter and refuge by powerful men who would take them in and protect them'.[41] The royal ordinance issued on 20 November 1692 once again reiterated the provisions of earlier legislation; but it included the observation that the failure to enforce the laws promulgated by Charles II's predecessors should be attributed to 'the laxity of those Justices responsible for enforcing the said laws, whose negligence should have been punished with the severity demanded by the importance of the purpose for which these laws were intended'.[42] Tightening significantly the procedures henceforth to be followed, it went on to insist that any such failure on the part of the justices in the future would not only be treated as an impeachable offence, but that those found to be in dereliction of their duty to apprehend gypsy criminals would also be required to make good any damage resulting from the latter's delinquent behaviour. Finally, a royal ordinance issued by Charles II in Madrid on 12 June 1695 offered any member of a gypsy gang caught in open country with firearms, and therefore automatically subject to the death penalty, a pardon, provided he handed over at least one of his confederates to the authorities. Any group of three or more individuals would constitute such a gang for the purposes of the law. And in a further indication of the sense of frustration felt by the authorities in Madrid, the ordinance took aim at nobles and commoners alike, adding, 'we understand that the continuing presence of gypsies in these Kingdoms has depended upon the favour, protection and help they have received from people of different social classes'. The ordinance went on to stipulate the severe penalties to be applied to such individuals: 'if noble, he shall be fined 6000 ducats, half of this to be applied to our royal exchequer and half to legal costs; and if a commoner, he is to be condemned to ten years in the galleys'. Meanwhile, any local justices failing to comply with the provisions of the new ordinance were to be removed and debarred from office in perpetuity, while half their assets were to be confiscated to help defray the crown's expenses. Two depositions supplied by individuals regarded as above suspicion, or three supplied by gypsies, even under torture, were to be regarded as sufficient evidence against such men. Some justices were clearly suspected of effectively harbouring gypsies, as the ordinance adds, 'we instruct any of the said Justices who hears of another who tolerates the presence of non-sedentarized gypsies in his area of jurisdiction [. . .] to inform himself of the circumstances and send the information to the Council or to the Supreme Court for his area, so that the law may take its course'.[43] Where gypsies were apprehended, they could expect severe penalties during the reign of the last Habsburg. The decree of 21 July 1673 had, for example, insisted that boys of 12 and over found in the company of vagrant gypsies should be sent to the galleys. Even before this, in 1672, three gypsies, one of whom was 13 years old, were sentenced in the capital to six years in the galleys for theft, with two others being sent to the mines at Almadén for four years.[44] Ten years later, two brothers from Aranda de Duero, Sebastián and Manuel de Avendaño, were put to the oar for six years by the *corregidor* of Palencia merely 'for saying they were gypsies and that they spoke the gypsy tongue'. Their sentence was later upheld by the *Real Chancillería* in Valladolid.[45]

But change was in the air as the seventeenth century drew to a close. These were the dying days of Habsburg Spain. Charles II, the last of the *Austrias*, as the Spanish say, had failed by either of his two marriages to provide an heir to the Spanish throne, and the question of the succession now came to dominate the political agenda. The king's physical and mental debility had for most of his reign kept him away from the business of government, which was instead managed by his ministers. It is true that this unprecedented situation posed challenges. In the early years there was no powerful *valido*, no commanding presence like Olivares to hold the centre stage and steer government policy. Even the later *valimientos* of the Duke of Medinaceli and the able Count of Oropesa were characterized by a proneness to factionalism and infighting that inevitably led to delays, indecision, and a certain disarray in the administration of the nation's affairs. Yet the government of Spain was neither as inert nor as inefficient during this period as it has sometimes been painted, especially during the last two decades of the seventeenth century. After 1680, both Medinaceli and Oropesa made serious attempts to stabilize the monetary system, restrain state expenditure, reform the public administration and fiscal arrangements, and even to curb the still burgeoning numbers of false vocations to the Church. As far as the gypsies were concerned, ministers now began to take an even harder line than had their predecessors, and one detects the first, ominous signs of a new, and even newly efficient determination to see the gypsy problem finally brought under control. The ordinance of 1692, referred to earlier, had continued to take the line adopted in 1619, insisting loftily that 'it has never been thought that true gypsies [*gitanos* or Egyptians] existed in these our Kingdoms', and had introduced new and tighter measures, including reporting procedures, designed to ensure compliance. Three years later, the lengthy ordinance of 1695 tightened the noose even further. Acknowledging the difficulties involved in the prosecution of gypsy thieves, it further reduced the burden of proof, so that a statement from the victim plus just one corroborating statement by a person of good name would henceforth be regarded as sufficient to secure a conviction. It also ordered a census of Spain's gypsies, notwithstanding the fact that the question of how precisely they were to be defined clearly remained problematic, as a later clause of the ordinance reveals:

And so that there is no doubt about who should be considered a gypsy for purposes of the provisions and penalties set out in this ordinance, we declare that any man or woman apprehended who is dressed in the manner favoured until now by these people, or who may be proven to have used the language known as *jerigonza*, will be deemed to be a gypsy for the said purposes; and the same is to be understood in the cases of those held and reputed to be gypsies by common consent attested to by at least five witnesses in the villages where they reside.[46]

In order that the census might be carried out, gypsies were instructed to present themselves within 30 days to the justices of the towns where they were resident, regardless of whether or not the town in question fell under royal jurisdiction. They were to state under oath their names, ages, and marital status, as well as the names and ages of any children. They must also declare their occupations, all the weapons they owned of whatever type, 'both offensive and defensive', and whether these were held in their homes, or elsewhere, or in the care of another person. Finally, they must declare all the horses, mules, and other animals in their possession, whether intended for personal use or for sale or exchange. No record exists today of this census and it may well be that it was never completed. Philip III's ordinance of 1619 had demanded that gypsies take up settled residence in towns of more than 1000 households. That figure was now reduced to 200, in recognition of the fact that many gypsies were already leading relatively settled lives in communities considerably smaller than those to which earlier legislation, quite unrealistically, had demanded that they move. This was a rarity, a sensible if modest concession to the status quo, to pragmatism. It was not destined to last. The ordinance also suggested that one of the reasons for the failures of previous legislation may have been that 'the multiplicity of these same laws makes them hard to comprehend and hinders simple compliance with what is demanded by them'. The 1695 ordinance set both the scene and tone for a new century. The changes it would bring to the fortunes of Spain's gypsies would certainly not happen overnight. Long established patterns of resistance, active and passive, to the crown's attempts to control them were far too deeply ingrained for that. Nonetheless, with fundamental changes to the way the nation was governed and a newly efficient centralization of state power, the 1700s would eventually witness the most fearsome crackdown ever visited on them. And then, paradoxically, it would also give way in 1783 under the 'enlightened despotism' of Charles III to a kind of reform and repeal of some of the more repressive aspects of past legislation.

9

The Bourbon Period

Forging a modern state

The last Habsburg, the unfortunate Charles II 'The Bewitched', died on 1 November 1700. His two marriages, to Maríe-Louise of Orléans, who had died in 1689, and Mariana of Neuburg, had failed to produce an heir to the Spanish throne. The thirteenth clause of his will, drawn up on 3 October after considerable vacillation, accordingly named a French prince, Philip, Duke of Anjou, as his successor, following a majority recommendation by the Council of State. The choice of Philip, the grandson of Louis XIV of France and María Teresa, daughter of Philip IV of Spain, grandly ignored a provision in his grandparents' marriage contract which had stipulated that none of their descendants might ascend to the Spanish throne. His accession later that month as Philip V, king of Spain and all its European and overseas possessions, marked the beginning of a long period of *rapprochement* between France and Spain, which had so recently (1689–97) been at war. It would last until the Napoleonic Wars once again plunged the two nations into conflict. The transfer of royal power had, however, been anything but smooth. The Austrian Archduke Charles's rival claim to the Spanish throne, backed by Mariana of Neuburg and the Admiral of Castile, was quickly supported by the Grand Alliance of the Hague formed by Austria, Great Britain, and the United Provinces and bolstered two years later by Portugal. The ensuing War of the Spanish Succession (1702–14) was to all intents and purposes a civil war, albeit one in which both sides, especially those supporting the Bourbon cause, relied heavily on foreign military assets. Opening up Spain's old fault lines, the war saw Catalonia, Valencia, Aragon, and Mallorca come out in support of Charles, Madrid occupied twice, albeit briefly, and Gibraltar and

Menorca occupied by the English before the Peace of Utrecht in 1713 and the Rastatt accords of September 1714 eventually acknowledged the legitimacy of the new Bourbon king. That same month, Barcelona, where Archduke Charles had initially established his court, had finally fallen after a two-month siege by joint French and Spanish forces. The outcome of the war had nevertheless already been assured by the death in 1711 of the Emperor Joseph, which had seen the Archduke Charles succeed to the Imperial throne. This uncomfortable turn of events had quickly persuaded the English and Dutch that it would be preferable on balance to have a Bourbon on the throne of Spain, provided he relinquished any claim to the French crown – which Philip duly did at Utrecht – than to see Austria and Spain once again united under a single ruler as in the great days of Spanish imperial expansion under Charles V.[1]

Now, under Philip V and his successors Ferdinand VI and Charles III, the governance of Spain would be developed and conducted largely according to French principles. The role of the state would be greatly enhanced and the rationalization and modernization of Spain's outdated political, legal-judicial, and fiscal structures would drive policy. Power would be concentrated at the centre in a remodelled, embellished, and modernized Madrid, and would reside in the person of the king and a handful of his ministers. Except for the Council of Castile, which could still muster considerable influence in the domestic sphere, Spain's old, broadly consultative and legalistic system of conciliar government fell into virtual desuetude, with power now concentrated instead in the *despacho*, or cabinet council, not least in the persons of the French ambassadors who attended it.[2] What under the Habsburgs had always remained a decidedly pluralist Spain of semi-autonomous regions now saw radical reforms, collectively known as the *Nueva Planta* (New Project), begun in 1707 and designed effectively to create, or rather force into existence, a unitary, monolithic, and, to the extent possible, uniform state. The *Cortes* of Castile had long since ceased to exercise any influence – those of Aragon and Navarre had fared little better – and were convened on only three occasions during the eighteenth century. In Aragon and Valencia, they were now abolished, as were their regional councils. Along with the removal of the institutions of government in regions which had opposed the Bourbon succession went suppression of their traditional privileges and *fueros*. Henceforth, Castilian law would apply in these areas and would be overseen by Castilian *corregidores* and high courts based on the Castilian model. In 1716, Catalonia, where Barcelona had held out against Philip to the bitter end, received similar treatment. The viceroys were to be superseded by Captain-Generals, who would rule the region on behalf of the crown along with a royal *Audiencia*, all related business, including that of the courts, henceforth being conducted in Castilian Spanish, a language still barely or not at all understood by significant numbers of people there.[3] Catalan universities were closed down and replaced by a new, royalist institution at Cervera. Only the Basque provinces and Navarre, which had supported Philip from the outset, retained their traditional *fueros* and law courts. These changes were accompanied by moves towards fiscal harmonization, with the introduction between 1714 and 1717 of a single property and income tax in Aragon, Valencia, and Catalonia.[4]

As far as Spain's gypsies were concerned, despite, or perhaps because of this continuing process of radical change, the new Bourbon monarch limited himself to following his Spanish predecessors' integrationist policy of enforced sedentarization, rather than attempting to emulate the more exclusionist policies adopted in France. There, legislation against gypsies had been introduced as long ago as 1539 by Francis I;[5] but a whole series of edicts had been enacted in the seventeenth century, in 1634, 1656, 1665, 1666, 1673, 1678, and 1682, and in the second half of the seventeenth century in particular, expulsion or condemnation to the galleys without benefit of any legal process whatsoever became the norm – though enforcement, as in Spain, was distinctly patchy.[6] Nonetheless, Philip V's royal ordinance of 18 August 1705 essentially limited itself to reiterating Charles II's 1695 ordinance, noting in particular that large gangs of gypsy bandits were continuing to terrorize small communities and travellers on the open road.[7] That same day, the municipal council of Madrid issued an order instructing *corregidores* and other law officers to look to the security of farm labourers and travellers, authorizing them to open fire on any bandit resisting arrest or refusing to lay down his arms, 'since the countryside and roads are infested with gypsies'.[8] A later ordinance, published in Madrid on 15 January 1717, again reiterated the 1695 ordinance, but is nevertheless interesting, principally for three reasons. First, despite the fact that it was for the most part copied verbatim from its 1695 predecessor, where that earlier document routinely referred to *gitanos*, in the 1717 ordinance no fewer than 17 of those references were amended to read 'those known as gypsies' ('los que se dizen gitanos'), a small but telling reflection of continuing official uncertainty about how exactly gypsies were to be defined.[9] Second, to clause 4 of the 1695 ordinance, which had once again insisted that gypsies devote themselves to work on the land and engage in no other commerce or trade of any kind, it added the phrase 'especially that of blacksmithing', in recognition of the fact that many gypsy families had continued regardless of previous legislation to earn their living in precisely this traditional way. Third, and by far the most important, it reversed the provision of Charles II's 1695 ordinance which had stipulated that gypsies living in communities of as few as 200 inhabitants should no longer be criminalized for so doing. The ordinance argued that this legislative volte-face was necessary because the fact that gypsies had since 1695 been allowed to reside in smaller settlements of their own choosing and without adequate supervision meant that many had been able to slip in and out of these places to join up with bandit groups, this amid continuing and widespread uncertainty on the part of the authorities about precisely which gypsies were resident where. The ordinance accordingly listed 41 towns where gypsies were within four months of publication required to take up – and, of course, be granted – residence. These were: Toledo, Guadalajara, Cuenca, Ávila, Segovia, León, Toro, Palencia, Aranda de Duero, Burgos, Soria, Ágreda, Logroño, Santo Domingo de la Calzada, San Clemente, Ciudad Real, Chinchilla, Murcia, Plasencia, Cáceres, Trujillo, Córdoba, Antequera, Ronda, Carmona, Jaén, Úbeda, Alcalá la Real, Oviedo, Orense, Betanzos, San Felipe, Orihuela, Alcira, Castellón de la Plana, Calatayud, Tarazona, Teruel, Daroca, Berja, and Barbastro.[10] Madrid was, of course, conspicuous by its absence, though its exclusion was entirely consistent with the crown's repeated attempts since the days of Philip II to expel gypsies from the capital. These had met with little success, however, and as late as 1747 Ferdinand VI would complain about the large numbers of gypsies there.[11] Gypsies now failing to comply with the new ordinance would incur penalties of between six and eight years at the oar for men and 100 lashes and internal exile for women, though the use of galleys, overtaken by developments in naval technology, would in fact be abolished as a form of corporal punishment on 28 November 1748, the *forzados* subsequently being relocated to other prisons or the mines at Almadén. Once settled, clause 12 stipulated that gypsies were only to leave their towns or villages of residence in order to engage in agricultural labour, the only form of work permitted to them. Those wishing for some personal reason to travel elsewhere must first seek permission to do so from a magistrate, who, if convinced of the need, would issue a written licence valid for a specified period. One entirely predictable effect of the ordinance, just as had been the case in 1633, was the uprooting and disruption of gypsy families who had already managed, against the odds, to establish themselves in other towns and villages as previous laws had demanded. There were, however, a significant number of cases in which the continued presence of gypsy families already settled in towns not included in the 1717 list was permitted, though normally only where petitions to the Council of Castile from families who found themselves in this situation were supported by the authorities of the town in question.[12]

The 1717 ordinance was reiterated in 1726, 1727, 1731 and, with amendments, in 1738, 1745, and 1746, a testament, despite Spain's newly authoritarian climate, to its continuing inefficacy. This was in part due to the difficulties inherent in the dissemination of clearly understandable information about new variations on old laws among an often illiterate populace, especially in more remote areas. Stark evidence of such public ignorance of legislation against gypsies was provided in 1718 when the *alcalde mayor* and governor of Gata, Bernardo Ventura de Capua, a much-feared gypsy hunter, descended on the village of Ceclavín, some 50 kilometres north-west of Cáceres near the Portuguese border. His questioning of the inhabitants, including the village notary and its virtually illiterate mayor, whom he accused of failing to implement the new ordinance, revealed not only that local gypsies were continuing to trade in horses, but that no one in the village was aware that this was against the law. The mayor had signed the official authorization required by legislation from the days of Philip II for the gypsies to be able to leave the village and conduct their business.[13] But he had not understood it, simply believing them when they told him they wanted to leave in order to collect a debt. No one in the village, including the notary, had heard of the 1717 ordinance.[14] A year later, Ventura de Capua heard how various bands of gypsies had traded horses and mules in the village of Zalamea in the full knowledge of its *alcalde*, who had never attempted to intervene or arrest them.[15] The picture was similar elsewhere, and Ventura de Capua was almost as zealous in his harrying of local justices who failed to enforce the law, whether through ignorance or wilful negligence, as he was in the pursuit of gypsies. In the summer of 1719, after a detailed investigation, he ordered the *alcaldes* of Zalamea, Azuaga, Guadalcanal, and Berlanga to appear personally before the Council of Castile in Madrid. There they would answer the charge that they had allowed such activities involving gypsies to continue under their very noses, although one, an elderly *alcalde* of Berlanga, Pedro Sánchez, was ultimately excused the journey after explaining that a serious groin injury had left him quite unable to ride.[16] Ventura de Capua's activities in Extremadura were later matched in La Mancha by those of Tomás Cesareo, a commissioner of the Council of Castile charged primarily with the investigation of tobacco smuggling, but who, like his predecessor, was also keen to pursue gypsies, those who traded with them, and allegedly negligent law officers alike. His high-handed activities continued for some 15 years between 1730 and 1745, despite the occasional slap on the wrist from the Council of Castile as it responded to a flood of complaints. These came from the Church, various *corregidores*, and a number of local justices, who accused Cesareo of exceeding his authority as well as various other questionable or even illegal practices.[17]

The screw was gradually being tightened in other ways, too. The 1726 reiteration had forbidden complaints about lower justices by gypsies, in practice usually women protesting the treatment of their menfolk, from being referred to higher tribunals, the *Chancillerías* and *Audiencias*. In 1731 local justices were reminded once again of their obligation, set out in the ordinances of 1692, 1695, and 1717, to conduct periodic inspections of gypsy homes to search for weapons or other prohibited items; but they were now instructed to take the necessary measures to ensure that such inspections were carried out unannounced. The 1738 ordinance sought to limit any discretion available to justices locally in respect of how and to whom they should apply its provisions, instructing them to collect and send to the Public Prosecutor any licences previously granted to gypsies by the Council of Castile permitting them to remain in their current place of residence.[18] They were to do so even in cases where the beneficiaries of such licences were described therein as 'Old Castilians', a phrase clearly designed to acknowledge in such families a degree of genuine acculturation not usually associated with the integrationist euphemism 'New Castilians' which had begun to be used of gypsies after Philip IV's 1633 prohibition of the term *gitano*.[19] That said, such documents had never guaranteed much protection. When the previously mentioned governor of Gata, Don Bernardo Ventura de Capua, came upon a couple accompanied by two children of 12 and two years of age at the fair at Medellín (Extremadura) in December 1718, he became doubly suspicious of them precisely because the man was carrying such papers. Why would he have such documents with him, asked the *alcalde mayor*, unless, despite the man's denials, the four were in fact gypsies? The latter replied that he needed them because of his dark skin, which could give the authorities an erroneous impression of his background. Ventura de Capua was not impressed and gaoled them anyway, sequestrating their four donkeys and a few other, wretched belongings.[20]

Finally, on 30 October 1745 at El Escorial and 7 February 1746, just months before his death, Philip V reiterated and amended the 1717 and 1738 ordinances yet again, noting that gypsy banditry on Spain's roads remained a serious problem.[21] Authorities across the country were accordingly instructed to publish an edict giving gypsies 15 days to return to their designated place of residence, after which time those failing to comply would be declared bandits. Gypsies who left the towns and villages assigned to them were declared 'incorrigible rebels and enemies of the common peace'.[22] Toughening similar provisions of 1695, 1708, and 1717, clause 14 of the 1746 ordinance now stipulated that those declared bandits and found to be carrying arms could be summarily executed, a significant harshening of the same clause in the 1717 ordinance, which had insisted that the death penalty in such cases be confirmed either by the Council of Castile for gypsies found within ten leagues of Madrid, or by the relevant *Chancillería* or *Audiencia* elsewhere.

The numerous petitions sparked by the 1717 ordinance from gypsies requesting permission to remain in a particular town and village reveal that many families were already living sedentarized or semi-sedentarized lives. When Pedro Gómez, his wife Teresa Victoria and their children, together with the widow Manuela Victoria, her children, and a number of other gypsies jointly petitioned the Council of Castile for the right to remain in Coca, they stated that they had been living there quietly for four years, the men working on the land or collecting firewood to sell when work was in short supply, while the women made stockings and items of household linen.[23] But such petitions to the Council could also reveal just how difficult it was fully to comply with the harsh requirements of the law, especially for gypsy families for whom occasional mobility was quite simply an economic necessity. Sometimes, as shown by the 1783 census, some travel was essential if gypsies were to continue to exploit the few opportunities available to them by taking seasonal work harvesting olives and other crops. Many were obliged to alternate work as day-labourers with begging when the season was over. Others combined a semi-sedentarized existence with long absences during which they would engage in buying, selling or exchanging what their neighbours commonly assumed to be stolen horses, mules and donkeys, or other goods.[24] There were times, too, when moving on was the only option available, simply because any downturn in the local economy of often wretchedly poor rural villages, whether as a result of failed harvests or the alienation of land, could be enough to force gypsy and non-gypsy families alike onto Spain's roads in search of new opportunities. Such was the case of a group of gypsies resident in Curiel de Duero just north of Peñafiel. Ana Salazar, her niece María Salazar, Diego Hernández and his son and daughter, as well as various others, all of whom described themselves as 'Old Castilians', had been resident in the village for a few years 'living quiet and ordered lives, without giving their neighbours any cause for complaint or scandal, and supporting themselves most honourably by their own efforts and working at whatever came their way', as the petition drawn up for them by a notary put it.[25] Now, however, times had changed, and, like other, non-gypsy residents of the village who had been forced to leave, they found they were no longer able to support themselves there. Instead, they now requested permission to move to Logroño or Segovia, where, they thought, they would be able to find work. Gypsy women, like the men, worked as and when they could, spinning and sewing, washing clothes or, especially in southern Spain, making and selling fritters.[26] But the arrest of their menfolk could bring particular hardship. When in 1735 Catalina Bustamante requested permission to reside in Santo Domingo de la Calzada, she did so on the grounds that the five-year sentence being served by her husband and nephew in the galleys had reduced her to begging in order to support herself and her three children. The Council acceded to her request.[27]

By 1746, it had become clear that the original list of 41 towns designated for settlement by gypsies would have to be extended. The currently designated towns were far too few in number to allow what clause 7 of Philip V's ordinance of 7 February that year now stipulated should be a settlement ratio of one gypsy to every 100 non-gypsy families. Representations had been made to the Council of Castile by Segovia, Plasencia, Trujillo, Murcia, Ronda, Seville, and other towns in an attempt to see the numbers of gypsies settling therein reduced, in part because such concentrations would be difficult to control, but also because the towns in question were simply unable to provide sufficient work of any kind for such an influx of people, let alone the agricultural labour to which the gypsies had been ordered to devote themselves. Carmona and Alcalá la Real in Andalusia claimed, for example, to have seen no fewer than 441 and 145 arrivals, respectively, numbers impossible for such small towns to manage. Even the *Asistente* of Seville, noting that a large gypsy population had long been resident in that city, complained that the numbers should now be controlled as a matter of urgency.[28] With the death of Philip V on 9 July 1746, it fell to his son Ferdinand VI to issue a new royal ordinance, just ten days after his accession to the throne. In it, he designated an additional 34 towns to be added to the 1717 list of 41. Of these, nine were in Andalusia, reflecting the concentration of gypsies in southern Spain. They were, notwithstanding the *Asistente*'s concerns, Seville, Granada, Andújar, Écija, Guadix, Baza, Mancha Real, Baeza, and

Puerto de Santa María, where a year earlier the governor, Diego de Cárdenas, had imprisoned all 77 gypsies resident at that time in the town, those men strong enough to survive the experience subsequently serving for up to 20 years in the hellish mines at Almadén. Elsewhere, towns newly designated were Cieza, Hellín, Lorca, Albacete, Almansa, Yecla, Villena, Valencia, Alicante, Villarreal, Morella, Alcoy, Zaragoza, Ejea de los Caballeros, Barcelona, Gerona, Lérida, Tortosa, Villafranca del Panadés, Requena, Villanueva de los Infantes, Valladolid, Villanueva de la Serena, Zamora, and Zafra.[29] Clause 2 noted that residence in any given town should in the first instance be granted to gypsies who came from there, the reason given being that their neighbours, accustomed to their ways, would be better able to monitor their activities and ensure their 'uniformity in dress and language, without permitting them any distinctiveness whatsoever'. At any event, gypsy families were not to be permitted to live together or even in the same *barrios* (clause 3). Once settled, they must pay all crown and municipal taxes, 'to which end they may engage in all those occupations and kinds of work which are legal and not prohibited by Royal Ordinance', an expansive phrase which, as we have seen, actually meant agricultural labour and nothing else (clause 4). Those designated to new places of residence were to be granted the relevant travel permits by local *corregidores*. These must contain the names and descriptions of those travelling, as well as the precise number of days needed for the journey (clause 5). A copy must also be sent to the authorities in the town to which they were travelling so that they might know whom to expect and precisely when to expect them (clause 6). Within two months, justices from the towns listed were to provide the Council of Castile with accurate and detailed records of gypsy families settled in each place (clause 8).[30] One cannot assume that these records were in every case complete or accurate, or that they represented the national picture. But they were certainly far more comprehensive than anything previously available to the Council. The centralization or Castilianization of authority in Bourbon Spain ensured that the 1746 ordinance was implemented with a new efficiency unimaginable under the Habsburgs. It had not been a complete success, by any means, and there are good reasons for believing that many gypsies continued to live itinerant or semi-itinerant lives, while others remained in the non-designated towns and villages where, in some cases, they had been based for over two centuries. Nonetheless, records submitted by the towns to the Council of Castile as required by the ordinance showed that 881 gypsy families had now taken up residence in 54 of the 75 designated towns in approximately the correct ratio of gypsies to non-gypsies.[31] There were, however, those who quickly saw this as an unprecedented opportunity, and it would not be long before the information collected would be turned to a new use as sinister as it was cruel.

Crackdown

On 23 August 1746, some six weeks after the promulgation of Ferdinand VI's new ordinance, Gaspar Vázquez Tablada, Bishop of Oviedo, was appointed Governor of the Council of Castile. Less than a year later, on 5 July 1747, convinced that the gypsies had not yet been reduced to sufficient docility by the new measures, he approached the king privately with two suggestions designed to resolve the issue once and for all. His first proposal, which may have been influenced by the writings of Fernández Navarrete, Salazar de Mendoza, and Sancho de Moncada over a century earlier, was that all gypsies be expelled from Spain, any who returned being automatically and irremissibly condemned to death. His second, only marginally less radical suggestion, which may have owed something to the royal decree of 1673 which had ordered all vagrant gypsy males of over 12 years of age to be rounded up and sent to the galleys,[32] was that they should be imprisoned *en masse* and forced to work productively both to finance their own incarceration and for the benefit of the nation.[33] Such an operation, he argued, would necessarily have to be conducted in conditions of great secrecy, at night; and its success would depend on both the element of surprise and carefully synchronized action involving both civil and military authorities across Spain. Should such action be taken, two recent developments would make success much more likely than had hitherto been the case. First, the 1748 concordat with Rome meant, to all intents and purposes, that gypsies would no longer be able to avoid arrest by claiming ecclesiastical sanctuary. Second, the operation would be made easier by the availability of the registers of gypsy families compiled in the aftermath of Ferdinand's ordinance of the previous year. The initiative would, that is to say, be directed primarily against sedentarized families, against those who had obeyed rather than resisted the crown's demands, though operations would also, in the event, extend to some towns not listed in either the 1717 or 1746 ordinances, including Madrid, where 90 gypsies were eventually arrested.

On 30 July 1749, an order was duly issued to take into custody all the gypsies who could be apprehended across the length and breadth of Spain. Vázquez Tablada had instigated the move, although planning for the vital military involvement in the round-up was carried out under the direction of the Marquis of Ensenada. Using the records now held by the Council, Vázquez Tablada supplied a list of 54 towns where the round-up was to be carried out. Twenty-one of the 75 towns originally designated for occupation by gypsies in the 1717 and 1746 ordinances did not, therefore, appear. These included Betanzos, Orense, and Oviedo in north-west Spain, where gypsy numbers had always been negligible. Less easily explained, however, are the omissions of Barcelona, Gerona, and a number of other Catalan towns designated, as well as Valencia, Albacete, Alicante, Alcoy, and Cieza in the east, and Valladolid, Teruel and even Guadalajara, where one might have expected to see evidence of at least a small settled gypsy population after 1717. Whatever the reason for the failure to include these towns and cities, it is hard to believe that there were no gypsies at all to be found in any of them, especially when towns such as Aranda de Duero, Santo Domingo de la Calzada and Mancha Real, which did figure in the Council of Castile's list, were recorded as having just one gypsy family in each case. Certainly the list should not be taken as a reliable indicator of Spain's gypsy population, since it included neither families who had continued to reside in other, unlisted towns, nor those who still lived largely itinerant lives and whose numbers may now have been swollen by others determined to regain some control over their lives. One curious document from the 1780s, allegedly discovered by an army colonel, one Benigno González García, purports to offer what is probably a second-hand description of events between 1740 and 1750 in Triana, a suburb of Seville and home to many gypsies. Describing how soldiers arrested most of the city's gypsies in 1749 on the orders of the king, it claims that two were shot dead attempting to flee on horseback and another wounded, while yet another drowned in the River Guadalquivir in front of his wife and two young children. Those seeking sanctuary in church were prevented from doing so. But the author adds that the gypsies living in a shantytown near the monastery of La Cartuja did in fact manage to escape, abandoning all their possessions.[34] Certainly the list of sedentarized gypsies furnished by Vázquez Tablada revealed a marked concentration in the south, principally in El Puerto de Santa María with its 157 families and Seville with its 130, but also in Lorca (47 families), Écija (35), Granada (32), Antequera (22), and elsewhere. Based on this information, sealed orders were prepared and distributed to the *corregidores* of the 54 towns listed. In each case, the *corregidor* was given overall responsibility for ensuring the success of the operation, but was also charged with the capture at his own expense of any gypsies slipping through the net. Each envelope contained a copy of the Apostolic Nuncio's new instructions in respect of ecclesiastical sanctuary, should it be required, and a separate set of orders to be handed by the *corregidor* immediately the envelope was opened to the commanding officer of the troops enlisted to round-up and guard the prisoners as they were taken to their places of incarceration. Little was left to chance, with the troops often matching in number those to be apprehended. In Murcia, for example, over 160 cavalry and infantrymen were sent under Lieutenant-Colonel Lorenzo Bécar to apprehend the city's 49 gypsy families.[35]

Ensenada, however, was not satisfied with the initial results of the round-up, and, with Vázquez Tablada, whom he blamed for its deficiencies, having been replaced by yet another prelate as Governor of the Council, the marquis now assumed responsibility for the exercise himself, issuing new, detailed orders for its completion on 12 August 1749. Once apprehended, the gypsies were inventoried and their property seized for subsequent auction. The men, together with boys of over seven years of age, were separated from the women. According to Ensenada, Vázquez Tablada had raised no objection to the separation of wives from their husbands,[36] doubtless because such separation was essential to a project almost certainly designed to ensure extinction. The women and younger children were to be held in establishments that were part gaol, part factory in Seville, Valencia, and Zaragoza, where it was intended that they would spin yarn to pay for their upkeep. The men were destined for hard labour in penal colonies or, in most cases, the arsenals of La Carraca (Cádiz), then being extended, Cartagena, where they slept in decommissioned galleys, and for some, eventually, La Graña (El Ferrol). Boys of over seven years of age were sent with them, 'so that they might learn some trade'.[37] The precise number of gypsies detained is unknown. The Public Prosecutor Pedro Rodríguez de Campomanes later estimated the figure to have been more than 9000, though it may have been as high as 12,000.[38] The strict secrecy that had surrounded every aspect of the operation had certain disadvantages, too. When on 7 August, a week after the arrests, the authorities in Málaga were suddenly informed that there was insufficient prison space available for the large influx of detainees and that they must therefore accommodate a number of gypsy women and children in the city's Alcazaba fortress, this was the first they had heard of the matter. Unable to meet the request, since the fortress was already being used as a gunpowder store, the impecunious city council was left to make piecemeal and wholly unsatisfactory arrangements for the 1000 or more gypsies who were eventually brought there.[39] Meanwhile, the governor of the arsenal at La Carraca made it abundantly clear that he did not want a gypsy workforce who were 'weak and idle by nature', as he put it. He wrote to Ensenada repeatedly to complain that he had neither the money to feed them, nor the space to accommodate them, nor yet sufficient men to guard them.[40] He was obliged, he said, to have them work alongside paid day-labourers, so that they might learn the skills needed for the work there. And how anyway could gypsies, weighed down by their shackles and chains, possibly be used to repair rigging or perform other tasks, skilled or otherwise, requiring a certain mobility? His fears that he was sitting on a powder-keg were well founded. After one revolt, when the gypsies turned on their guards with improvised weapons, the governor, unable to extract from the prisoners any information about who had been responsible, resorted to constructing a gallows outside the huts where, chained to the walls as they always were at night, his charges might contemplate the consequences of any further disturbance.[41]

It was becoming clear, however, that the situation was unsustainable. On 7 September 1749, just six weeks after the first arrests, amid numerous protests to the king from gypsy prisoners who argued that they had always lived peacefully within the law and could prove it, as well as from other, ostensibly reputable individuals, including parish priests,[42] Ensenada ordered a board to be established to look into whether some of those imprisoned should in fact have been granted exemptions. As discussions continued about what was ultimately to be done with the gypsies, including the suggestion that they might be sent to Spain's colonies in the Americas, the Council reversed its position on those to whom its predecessors had granted letters acknowledging their status as 'Old Castilians'. It had previously instructed that those possessing such letters were not to be exempted from arrest. Now, such 'formal declarations that they are not gypsies', as Ensenada put it, were to be taken into account as part of secret reports designed to establish whether such individuals had indeed lived decently and worked as others did, as they had claimed.[43] Meanwhile, the sale of their possessions should be suspended, pending the outcome. As a result, on 28 October, those who should not according to such criteria have been arrested were ordered to be returned to their places of residence. Politics accordingly attempted to rewrite history with the patently absurd assertion that

> not all those who through name or origin are said to be gypsies were included in his Majesty's Royal Order, which from the outset was only intended to bring about the detention of those who are pernicious

and inclined to wickedness, and not those who have managed because of their conduct to confute the evil resonances of that criminal name.[44]

Those returned were in theory to have their belongings restored to them, though much had in fact already been sold off. In Carmona, the *corregidor* issued such an order in 1750, adding that those of the 16 gypsies involved whose tools could not be returned to them should receive compensation in cash, while blacksmiths, many of whom, along with bakers, were reclaimed from captivity by their neighbours, should be provided with coal to re-start their forges. Despite the releases, on 28 December 1750 the governor of La Carraca could still complain that of the 1193 gypsies originally sent there, only 534 had been returned to their towns, though 14 had meanwhile died in captivity. On 15 September the following year, he reported that the prisoners themselves attributed their continuing detention to the fact that local magistrates, reluctant to return confiscated belongings or to provide compensation where these had been sold, were unwilling to vouch for them. His report echoed similar comments made to Ensenada by the commandant at Cartagena two months earlier.[45] In 1757, the governor wrote to the Council of Castile requesting it to authorize the release of La Carraca's remaining gypsies and citing documents presented to him attesting to their good character. His request was denied.[46]

Some of those detained had meanwhile managed to escape. Indeed, the Governor of Almagro reported that it was escapees from the arsenals who accounted for most of the gypsy bandits operating in the areas around La Roda, El Bonillo, and other villages in La Mancha, allegedly supported in their activities by a priest, one Pascual Carrión.[47] In the end, however, after complaints from the arsenals and other places of detention that continued incarceration of the gypsies was no longer of any benefit whatsoever, that many had become sick and required constant medical attention, and that remaining numbers were anyway small (some 165), a general pardon was granted by Charles III four years after his accession to the throne on the death of his half-brother Ferdinand. The order was communicated to the Council of Castile by the Secretary of the Navy on 16 June 1763. It had taken 14 years, and, even then, 2 further years were to elapse, much to the displeasure of the king, before all those remaining in Cádiz and Cartagena were finally liberated.

'Enlightened despotism': Towards reform

Spain's age of 'enlightened despotism' had between 1749 and 1765 shown the despotic side of its Janus face all too plainly. And it had done so to disastrous effect, not just for the gypsy men, women, and children who suffered so terribly in the years following the 1749 round-up, but also, ultimately, for the crown's fundamentally unworkable policies towards them. With the accession of the reformist Charles III in 1759, in a Spain moving into a new phase of population growth and economic expansion, official policy towards the gypsies was to see important changes. There would, it is true, be a good deal of continuity in so far that the primary aim of published government policy remained the assimilation of this pariah minority to mainstream society. But the new policy would nevertheless mark a radical departure from many of the more repressive aspects of previous legislation, which had if anything served to obstruct the progress of the assimilationist agenda. Charles III was described by Sir Charles Petrie as 'the perfect type of the benevolent despot of the eighteenth century'. Yet despite Petrie's additional observation that 'although the new King of Spain was thoroughly imbued with the ideas of the French Encyclopaedists, he was not always sufficiently acquainted with the outlook of the ordinary Spaniard', Charles and his ministers did in the end come to the view that it was marginalization itself that lay at the heart of the gypsy problem.[48] This is not to suggest that the new policy eventually introduced in 1783, relatively tolerant though it undoubtedly was, reflected any warming of official attitudes towards the gypsies. Rather the new approach was what might be termed resignedly pragmatic. The decision taken in 1763 to release the last of the gypsies incarcerated 14 years earlier had ushered in a 20-year period of consultation and reassessment. Two separate recapitulative reports were produced for Charles III by the Public Prosecutors Campomanes and Lope de Sierra Cienfuegos on 26 October 1763 and 12 May 1766, respectively. While neither report recommended any softening of the government's line on gypsies at this stage, both nevertheless foreshadowed in some ways the changes to come. Campomanes, for example, while still taking a distinctly hardline approach, nevertheless noted that land vacated with the departure of the *moriscos* had not, 'as would have been advisable', been shared out among the gypsies. This, plus the fact that the latter were nevertheless permitted only to engage in agricultural labour, had inevitably meant that 'the decision to sedentarize them had no effect and they continued to roam in troops as before'.[49] And, he observed, albeit with evident exaggeration,

The gypsies are considered incorrigible thieves. Nobody wants them as servants for fear that they will rob them and steal their livestock. Nobody uses them on the land, or wishes to trade with them, regarding them as people without religion, whose word cannot be trusted, and as vile and despicable individuals.[50]

There is clear acknowledgement here of the sheer impracticality of legislation which had effectively required all gypsies, almost all of whom had no land of their own and were commonly regarded as untrustworthy idlers, to seek employment as agricultural labourers, work which was anyway largely seasonal, from their non-gypsy neighbours. Campomanes identified this as a fundamental contradiction running through much previous legislation, though one should stress that his analysis was based firmly on practical rather than humanitarian concerns. He railed in particular at the protection afforded to gypsies by others, including the regular and secular clergy, twice describing such behaviour as 'incredible'. Gypsies who had settled had, he thought, merely used this as a cover for their other, illegal activities, and in particular as a way of providing themselves with alibis when necessary, and he inclined to the view that expulsion or physical extermination would have been the only truly effective ways of solving the problem. As things were, he favoured sending vagrant gypsies to the colonies, to Louisiana, Cuba, Puerto Rico, Trinidad, Santo Domingo, Venezuela, the Bay of San Julián in southern Argentina, or the Juan Fernández Islands, far out in the Pacific due west of the Chilean capital Santiago. Lope de Sierra's report, produced three years later, merely concurred for the most part with Campomanes's findings. The reports were discussed by the Council of Castile on 22 February 1771, though no conclusions were reached. The President of the Council, Pedro Pablo Abarca de Bolea, Count of Aranda, indisposed on that day, sent instead a written opinion in which he expressed the view that gypsy children, once weaned, should be separated from their parents and educated in charitable institutions. Of those of over 15 years of age, women should be sent to colonies on the American mainland, while gypsy men should be sent instead to islands. Both sexes, kept firmly apart, would then conveniently intermarry with the continent's indigenous peoples.[51]

However, it was another report of 29 January 1772, written by Campomanes and Pedro Valiente, also a member of the Council, which finally served as a basis for the reformist legislation of September 1783, though only after certain of its recommendations had been rejected. The report proposed, for example, not just transportation to the Americas, but also that delinquent gypsy youths be drummed into corrective naval service, after which they might be employed in shipyards, sail-making, or other related activities. For this reason, it was eventually sent for approval in August 1775 by the Minister of Justice, Manuel de Roda, to Fray Julián de Arriaga, at that time responsible both for the navy and the American colonies. In 1776, before he could respond, Arriaga died, to be replaced in the colonial role by José de Gálvez. Prompted once again by Roda after eighteen months, Gálvez declared himself in 1777 roundly opposed to any disruptive gypsy presence in Spain's overseas possessions, especially at a time when England's colonies were in a state of potentially contagious revolutionary ferment. Meanwhile, responsibility for the navy had passed to Pedro González de Castejón, who on 23 February 1778 made no secret of his contempt for what he evidently regarded as a landlubber's proposal that young gypsy men might usefully serve with the Spanish fleet.[52] Modern warships were not like the galleys, the Marquis reminded the Council, and far from inculcating a sense of discipline in the gypsies, he worried that it would be naval discipline itself that would suffer, were such a policy to be implemented.[53] The Campomanes-Valiente report estimated Spain's gypsy population at 10,000 individuals, though for reasons similar to those stated earlier, this figure should be treated very warily. And it insisted once again that the protection of gypsies, often by members of the nobility, had been the principal reason for the failures of previous legislation. Crucially, however, it also argued that it was the very exclusion of gypsies from all manner of trades and professions that had contributed to their extreme social marginalization; and it was this, 'indirectly', as the report put it, together with the fact that they had been unable to educate their children, who were consequently 'full of vices and bad habits', that had forced them of necessity to continue with their careers of crime.[54]

Progress had been slow, to be sure, but the report was brought back to the Council of Castile in May 1782. The result was the promulgation by Charles III on 19 September the following year of a new royal ordinance which overturned much that was repressive in earlier legislation, but whose *dirigiste*, utilitarian thrust would nonetheless exact an exorbitant price. In it, the monarch drew attention initially to the effects of the recent war with England, which had brought together 'large gangs of vagrants, smugglers and villains who have infested the roads'.[55] Although not mentioned specifically, the long siege of Gibraltar, which had lasted from 1779 to 1782 had certainly led to a spate of desertions on both sides, and the ordinance went on to blame the gypsies for providing the very model for the behaviours now embraced by such groups, including deserters from both the Spanish army and navy.[56] After citing as the guiding precedent for this new legislation the 1619 and 1633 ordinances promulgated by Philip III and Philip IV, respectively, clause 1 declared that 'those who are called and known as gypsies, are not so, either by origin or nature ["ni lo son por origin, ni por naturaleza", the exact phrase used in 1633], nor do they proceed from any infected root whatsoever'. Clause 2 forbade once again the gypsies' language, dress, and itinerant way of life, while clause 3 prohibited not just the use of the term *gitanos* but also its equally stigmatizing replacement 'New Castilians' (*castellanos nuevos*). But it was clause 5 that ushered in change, ordering now that gypsies conforming to the requirements of clause 2 be allowed henceforth to take up the occupation of their choosing and that they be admitted to guilds without any legal or other form of impediment being placed in their way. Clause 7 gave 90 days for 'vagrants of this or any other class' to take up residence in towns or villages chosen by themselves, 'except, for the time being, the Court and Royal Places'. Clause 8 returned to the question of occupations, imposing certain restrictions: 'it is not enough for them to work only as shearers, or as dealers at markets and fairs, still less to run country inns in remote, uninhabited places'. Gypsies would, however, be permitted to work as innkeepers in towns and villages, unless compelling evidence could be adduced to show that they were themselves criminals or had ever sheltered such individuals. Clause 9 provided that those giving up their old way of life, dress and language, but who failed to devote themselves to honest work, were to be regarded as vagrants and treated exactly like other Spaniards, as were those subsequently found guilty of crimes, who were to be 'pursued, prosecuted and punished like other offenders, with no differentiation whatsoever'.

For gypsies who failed to observe the ordinance the penalties were, however, to be severe. Those refusing to abandon their old ways were to be apprehended (clause 11), their details passed to the appropriate *corregidor* and thence to the *Sala del Crimen* (criminal court) for the area (clause 12). The *Sala*, having verified the offence, would immediately order a 'small' representation of the Arms of Castile to be burned into the prisoner's back. Branding irons for the purpose were to be held in readiness in the principal town of each district (clause 13). This would replace 'for now' the sentence of death for a first offence as well as notching of the ears, a historical penalty probably not imposed for almost a century and a half and even then only very rarely (clause 15). The resulting scar would be used to identify recidivists, who, as they should have been informed when branded, were to be condemned, without possibility of remission, to death (clause 20). Children under 16 years of age were to be exempt, but were to be separated from their parents, sent to 'workhouses or houses of instruction', and entrusted to the care of parochial charitable boards to be established by the Council of Castile (clauses 16, 17, and 18). Justices failing to enforce the law would be liable to removal from office and the imposition of heavy fines.

Anyone helping, receiving stolen goods from, sheltering, or otherwise protecting gypsy 'vagrants and criminals' would incur a fine of 200 ducats for a first offence, 400 for a second, and up to 1000 for a third. Those unable to pay – here the ordinance's ostensibly egalitarian façade begins to crumble – would instead serve three, six, or ten years, respectively, in one of Spain's North African penal colonies (clause 31). Money collected through fines was to be divided equally between the Treasury, the judge imposing the sentence, and, not least, the informant (clauses 28 and 30). Where members of the clergy were found to be involved in such activities, justices were authorized to confiscate and sell their belongings in order to realize the fines imposed. Where poverty made this impossible, however, the matter must be referred to the Council before any prison sentence might be imposed (clause 32). Finally, the ordinance announced a general amnesty for gypsies, including deserters and smugglers, accused of all but the most serious of offences, such as '*lèse-majesté* divine and human', murder, and theft from a church or involving violence, subject, of course, to general compliance with the new law's demands (clause 35).

In both the census records compiled in the wake of the 1783 ordinance and earlier, amid the flurry of protests by individuals identified as gypsies in 1717 and 1746, are to be found repeated claims by those so classified that they were in fact mulattos, mestizos, negroes, or simply Spaniards whose lowly professions, dubious way of life, or mixed marriages had led the authorities to categorize them incorrectly as gypsies.[57] To take just three examples, in one case registered in Guadix in 1746, Antonio Domingo Lisalde, husband of the gypsy Francisca de Malla, declared himself to be in fact a 'Berber', while in another, Fernando Carrillo assured the authorities in Córdoba in 1717 that although a gypsy on his father's side, his mother had been Galician. In Cádiz, Vicente Nuñez objected that he had no idea why he had been imprisoned, 'because neither the deponent nor his ancestors are or ever have belonged to those known as gypsies, their line of descent in fact going back to the island of Puerto Rico'.[58] It is difficult at this remove to know how many of these claims were genuine, though one can hardly ignore the oppressive and threatening circumstances under which they were made.

They are, however, entirely consistent with repeated claims dating back to the 1470s that outsiders were frequently accepted by the gypsies into their communities. Nor were mixed marriages nearly as uncommon as has sometimes been asserted. Antonio Gómez Alfaro has, for example, identified about a hundred cases in Andalusia between 1783 and 1785, with one non-gypsy male marrying a gypsy female for every three gypsy male to non-gypsy female marriages in Granada, a situation reversed in Seville, while numbers for Córdoba were about equal.[59] The census records' physical descriptions of those who did not deny their status as gypsies, whilst by no means conclusive, nevertheless lend weight to the view that there had been a significant degree of racial mix over the centuries, and range from those whose skin was described as being black to a surprising number of others described as having blonde hair and blue eyes.[60] Overall, the census recorded 9875 gypsies in Castile, of whom 80 per cent, 7933, lived in Andalusia. There is no official figure for Aragon or Navarre, though Gómez Alfaro's studies of registers for these regions in Madrid and Simancas led him to estimate the national grand total at around 11,000.[61] Yet even when one takes account of the fact that non-gypsy husbands of mixed marriages and their children were in most places excluded from the figures, this seems an improbably low total, representing only just over 0.1 per cent of a total Spanish population reckoned at 10.4 million in 1787.[62] It seems likely, therefore, that it was arrived at only after a considerable winnowing out over the years since 1717 on grounds such as those just discussed of many of those previously regarded by the authorities, and probably by many of their neighbours, as gypsies. It would also have been difficult or impossible for the authorities to include in the census those groups who stubbornly continued to live semi-sedentarized or even wholly itinerant lives.[63] And it would be surprising if their numbers had not now been swollen by others, who, mindful of the brutal use to which the registers had been put in 1749, preferred to flee their places of residence and take their chances in open country. This, after all, is what had reportedly happened in Triana in 1749 and earlier, in 1745, when news reached Seville of Philip V's ordinance of 30 October that year permitting the summary execution of gypsies carrying arms.[64]

Until his death on 14 December 1788, Charles III's 1783 ordinance excited a good deal of further debate about how best its essentially util-itarian aims might be achieved. There were, it is true, those *corregidores* and *alcaldes* who favoured toughening certain aspects of the legisla-tion, and later monarchs would still heed such voices on occasion. But others were now making themselves heard, too, actively advocating true integration of the gypsies to Spanish society. They did so amid much discussion of the pressing need for education, of the cultural rather than racial nature of difference, and of the duty of every subject, even, with France poised on the brink of revolution, of every 'citizen', to make a useful contribution to society.[65] In one sense at least, the new ordinance had represented a watershed, in that it had provided for the first time a legal framework within which, at least in theory, the sedentarization and social integration of this pariah group might finally become economically viable. Gone now were most of the harsh and ultimately unworkable restrictions of those old laws which had for almost two centuries stubbornly insisted that gypsies support themselves only through agricultural labour. Given that such work was at best only sporadically available in any given locality, these had effectively made their physical survival contingent on resort to other activities, most of which, including almost all their traditional occupations, had already been outlawed. Now, too, they could choose to live wherever they wished, except for those few areas where there were royal residences. Change came with a price, however. Self-avowedly guided by the spirit of the 1619 and 1633 ordinances of Charles III's Habsburg predecessors, and despite the winnowing process referred to earlier, the new law had also insisted – the irony could hardly be more acute – on depriving those now unspokenly identified as *gitanos* of any claim whatsoever to a separate ethnic identity. It amounted, that is to say, to a form of inverted racism.

It is undeniable, however, that there had at last been a kind of sea change. A new, inchoate sense of realism, of pragmatism, had finally begun to inform government policy towards the gypsies. The world did not change overnight, to be sure, and the years that followed saw much reversion to the *status quo ante* as far as the gypsies' always marginal activities and ever antagonistic relations with the authorities were concerned. But the grounds of the debate had now decisively shifted and the failures of past legislation, especially after the government's ignominious retreat following the 1749 round-up, were widely acknowledged. The benighted attitudes of the past had, that is to say, become quite simply unsustainable. In that sense, Charles III's 1783 ordinance may therefore be said to have marked the beginning of the modern era for Spain's gypsies. As such, it represents an appropriate point at which to draw a line under the historical narrative for the early modern period.

Conclusion

The almost six centuries-long history of Spain's gypsies has frequently been characterized as one of more or less unrelenting oppression, of 'systematic discrimination, persecution and marginalization', in the words of a 1991 report for the non-governmental organization Asociación Nacional Presencia Gitana.[1] It is, of course, undeniably true that laws against gypsies in Spain over the early modern period became increasingly oppressive, stigmatizing and indiscriminate. Yet it is also clear that this trajectory was at once cause and consequence of the fact that for over 200 years the crown showed itself largely incapable of enforcing its own legislation with anything approaching the efficiency seen in 1749, the year of the savage round-up presided over by the Bourbon Ferdinand VI. One reason for this was that despite royal pretensions to absolute authority in 'these our kingdoms', early modern 'Spain' was never a unitary state, at least until centralization of power with the Bourbon reforms of the eighteenth century began finally to impose a new political and legislative template on the peripheries. As a result, the crown's *executive* power, its ability to translate edict into effective action on the ground was in reality quite extensively circumscribed, notwithstanding the fact that the monarch's theoretical authority as providential guarantor of justice and stability in an uncertain and dangerous world was almost universally acknowledged. For most of the period, Spaniards of every stripe and estate continued in practice to weigh their own local interests and traditional privileges against the demands of the crown and its councils, which were thus constantly reminded both of the limits of their power and the duties they owed to the kingdoms. Even at the heart of empire, in Castile itself, large areas remained under the jurisdiction of the nobility and the Church, with the military enjoying its own, powerful *fuero*, defended robustly by the Council of War,[2] while tensions relating to rights of cognizance periodically surfaced even between the *Chancillerías* and the Council of Castile. Taken together, these effectively ensured that the royal writ was always liable to run a less than certain course even across the peninsula's heartlands. Lack of resources for the pursuit, incarceration and transport of gypsies further compounded these difficulties, as did ignorance of the law, especially in remote rural areas.

There was also, of course, another, crucially important side to the story; for it is equally clear that for much of the period considerable active support and protection was given to the gypsies by other Spaniards. As the crown busied itself creating new crimes of the gypsies' traditional occupations and itinerant or semi-itinerant way of life, so, unsurprisingly, it created new criminals. The gypsies' need to transgress in order to survive was from an early stage ensured by the severity of legislative provisions which, had they been fully observed even by those who had ostensibly become sedentarized, would have made an already precarious existence next to impossible. Even if draconian limitations had not been placed on their freedoms of choice and movement, sedentarized gypsies, like so many of their non-gypsy neighbours, were anyway perfectly likely to find themselves forced by deteriorating economic conditions to return to the life of vagrancy so comprehensively forbidden to them. Meanwhile, once again unsurprisingly, gypsies were frequently protected by local clergymen, at least until 1748, after which date an agreement with Rome ensured that ecclesiastical sanctuary could no longer be used to cock a snook at the civil authorities. They were helped, too, by elements of the nobility, especially south of the Tagus where most gypsies had eventually gravitated, as well as by other Spaniards who, for one reason or another, variously sympathized with, feared, or stood, corruptly or otherwise, to gain something from them.

As to the gypsies themselves, while for some, probably most, gypsy lineages or *razas* endogamy was the norm, others are known to have countenanced mixed marriage, and by no means always between gypsy men and non-gypsy women. Some gypsies, especially those periodically involved in banditry, clearly accepted others, including for obvious reasons deserters and criminals well-versed in the use of weapons, into their companies. Yet despite the banditry that plagued some areas, it is quite clear that relations between gypsies and non-gypsies were by no means always and everywhere antagonistic, although they were almost certainly prone, then as now, to quite radical instability. As it was, by the end of the second decade of the seventeenth century, Spain's gypsies had officially been designated a home-grown criminal underclass, wayward Spaniards with, by implication, no real claim to a separate ethnic identity. This position and the government's henceforth increasingly integrationist policy were driven largely by political expediency in a Spain now officially purged of its allegedly problematic ethnic minorities and which anyway seemed incapable of resolving the gypsy question by anything other than this most cosmetic of methods. Repeated attempts to prohibit the outward signs of difference, such as dress and language, can of course be traced back to the time of Charles V. And as legislators throughout the period continued to avoid identifying gypsies in specifically racial terms, what was effectively an attempt to deny their ethnic identity itself came to constitute a form of racist exclusion, of symbolic expulsion. Ironically enough, it would be a denial encapsulated in its most developed form in 1783 in the very royal ordinance which finally lifted many of the repressive provisions of earlier legislation.

Notes

Introduction

1. *The Spanish Gypsy: The History of a European Obsession* (University Park, PA: Pennsylvania State University Press, 2004), p. 4.
2. Angus Fraser, *The Gypsies* (Oxford: Blackwell, 1992), p. 299.
3. Paloma Gay y Blasco, 'A "Different" Body? Desire and Virginity Among Gitanos', *The Journal of the Royal Anthropological Institute*, 1:3 (1997), 517–35 (p. 520).
4. *Economy and Society* (New York: Bedminster Press, 1968), p. 389.
5. *La diferencia inquietante: Viejas y nuevas estrategias culturales de los gitanos* (Madrid: Siglo Veintiuno, 1997), pp. 239–45.
6. *Spain's Road to Empire: The Making of a World Empire 1492–1673* (London: Penguin, 2002).
7. *Cartas marruecas; Noches lúgubres* (Madrid: Cátedra, 1998), pp. 100–6.

1 The early years

1. Miguel de Cervantes, in *Novelas ejemplares*, 3 vols (Madrid: Castalia, 1982), I, pp. 73–158.
2. For a more specific treatment of this topic, see Richard J. Pym, 'The Pariah Within: Early Modern Spain's Gypsies', *Journal of Romance Studies*, 4:2 (2004), 21–35.
3. ACRV, *reg.* 2483, fol. 136r. Angus Fraser notes that the same Count Thomas was ten years later granted 23 florins by Blanca of Navarre before departing the kingdom via Canfranc, which was with Roncevalles, one of the two main crossings into France for pilgrims returning from Santiago de Compostela. At the border, he produced the original safe-conduct, which had exempted his group as pilgrims from all tolls and other imposts. It produced the desired effect, though the gypsies still had to go through the motions of declaring their five horses, five silk robes, and four silver goblets (*The Gypsies*, p. 76; Bernard Leblon, *Los gitanos de España*, Barcelona: Gedisa, 1985, p. 18).
4. As Fraser notes, it is possible that some gypsies, described as 'Tartars', may have appeared in Lower Saxony as early as 1407, or in Basle in 1414. The scant evidence must, though, be deemed far from conclusive (*The Gypsies*, pp. 61–2).
5. Angus Fraser, 'Juridical Autonomy among Fifteenth and Sixteenth Century Gypsies', *The American Journal of Comparative Law*, 45:2 (1997), 291–304 (pp. 292 and 295).
6. Fraser, *The Gypsies*, p. 72.
7. Fraser notes that the German cartographer, mathematician and Hebraist, Sebastian Münster, claimed in his *Cosmographia universalis* of 1544 to have

seen such a letter from the Emperor Sigismund issued to the gypsies at Lindau (*The Gypsies*, p. 64).

8. Fraser, 'Juridical Autonomy', pp. 292–3.

9. *The Waning of the Middle Ages* (Harmondsworth: Penguin, 1968 [1924]), pp. 17–18.

10. A document discovered by Amada López de Meneses in the Archivo de la Corona de Aragón (ACA) dated 26 November 1415 in Perpignan (Real Chancillería, *reg.* 2452, fol. 82r–v) has been cited by San Román (*La diferencia inquietante*, p. 7) and Capdevila y Orozco (*Errantes y expulsados: normativas jurídicas contra gitanos, judíos, y moriscos*, Córdoba: Francisco Baena, 1991, pp. 17–18) as evidence of an earlier gypsy presence in the peninsula. A letter of safe-conduct issued by the future Alfonso V to Thomas, son of Duke Bartholomew de Sabba, it authorizes Thomas to undertake a pilgrimage to the tomb of St James at Santiago as well as other shrines. The Duke, though, is reported to hail from Ethiopia, not Egypt or Little Egypt ('Thoma, filius, ut asserit, ducis Bartholomei de Sauua, Indie majoris Ethiopie'), even if the insertion of 'so he claims' seems to imply a certain scepticism about his story on the part of the writer. Given the number of pilgrims, genuine and false, and from points far and wide, who travelled the pilgrim route to Santiago (J. N. Hillgarth, *The Spanish Kingdoms 1250–1516*, vol. II; *Castilian Hegemony 1410–1516*, Oxford: Clarendon Press, 1978, p. 121), any presumption that Thomas de Sabba was a gypsy must be deemed speculative. Were the claim to be true, on the other hand, his would hardly have been the first such incursion.

11. For the exalted status associated with the use of 'don' during this early period, see Américo Castro, *España en su historia* (Buenos Aires: Losada, 1948), p. 540.

12. ACRV, *reg.* 2573, fol. 145v.

13. AGS RGS, VIII, fols 1150–2.

14. Hillgarth, *The Spanish Kingdoms*, II, p. 121. The fact that others, including vagabonds and the criminally inclined, were also adept at using the pretext of pilgrimage to maximum advantage was eventually recognized in law one hundred and fifty years later in Philip II's ordinance of 1590. It demanded that all would-be pilgrims henceforth obtain a license in advance of their journey from the diocesan or civil authorities (David E. Vassberg, *The Village and the Outside World in Golden Age Castile*, Cambridge: Cambridge University Press, 1996, p. 163). Even in 1534, at the *Cortes* of Madrid, Charles V had noted concerns about the increasing numbers of foreign idlers and vagabonds masquerading as pilgrims (Leblon, *Los gitanos*, p. 24). See also Manuel Colmeiro (ed.), *Cortes de los antiguos reinos de León y Castilla*, vol. 4 (Madrid: Sucesores de Rivadeneyra, 1903), p. 253.

15. Fraser, 'Juridical Autonomy', p. 299.

16. Luis Suárez Fernández, *Nobleza y monarquía: Puntos de vista sobre la historia política castellana del siglo XV* (Valladolid: Universidad de Valladolid, 1975), p. 191. The Order of Santiago was one of the three principal military orders founded in Castile in the twelfth century as part of a continuing effort to re-focus Christian efforts on the recovery of Muslim Spain for Christendom. The others were those of Calatrava and Alcántara. Whilst not the oldest – that distinction belonged to the Order of Calatrava, founded in 1158 – the

Order of Santiago nevertheless enjoyed special prestige in a nation that regarded St James as the very symbol of its martial prowess.

17. Hillgarth, *The Spanish Kingdoms*, II, p. 64.
18. *Hechos del Condestable don Miguel Lúcas de Iranzo (crónica del siglo XV)*, ed. Juan de Mata Carriazo (Madrid: Espasa-Calpe, 1940), pp. 97–8.
19. *Hechos del Condestable*, p. 416.
20. Manuel Martínez Martínez, 'Los gitanos en el sureste peninsular de los siglos XV y XVI', *Boletín del Instituto de Estudios Almerienses*, 14 (1995), 91–101 (p. 91).
21. María Helena Sánchez Ortega, *Los gitanos españoles: el período borbónico* (Madrid: Castellote, 1977), pp. 78–9.
22. Angus MacKay, *Spain in the Middle Ages: From Frontier to Empire, 1000–1500* (Basingstoke: Macmillan, 1977), p. 186.
23. Palencia, himself of 'Old Christian' stock, wrote of the anti-*converso* rioters in Seville in 1474 that 'No person of standing doubted that those thieves would declare heretics anyone they thought rich' (Hillgarth, *The Spanish Kingdoms*, II, p. 415).
24. Simon Barton, *A History of Spain* (Basingstoke: Palgrave Macmillan, 2004), p. 85; Hillgarth, *The Spanish Kingdoms*, II, p. 414. The fifteenth century also saw anti-Jewish rioting in Toledo in 1449, in Seville in 1465, and again in Toledo in 1467.
25. So sweet does the pill appear to have been that on a number of occasions in the fifteenth century, Castile rejected offers from Portugal of military assistance from Ceuta to help put an end to the emirate of Granada. See Richard Hitchcock, 'Muslim Spain (711–1492)' in *Spain: A Companion to Spanish Studies* (London: Routledge, 1973), pp. 41–63 (p. 57).
26. Huarte de San Juan, *Examen de ingenios* (Madrid: Cátedra, 1989), p. 523.
27. Lou Charnon-Deutsch, *The Spanish Gypsy*, p. 5.
28. 'The gypsies say they are from Egypt, and that they wander the world as pilgrims exiled from that land as a punishment for the crime they committed by not taking in and cherishing the Virgin Mary and her Most Sacred Son when he was fleeing the wrath of Herod the Ascalonite', *Libro primero de la vida y milagros del glorioso Confessor Sant Ginés de la Xara* (Murcia: Agustín Martínez, 1607), fol. 5. Copy consulted: BNM 3/6491.
29. *Restauración política de España* (Madrid: Instituto de Estudios Fiscales, 1974 [1619]), p. 213. It has sometimes been suggested, as, for example, by Jean Paul Clébert (*Los gitanos*, Barcelona: Orbis, 1965, p. 109), that some of Spain's gypsies may have arrived via North Africa. Unfortunately, the lack of evidence ensures that this must remain mere conjecture, though the possibility cannot, of course, be altogether discounted.
30. *Memorial de el hecho de los gitanos* (Toledo?: n.p., 1618), AGP, VII/357, fol. 10.
31. Judith Okely, *The Traveller Gypsies* (Cambridge: Cambridge University Press, 1983), p. 3.
32. Fraser, *The Gypsies*, p. 82; Leblon, *Los gitanos*, p. 12. For a full account of the gypsies' progress through Greece and the Balkans, the reader is referred to Chapter 3 of Fraser's *The Gypsies*.
33. One of them was the German knight Arnold von Harff, who visited Modon in 1497 and claimed that there were about 300 households of 'poor black naked people [. . .] called gypsies' living on the outskirts who came from a

region called Gyppe 40 miles to the north of the city (Fraser, *The Gypsies*, p. 53). Von Harff also went to Santiago de Compostela, and, unimpressed, recorded in 1499 that when he had demanded sceptically to see the body of St James, he had been assured by the clergy there that his doubts would cause him to 'become mad, like a mad dog' (Hillgarth, *The Spanish Kingdoms*, II, p. 122).

34. *The Gypsies*, pp. 53 and 54. That both groups shared a common origin is also suggested by testimony given by the gypsy Isabel Hernández to the Inquisition in Cuenca in 1580, in which she claimed that although there were two groups, the 'gitanos' and the 'grecianos', her knowledge of 'gitano' beliefs in an afterlife as a kind of utopian version of life on Earth had been gleaned from a 'greciano gentleman' (Sánchez, *La diferencia*, p. 74).

35. López de Meneses, *La inmigración gitana*, p. 239.

36. Franz Babinger, *Mehmed the Conqueror and his Time* (Princeton, NJ: Princeton University Press, 1978), p. 95.

37. I. A. A. Thompson, 'A Map of Crime in Sixteenth-Century Spain' in *The Economic History Review*, 27:2 (1968), 244–67 (p. 258).

38. Hillgarth, *The Spanish Kingdoms*, II, pp. 128 and 130–1.

39. Barton, *A History of Spain*, p. 71; Hillgarth, *The Spanish Kingdoms*, II, p. 131.

40. Henry Kamen, *The Spanish Inquisition: An Historical Revision* (London: Phoenix, 1998), p. 4.

41. For more on *convivencia* and its breakdown, the reader is referred to Chapter 4 of Hillgarth's *The Spanish Kingdoms*, II, pp. 126–69, and Barton's *A History of Spain*, pp. 69–72.

42. Barton, *A History of Spain*, p. 70.

43. Hillgarth, *The Spanish Kingdoms*, II, p. 126; D. W. Lomax, *The Reconquest of Spain* (London: Longman, 1978), p. 169.

44. (Buenos Aires: Editorial Losada, 1948). There is an English translation of this work, *The Structure of Spanish History* (Princeton, NJ: Princeton University Press, 1954).

45. (Buenos Aires: Sudamericana, 1956).

46. María Moliner, *Diccionario de uso del español*, 2 vols (Madrid: Gredos, 1988), I, p. 760.

47. *España en su historia*, pp. 541–2 and 211–14. See also Felipe Fernández-Armesto, *Ferdinand and Isabella* (New York: Taplinger Publishing Company, 1975), p. 168, and Thomas F. Glick, *Islamic and Christian Spain in the Early Middle Ages* (Princeton, NJ: Princeton University Press, 1979), p. 5.

48. Sánchez-Albornoz is cited in Thomas F. Glick's *Islamic and Christian Spain*, p. 5. Miguel de Unamuno, *En torno al casticismo* (Madrid: Austral, 1991), p. 51. Spain's loss of Cuba, Puerto Rico and the Philippines, the last remnants of its empire, in 1898 sparked a number of writers, including Unamuno, to engage in a rather lugubrious quest to define 'true' Spanishness (*casticismo*), a process typically characterized, not for the first or last time in Spanish writing, by a retreat from the unpalatable facts of history into Castile-centred myth.

49. J. N. Hillgarth, 'Spanish Historiography and Iberian Reality', *History and Theory*, 24:1 (1985), 23–43, p. 33.

50. 'Spanish Historiography', p. 34.

51. Kamen, *The Spanish Inquisition*, p. 34.

52. For a more detailed discussion of these issues, the reader is referred to Chapter 9 of Felipe Fernández-Armesto's *Ferdinand and Isabella*, 'Unbelief, Heresy and the Church', pp. 164–83.

53. Kamen, *The Spanish Inquisition*, p. 4.

54. See Trevor J. Dadson, 'Un Ricote verdadero: el licenciado Alonso Herrador de Villarrubia de los Ojos de Guadiana – morisco que vuelve', *Actas del VI Congreso de la Asociación Internacional Siglo de Oro* (Burgos-La Rioja: Iberoamericana-Vervuert, 2004), 601–12; 'Convivencia y cooperación entre moriscos y cristianos del Campo de Calatrava: de nuevo con Cervantes y Ricote', in *Siglos dorados: Homenaje a Augustin Redondo*, vol. I (Madrid: Castalia, 2004), pp. 301–14; 'Literacy and Education in Early Modern Rural Spain: The Case of Villarubia de los Ojos', *Bulletin of Spanish Studies*, LXXXI: 7–8 (2004), 1011–37; and 'Official Rhetoric Versus Local Reality: Propaganda and the Expulsion of the *Moriscos*', in *Rhetoric and Reality in Early Modern Spain*, ed. Richard J. Pym (Woodbridge: Tamesis, 2006), pp. 1–24.

55. An analogous, markedly unstable form of *convivencia* between Spanish gypsies and their non-gypsy neighbours in present-day Andalusia has been discussed at length by Manuel Ángel Río Ruiz in his study *Violencia étnica y destierro: dinámicas de cuatro disturbios antigitanos en Andalucía* (Granada: Maristán, 2003).

56. See, for example, Leblon, *Los gitanos*, p. 17 and San Román, *La diferencia*, p. 8.

57. Not all the later arrivals, however, abandoned the appellation 'gypsy count' (see, for example, ACRV, *reg.* 3805, fol. 162r). Indeed, the term was still used in the seventeenth century, as for example in Covarrubias's 1611 dictionary, the *Tesoro de la lengua* and Salazar's *Memorial de el hecho de los gitanos* of around 1618.

58. See for example the safe-conducts granted to Francisco of Negropont, dated 26 January 1491 in Barcelona (ACRV, *reg.* 3802, fol. 170) and to Nicolás of Negropont 'Count of Egypt' on 25 November 1499, also in Barcelona (ACRV, *reg.* 3805, fol. 162r).

59. AGS RGS, I, fol. 98v, letter dated 25 January.

60. Archivo de la Pahería de Lérida, *reg.* 823, fols 71–4 and Archivo Municipal de Castellón, *Lib. Cons.* 73, cited in López de Meneses, 'La inmigración gitana', pp. 248–9.

61. ARCV, *reg.* 3390, fols 157v–158r.

62. López de Meneses, 'La inmigración gitana', p. 261.

63. AGS RGS, IV, fol. 13.

64. *Memorial de el hecho de los gitanos*, fol. 6.

65. One such Latin text may be consulted in Fraser, 'Juridical Autonomy', p. 295. See also ACRV, *reg.* 3371, fols 39v–40r; *reg.* 3385, fols 157v–158r; *reg.* 3386, fols 37v–38r; *reg.* 3514, fols 17v–18r.

66. *Los códigos españoles concordados y anotados* (Madrid: M. Rivedeneyra, 1847–51); *libro 8, título 17, ley 4* 'Que no se recepten malhechores en las fortalezas, y casas fuertes', 1480, Toledo.

67. Sharon Bohn Gmelch, 'Groups that Don't Want In: Gypsies and Other Artisan, Trader, and Entertainer Minorities', *Annual Review of Anthropology*, 15 (1986), 307–30 (317). See also San Román, *La diferencia*, pp. 101–2.

68. Vassberg, *The Village*, p. 6.

69. See, for example, Jerónimo de Alcalá Yáñez, *Alonso, mozo de muchos amos* (1624–6), a work known in its later editions as *El donado hablador* (Madrid: Aguilar, 1980), pp. 197–8; Sancho de Moncada's 1619 *Restauración política de España* (Madrid: Instituto de estudios fiscales, 1974), p. 214; and *Actas de las Cortes de Castilla* (Madrid: Sucesores de Rivadeneyra, 1887), vol. XXVI, pp. 163–5, *Cortes* of Madrid 8 November 1610.
70. Capdevila y Orozco, *Errantes y expulsados*, p. 34. See also Paloma Gay y Blasco, 'Gitano Evangelism: The Emergence of a Politico-Religious Diaspora' (paper at the 6th EASA Conference, Krakow, 26–9 July 2000), p. 6. The American anthropologist Sharon Bohn Gmelch described gypsies as 'self-employed opportunists who use generalist strategies and spatial mobility to take advantage of marginal economic opportunities' ('Groups that Don't Want In', p. 310).
71. *Memorial de el hecho de los gitanos*, fols 11–12.
72. Fraser, *The Gypsies*, p. 97.
73. *Libro de acuerdos 1464–1485*, vol. 1 (Madrid, 1932), p. 31 cited in López de Meneses, 'La inmigración gitana', p. 249.
74. Luis Astrana Marín, *Vida ejemplar y heroica de Miguel de Cervantes Saavedra*, 7 vols (Madrid: Reus, 1948), I, p. 129.
75. Astrana Marín, *Vida*, I, p. 131.
76. AHN N, Osuna, *leg.* 1761, cited in Astrana Marín, *Vida*, I, p. 132.
77. That a prelate should behave in this manner was not at all unusual for the period (see Elliott, *Imperial Spain*, p. 103), though the role-model represented by Martín de Mendoza's illustrious father would hardly have suggested restraint in such matters to his son.
78. For a detailed, if not always comprehensively referenced account, the reader is referred to Astrana Marín's *Vida*, pp. 129–58. See also Jean Canavaggio's *Cervantes* (Madrid: Austral, 2003), pp. 51–2, Leblon's *Los gitanos*, p. 20; and Krysztof Sliwa and Daniel Eisenberg's 'El licenciado Juan de Cervantes, abuelo de Miguel de Cervantes Saavedra', *Cervantes*, 17:2 (1997), 106–14 (p. 106).

2 Under one God

1. Fernández Navarrete, *Conservación de monarquías y discursos políticos sobre la gran consulta que hizo el señor Rey don Felipe Tercero dedicada al Presidente y Consejo Supremo de Castilla por el licenciado Pedro Fernández Navarrete, Canónigo de la iglesia apostólica del señor Santiago, capellán y secretario de sus Magestades y Altezas, consultor del Santo Oficio de la Inquisición*, ed. Michael D. Gordon (Madrid: Instituto de Estudios Fiscales, 1982 [1623]), p. 76. Navarrete is here citing Justinus's *Epitome to the Philippic History of Pompeius Trogus*, book 44, which claimed of the Iberians that 'their minds are inured to contempt of death. A strict and parsimonious abstinence prevails among them all. They prefer war to peace; and, if no foreign enemy offers himself, they seek one at home. Many have died under torture, to conceal what has been entrusted to them; so much stronger is their love of honour than of life.' (Trans. John Selby Watson, London: George Bell and Sons, 1886, p. 291.)
2. Hillgarth, *The Spanish Kingdoms*, II, p. 506.

3. *Crónica de los señores Reyes Católicos don Fernando y doña Isabel de Castilla y de Aragón* (Valencia: Benito Monfort, 1780), II, Chapter LI, pp. 95–6. Pulgar refers on a number of occasions in this text to the abuse of the poor by the powerful, as when he refers to 'tyrants who controlled fortresses from which they carried out robberies and caused damage in the villages', II, Chapter 1, p. 33.
4. James Casey, *Early Modern Spain: A Social History* (London: Routledge, 1999), p. 180; Barton, *A History of Spain*, p. 94.
5. Cited in Bartolomé Bennassar, *La España del Siglo de Oro* (Barcelona: Biblioteca de Bolsillo, 2004 [1982]), p. 75.
6. John Edwards, *The Spain of the Catholic Monarchs* (Oxford: Blackwell, 2000), p. 119.
7. Elliott, *Imperial Spain*, pp. 86–9.
8. Elliott, *Imperial Spain*, p. 90. The *Consejo Real* eventually evolved into the Council of Castile.
9. Henry Kamen, *Spain 1469–1714* (London: Longman, 1983), p. 30.
10. For a much fuller account of these developments, the reader is referred to Elliott's *Imperial Spain*, pp. 77–99, Kamen's *Spain 1469–1714*, pp. 1–61; and Barton's *History of Spain*, pp. 89–95.
11. Henry Kamen reckons the number to have been around 2000, considerably fewer than some estimates (*The Spanish Inquisition*, p. 60).
12. Barton, *A History of Spain*, p. 101.
13. Sánchez Ortega, *La Inquisición*, p. 406.
14. Fraser, *The Gypsies*, p. 299.
15. Ed. Faustino Gil Ayuso, *Textos y disposiciones legales de Castilla impresos en los siglos XVI y XVII* (Madrid: S. Aguirre, 1935), p. 12.
16. Fraser, *The Gypsies*, p. 98.
17. This was noted at the *Cortes* of Valladolid in 1544, where it was claimed that 'as thieves are commonly low and worthless persons or vagabonds or people of little honour', flogging not only had little deterrent value after it had been administered once, but that it was impossible to know whether a thief, once apprehended, had been flogged previously (Colmeiro, *Cortes de los antiguos reinos*, vol. 4, p. 266).
18. *The Mesta* (Port Washington, NY: Kennikat Press, 1964 [1920]), p. 42.
19. For the failings of traditional historiography in this regard, see Trevor J. Dadson, 'Official Rhetoric Versus Local Reality'.
20. The 1499 ordinance was once again confirmed in 1539, though now with increased penalties, the new provisions being reiterated yet again in 1542. Much the same can be said of anti-*morisco* legislation, which also saw repeated reiterations. See Joaquín Sanjuán's introduction to Pedro de Valencia's *Tratado acerca de los moriscos de España* (Málaga: Algazara, 1997), p. 18.
21. The *Cortes* of Madrid of 16 June 1610, for example received a petition from the *Mesta* asking for the gypsies to be expelled from Spain (*Actas de las Cortes de Castilla*, vol. XXVIII, Cortes de Madrid, de 1615, p. 396). In March 1633, a consultation document addressed to Philip IV from the Council of State noted the damage to livestock caused by gypsies and requested that the *alcaldes entregadores* of the *Mesta*, judicial officers responsible for the protection of transhumant herds, be encouraged to pursue gypsies beyond the boundaries of their own jurisdictions (AHN C, *leg.* 7133, *Mesta*).

22. Klein cites AHN Consejo Real, Expedientes, *leg.* 48, dated 1499 (*The Mesta*, p. 57, n. 2). All my attempts to locate this or any other document that might verify Klein's claim have proven unsuccessful, despite the dedicated assistance of archivists in the Archivo Histórico Nacional in Madrid and Toledo, and the Archivo General in Simancas.

23. ARCV, *Registro de Ejecutorias, caja* 0363.0032; ARCV, *Registro de Ejecutorias, caja* 0869.0017; AGS CC, *leg.* 728, fol. 5; Juan de la Plata, *Los gitanos de Jerez: historias, dinastías, oficios y tradiciones* (Jerez: Cátedra de Flamencología y Estudios Folklóricos Andaluces, 2001), p. 8.

24. AGS CC, *leg.* 196.

25. Elliott notes that in 1507 an average labourer's wage was 15–20 maravedís a day (*Imperial Spain*, p. 116).

26. Colmeiro (ed.), *Cortes de los antiguos reinos*, vol. 4, p. 437.

27. *La inmigración gitana*, p. 241n.

28. Colmeiro (ed.), *Cortes de los antiguos reinos*, vol. 4, pp. 515 (*petición* 128) and 618 (*petición* 122).

29. 'Ordenanzas reales de Castilla', *libro* 8, *título* 14, in *Los códigos españoles concordados y anotados*, 12 vols (Madrid, Julián Peña, 1872–84), vol. 6, p. 387.

30. Leblon, *Los gitanos*, pp. 26–7.

31. Casey, *Early Modern Spain*, p. 122.

32. Casey, *Early Modern Spain*, p. 36; Linda Martz, *Poverty and Welfare in Habsburg Spain: The Example of Toledo* (Cambridge: Cambridge University Press, 1983), p. 118. In New Castile it has been estimated that *jornaleros* desperately poor day-labourers, accounted for about 60 per cent of the peasantry, with some 25–30 per cent represented by *labradores*, independent farmers, most of whom were almost as impoverished as the *jornaleros*. The proportion of *jornaleros* tended to increase, albeit with local variations, as one moved south (John Lynch, *Spain 1516–1598: From Nation State to World Empire*, Oxford: Blackwell, 1991, pp. 150–1).

33. Elliott, *Imperial Spain*, p. 190.

34. *Los códigos españoles*, vol. 6, p. 387.

35. Elliott, *Imperial Spain*, p. 190; Martz, *Poverty*, p. 26. Elliott notes that the Dominican theologian, Domingo de Soto, argued in his 1545 *Deliberatio in causa pauperum* that any law depriving people of the right to beg if in dire need, moving around as necessary in order to do so, represented an offence to divine law. Martz points out that the law was not even printed until four years after it was first officially promulgated (p. 21). A later poor law enacted in 1565 no longer insisted that the poor return to their place of birth, though it did require them to prove they had confessed and communicated before being granted a begging licence (p. 33).

36. Vassberg, *The Village*, p. 156.

37. For the economic effects of the rapid expansion of Madrid after 1561 on its rural hinterland and, indeed, on other cities such as Toledo, see David Ringrose, 'The Impact of a New Capital City: Madrid, Toledo, and New Castile, 1560–1660', *The Journal of Economic History*, 33:4 (1973), 761–91.

38. BNM, R/14090.

39. *Novísima recopilación de las leyes de España, libro* XVII, *ley* II, *título* XVI (Madrid: n.p., 1805), p. 358. Copy consulted BNM 1/6724.

40. *Rerum Germanicarum historici clariss.* *Saxonia* (Frankfurt am Main: Andreas Wechel, 1580 [1520]), Book XII, Chapter 2, pp. 285–6.
41. Judith Okely, *The Traveller-Gypsies* (Cambridge: CUP, 1983), p. 4.
42. (Madrid: Juan González, 1631), fols 1 and 6. Copy consulted BNM, R/31436.
43. *Los gitanos*, p. 116. It should be noted that Leblon does not identify his source for the episode reported.
44. Ruth Pike, *Penal Servitude in Early Modern Spain* (Madison, WI: University of Wisconsin Press, 1983), p. 7.
45. *Novísima recopilación, libro XII, título XVI, ley II*, p. 358.
46. I. A. A. Thompson, 'Castile', in *Absolutism in Seventeenth-Century Europe*, ed. John Miller (London: Macmillan, 1990), pp. 69–98 (p. 77). In this chapter, Thompson explores the limits of royal power in Castile, describing the formulation *obedézcase, pero no se cumpla*, 'to which recipients of royal orders resorted again and again' (p. 77) as one of 'absolute obedience and limited compliance' (p. 96). See also Ruth Mackay, *The Limits of Royal Authority: Resistance and Obedience in Seventeenth-Century Castile* (Cambridge: Cambridge University Press, 1999), pp. 1–3.
47. Charles's reply read as follows: 'To this we reply to you that we are not aware that such documents have been issued in contravention of the said ordinance, nor shall we issue any such document in the future, and should one appear, we command that it be obeyed and not put into effect' (Colmeiro, *Cortes de los antiguos reinos*, vol. 4, p. 253).
48. Colmeiro (ed.), *Cortes de los antiguos reinos*, vol. 5, p. 253.
49. See, for example, J. H. Elliott, *The Count-Duke of Olivares: The Statesman in an Age of Decline* (New Haven and London: Yale University Press, 1986), p. 177; Henry Kamen, *Philip of Spain* (New Haven and London: Yale University Press, 1998), pp. 231–2; and Anne Dubet, 'Los arbitristas entre discurso y acción política: propuestas para un análisis de la negociación política', *Tiempos Modernos*, 9 (1999), 1–14 (p. 12).
50. *Philip of Spain*, p. 232.
51. (Antwerp: Hermanos de Tournes, 1659 [1597]), p. 382.
52. Martz, *Poverty*, p. 86.
53. *Amparo de pobres*, ed. Michel Cavillac (Madrid: Espasa-Calpe, 1975 [1598]), p. 10. Rivadeneyra, the full title of whose work (see below) makes clear from the outset its anti-Machiavellian credentials, argues that 'There is not one Reason of State, but rather two: one is weak and feigned; the other is firm and true; one is deceitful and diabolical, the other constant and divine; one makes a religion of the State, the other builds the State on religion; one is taught by politicians and based on vain prudence and wicked human methods, the other is taught by God' (*Tratado de la religión y virtudes que debe tener el príncipe cristiano para gobernar y conservar sus estados contra lo que Nicolás Maquiavelo y los políticos deste tiempo enseñan*, Barcelona: Viuda e Hijos de J. Subirana, 1881, p. 13). Another influential text in this connection was Giovanni Botero's 1589 *Della ragion di Stato*, in which the author was at pains to reject the more notoriously instrumental aspects of Machiavelli's vision.
54. Minutes of the *Cabildo* of 1 August 1594, cited by Pedro Herrera Puga in *Sociedad y delincuencia en el Siglo de Oro* (Madrid: La Editorial Católica, 1974), p. 68. Francisco de Ariño reported in his *Sucesos de Sevilla de 1592 a 1604*

that over two thousand beggars were eventually rounded up in Seville on 29 April 1597. Licences were then issued to the crippled or aged, while the others were ordered to find work within three days or expect a flogging (Casey, *Early Modern Spain*, p. 125).

55. Paul Slack described the situation in England thus, though his words could just as well have been written of Spain: 'Vagabonds became the scapegoats for all social problems. They were carriers of rumour, sedition, and disease, and they infected others with their "licentious liberty". The threat they posed by their needless idleness and reckless mobility seemed immediate and overwhelming' ('Vagrants and Vagrancy in England, 1598–1664', *The Economic History Review*, New Series, 27:3, 1974, 360–79, p. 360).

56. Helen Rawlings, '*Arbitrismo* and the Early Seventeenth-Century Spanish Church: The Theory and Practice of Anti-Clericalist Philosophy', in *Rhetoric and Reality in Early Modern Spain*, ed. Richard J. Pym (Woodbridge: Tamesis, 2006), p. 35.

57. *Amparo de pobres*, p. 177.

58. *Amparo de pobres*, p. 11.

59. A series of poor laws enacted between 1523 and 1565 sought to address the problem of the mendicant poor. Among the measures adopted was the introduction of begging licences. These were to be issued only after appropriate approval had been obtained from local ecclesiastical and legal representatives, and eventually only to the infirm or aged. Different forms of shelter (*albergues* or *hospitales*) were used to accommodate licenced beggars. See Casey, *Early Modern Spain*, pp. 124–5; Martz, *Poverty*, p. 86–8; and Vassberg, *The Village*, pp. 155–7.

60. *Amparo de pobres*, p. 114. Later, extolling the advantages of forcing healthy vagabonds either to work or serve in the galleys, Pérez de Herrera once again singles out elimination of the 'waywardness and indolence' of the gypsies as a major benefit to be obtained in the process (p. 171).

61. *Petición* 34, Colmeiro (ed.), *Cortes de los antiguos reinos*, vol. 5, p. 253.

62. Gil Ayuso, *Textos y disposiciones*, p. 4.

63. *Pragmática sobre los Vagamundos, Ladrones, Blasphemos, Rufianes, Testigos falsos, Inducidores, y Casados dos veces, y otras cosas*, BNM, R/14090 (26).

64. *Novísima recopilación, libro XII, título XVI, ley III*, p. 358.

65. Edwards, *The Spain of the Catholic Monarchs*, p. 57.

66. Casey, *Early Modern Spain*, p. 181.

67. *Política para Corregidores*, pp. 382–3.

3   The road to the sea

1. Robert S. Chamberlain, 'The Corregidor in Castile in the Sixteenth Century and the Residencia as Applied to the Corregidor', *The Hispanic American Historical Review*, 23:2 (1943), 222–57 (pp. 225–6).

2. San Román, *La diferencia*, p. 26.

3. David R. Ringrose, 'The Government and the Carters in Spain, 1476–1700', *The Economic History Review*, New Series, 22:1 (1969), 45–57 (p. 51). In 1626, Fernández Navarrete made the polemical claim that 'most Spaniards have become idlers, some feigning nobility, while others pretend to be beggars.

And it is a sight to behold all the streets of Madrid full of idlers and vagabonds, playing cards all day, waiting for the hour when they can go to the
convents to eat or go out to rob people's houses' (*Conservación de monarquías*,
p. 86).

4. Vassberg, *The Village*, p. 156. In his article 'Gitanos y moriscos: verdad
y ficción', on the other hand, Serafín Fanjul accepts Pérez de Herrera's
estimate (in *Actas del VIII Simposio Internacional de Mudejarismo. De mudéjares a moriscos: una conversión forzada*, 2 vols, Teruel: Centro de Estudios
Mudéjares, 2002, I, 7–25, p. 13).

5. I. A. A. Thompson has suggested that the acute difficulties faced by the
government throughout the second half of the sixteenth and most of the
seventeenth centuries in finding oarsmen for the galleys may indicate that
vagabondage was not quite the problem some imagined it to be ('A Map of
Crime', p. 261).

6. In his early study of vagabondage in Elizabethan England, Frank Aydelotte
noted that 'the life led by the wandering vagabonds was similar in many
respects to that of the gypsies, and there is much evidence that they were
closely associated in the popular mind. Almost every statute against rogues
and vagabonds includes "Egyptians" as well. There are several statutes
against English vagabonds disguising themselves as gypsies or wandering in
company with them, which indicates that there were some relations between
the two races.' (*Elizabethan Rogues and Vagabonds*, Oxford: Clarendon Press,
1913, p. 18).

7. A similar observation has been made by María Helena Sánchez Ortega in *Los
gitanos españoles*, p. 103.

8. See Sánchez Ortega, *Los gitanos españoles*, pp. 55–6 and Serafín Fanjul,
'Gitanos y moriscos: verdad y ficción', p. 9.

9. *Memorial de el hecho de los gitanos*, fol. 12. The word *rodela* normally
referred to a round shield. Here one assumes it must have referred to similarly shaped headwear designed to afford maximum protection from the
elements.

10. *Libro primero*, fol. 4.

11. AHN, *Sala de Alcaldes, libro año* 1592, fol. 346, cited by Antonio Gómez
Alfaro in 'Anotaciones a los censos gitanos de Andalucía', in *Actas del I
Congreso de Historia de Andalucía: Andalucía moderna, siglo XVIII* (Córdoba:
Monte de Piedad, 1978), 239–56 (p. 243). One is reminded of this, much
more recent description of Spanish gypsy women by American anthropologist Sharon Bohn Gmelch: 'In contrast to the neat, sombre dress and
rather reserved behaviour of the people around them, *gitanas* wear vividly
coloured clothing; their dress and hair styles are careless; and their body
movements and deportment are characterized by boldness, loudness, spon-
taneity, and violations of street etiquette.' ('Groups that Don't Want In',
pp. 322–33).

12. (Madrid: S. A. de Promoción y Ediciones, 1980 [1626]), p. 199.

13. AHN C, *leg.* 7, *exp.* 8, fol. 41.

14. AHN C, *leg.* 525, cited by Antonio Gómez Alfaro in 'Anotaciones', p. 243.

15. *Pregón general para la buena gobernación de esta Corte* (Madrid: Imprenta
Artesanal del Ayuntamiento de Madrid, 1585).

16. AHN, *Sala de Alcaldes de Casa y Corte* 1609, fol. 434.

17. AHN C, *libro* 1202, fol. 33.
18. *Novelas ejemplares*, 3 vols (Madrid: Castalia, 1982), I, p. 96.
19. Sánchez Ortega, *Los gitanos españoles*, p. 105.
20. Henry Kamen, *Spain in the Later Seventeenth Century, 1665–1700* (London: Longman, 1980), p. 282.
21. San Román, *La diferencia*, p. 58.
22. AHN C, *leg.* 49692, cited by Sánchez Ortega, *Los gitanos españoles*, pp. 150–1.
23. Antonio Gómez Alfaro, *The Great Gypsy Round-up: Spain: The General Imprisonment of Gypsies in 1749*, trans. Terence W. Roberts (Madrid: Editorial Presencia Gitana, 1993), p. 24.
24. AGS CC, *Diversos, leg.* 28, doc. 2, fol. 299, letter dated 6 September 1573.
25. AGS GA, *leg.* 272, fol. 164.
26. The enforcement of the *fueros* and royal pragmatic sanctions has been advanced as the reason for the scarcity of gypsies in the Basque region by Sánchez Ortega in *Los gitanos españoles*, p. 104. See also San Román, *La diferencia*, p. 25.
27. AHN CC, *leg.* 51422, *exp.* 6, letter dated 23 May 1674.
28. I. A. A. Thompson, 'A Map of Crime', p. 257.
29. J. H. Elliott, *The Revolt of the Catalans* (Cambridge: Cambridge University Press, 1963), pp. 116–25.
30. San Román, *La diferencia*, pp. 58 and 61–2.
31. San Román, *La diferencia*, p. 58.
32. Kamen, *Spain in the Later Seventeenth Century*, pp. 282–3.
33. AGI, Panamá, 236, *libro* 10, fols 113v–114r.
34. Sánchez Ortega, *Los gitanos españoles*, p. 105.
35. In a letter to María Bautista in Valladolid written in Seville on 29 April 1576 (*Obras completas, carta* 101:2, Madrid: Editorial de Espiritualidad, 1984), p. 1395. See also Antonio Domínguez Ortiz's introduction to Francisco de Ariño's *Sucesos de Sevilla de 1592 a 1604* (Sevilla: Servicio de Publicaciones, Ayuntamiento, 1993), p. xiii.
36. Sánchez Ortega, *Los gitanos españoles*, p. 105.
37. AGI, *Indiferente*, 427, *libro* 30, fols 326r–326v, dated 25 February 1581.
38. AGI, *Cartas de Audiencia*, Quito, 8, *reg.* 21, nos 56 and 59.
39. AGI, *Contratación*, 5272, No. 1, *reg.* 43, dated 13 March 1602.
40. Pike, *Penal Servitude*, p. 4.
41. AGS CC, *Diversos, leg.* 42, no. 16, letter dated 30 April 1501.
42. Writing of the period 1568–1638 in Seville, Ruth Pike noted that vagrancy was not usually prosecuted there as a stand-alone offence: 'Surprisingly, none of the men in the Sevillian records had been condemned for simple vagrancy although the laws provided for this. By 1552 the penalty for vagabondage had been increased to four years on the galleys for the first offence, eight for the second, and life for the third. Nevertheless, all those described as vagrants had also been convicted of some other offence, mainly theft. Moreover, it was standard practice to charge ruffians with vagrancy and wherever applicable, with resistance to arrest' ('Crime and Criminals in Sixteenth-Century Seville', *Sixteenth Century Journal*, 6:1, 1975, 3–18, p. 12).
43. 'Pragmática de los gitanos: Toledo, 30 de agosto de 1560, publicada en 11 de septiembre' in Faustino Gil Ayuso, *Textos y disposiciones*, p. 61.
44. *Petición* 88, Colmeiro (ed.), *Cortes de los antiguos reinos*, vol. 5, pp. 852–3.

45. Pike, *Penal Servitude*, p. 7; David Goodman, *Spanish Naval Power, 1589–1665* (Cambridge: Cambridge University Press, 1997), p. 217.

46. John Francis Guilmartin, *Gunpowder and Galleys: Changing Technology and Mediterranean Warfare at Sea in the Sixteenth Century* (Cambridge: Cambridge University Press, 1974), p. 101. See also by the same author 'The Galley in Combat', *MHQ: The Quarterly Journal of Military History*, 9:2 (Winter 1997), 20–1.

47. Guilmartin, *Gunpowder and Galleys*, pp. 226–7. The author notes, too, that at the battle of Lepanto, the number of rowers was increased to 200, an almost 40 per cent increase on those employed a quarter of a century earlier.

48. Fernand Braudel, *The Mediterranean and the Mediterranean World in the Age of Philip II*, 2 vols (Glasgow: Fontana/Collins, 1972), vol. II, p. 981; Kamen, *Spain's Road to Empire: The Making of a World Power 1492–1763* (London: Penguin, 2003), p. 156.

49. Braudel, *The Mediterranean*, II, pp. 1008–12.

50. Thompson, 'A Map of Crime', p. 246. Thompson estimated that perhaps as many as half of the *forzados* 'died in their chains' (p. 261); see also Pike, *Penal Servitude*, p. 23; Goodman, *Spanish Naval Power*, p. 158.

51. *Pragmática sobre los Vagamundos, Ladrones, Blasphemos, Rufianes, Testigos falsos, Inducidores, y Casados dos veces, y otras cosas* (BNM, R/14090 [26]).

52. Ruth Pike, 'Crime and Criminals', pp. 3–4. A good copy of Philip II's letter, in this case the copy sent to Sanlúcar de Barrameda, can be consulted in Simancas (AGS CC, *Diversos, leg.* 29, doc. 1, fols 187–8).

53. AGS CC, *Diversos, leg.* 28, doc. 2, fol. 564, letter dated 26 December 1572.

54. AGS CC, *Diversos, leg.* 28, doc. 1, fols 495–6, letter dated 21 December 1572.

55. AGS CC, *Diversos, leg.* 29, doc. 1, fols 465–6, letter dated 29 January 1573.

56. AGS CC, *Diversos, leg.* 28, doc. 1, fol. 798.

57. Pike, *Penal Servitude*, p. 16.

58. AGS CC, *Diversos, leg.* 28, doc. 1, fol. 799. This letter from Galicia cites additionally the extreme poverty of the region and, like others, insists on the under-funded insecurity of Spain's gaols.

59. AGS CC, *Diversos, leg.* 28, doc. 1, fols 324–5 and 766; doc. 2, fol. 309; *leg.* 29, fol. 362

60. AGS CC, *Diversos, leg.* 28, doc. 1, fol. 798 and doc. 2, fol. 548.

61. AGS CC, *Diversos, leg.* 28, doc. 1, fol. 859, letter dated 3 January 1573.

62. AGS CC, *Diversos, leg.* 29, doc. 1, fol. 25, letter dated 9 January 1573.

63. AGS CC, *Diversos, leg.* 29, doc. 1, fol. 761, letter dated 8 February 1573.

64. AGS CC, *Diversos, leg.* 29, doc. 1, fol. 627, letter dated 4 February 1573.

65. AGS CC, *Diversos, leg.* 29, doc. 1, fol. 586.

66. AGS CC, *Diversos, leg.* 29, doc. 1, fol. 209, letter dated 23 December 1572.

67. AGS CC, *Diversos, leg.* 29, doc. 1, fol. 190, letter dated 4 January 1573.

68. AGS CC, *Diversos, leg.* 29, doc. 1, fol. 123, letter dated 24 December 1572.

69. Vassberg, *The Village*, p. 15.

70. AGS CC, *Diversos, leg.* 28, doc. 1, fols 807 and 817.

71. One such complaint is found in a letter of 19 November 1639 to Philip IV from the *Junta de galeotes, esclavos, y gitanos* (AGS GA, *leg.* 3173).

72. AGS CC, *Diversos, leg.* 28, doc. 1, fols 432, 3, 716, 512 and 884.

73. AGS CC, *Diversos, leg.* 29, doc. 2, fol. 21.

74. AGS CC, *Diversos, leg.* 29, doc. 1, fol. 4, letter dated 19 January 1573.

75. AGS CC, *Diversos, leg.* 28, doc. 1, fol. 373, letter dated 16 January 1573; *leg.* 29, doc. 1, fol. 441, undated letter. Enrique de Guzmán was the father of Gaspar, who went on to become Philip IV's chief minister as the Count-Duke of Olivares.
76. AGS CC, *Diversos, leg.* 28, doc. 1, fol. 418.
77. AGS CC, *Diversos, leg.* 29, doc. 1, fol. 145, letter dated 29 December 1572.
78. AGS CC, *Diversos, leg.* 28, doc. 1, fols 277, letter dated 7 March 1573, and 765.
79. AGS CC, *Diversos, leg.* 29, doc. 1, fol. 359, letter dated 31 December 1572.
80. AGS CC, *Diversos, leg.* 29, doc. 3, fol. 10.
81. AGS CC, *Diversos, leg.* 29, doc. 2, fols 21 and 13. Fray Melchor de Huélamo complained bitterly about the gypsies' adoption of such distinguished names, citing as examples Malla and Maldonado and condemning their use as 'all lies'. See *Libro primero*, p. 110.
82. Pike, *Penal Servitude*, p. 5.
83. AGS GM, *leg.* 88, fol. 359, doc. 1.
84. Cited by Antonio Domínguez Ortiz in *El antiguo regimen: los Reyes Católicos y los Austrias* (Madrid: Alianza Universidad, 1974), p. 181.
85. Rodrigo Vázquez de Arce was a distinguished jurist and adviser to the King. A judge at the *Chancillería* in Granada before being appointed President of the Council of Finance, he was no dove. Before his unceremonial removal from office as President of the Council of Castile in 1599 by Philip III, he had been one of those who in 1582 suggested the possible expulsion from Spain of Valencia's *moriscos*; see Antonio Feros, *Kingship and Favoritism in the Spain of Philip III, 1598–1621* (Cambridge: Cambridge University Press, 2000), p. 201.
86. Kamen, *Philip of Spain*, p. 127.
87. AGS GM, *leg.* 88, fol. 359, doc. 2, letter dated 21 December 1578.
88. Braudel, *The Mediterranean*, p. 842, n. 18; Leblon, *Los gitanos*, p. 117; Vassberg, *The Village*, p. 144.
89. 'A Map of Crime', pp. 260 and 263. The document he cites is in the AGS GA, *leg.* 24, fol. 2.
90. Andrew S. Hess, 'The Moriscos. An Ottoman Fifth Column in Sixteenth-Century Spain', *American Historical Review*, 74 (1968), 1–21 (p. 15). Hess showed that in addition to sundry expressions of moral support, arms and ammunition were also supplied to the Alpujarras rebels from Algeria.

4 Years of crisis

1. Ed. J. P. Le Flem (Madrid: Instituto de Estudios Fiscales, 1975), p. 52.
2. Henry Kamen cites a 1597 report from Juan Fernández de Velasco, Constable of Castile and governor of Milan, in which the latter spoke of 'a general desire to expel the Spaniards' among Italians (*Philip of Spain*, p. 309).
3. Carla Rahn Phillips, 'Time and Duration: A Model for the Economy of Early Modern Spain', *The American Historical Review*, 92:3 (1987), 531–62, p. 545.
4. Casey, *Early Modern Spain*, p. 41; Elliott, *Imperial Spain*, p. 301.
5. Barton, *A History of Spain*, p. 120.
6. Ed. José L. Pérez de Ayala (Madrid: Instituto de Estudios Fiscales, 1991), p. 11.

7. *Memorial de la política necesaria y útil restauración a la república de España y estados de ella y del desempeño universal de estos reinos*, ed. José L. Pérez de Ayala (Madrid: Instituto de Estudios Fiscales, 1991 [1600]), pp. 14 and 88.

8. Elliott, 'Self-Perception and Decline in Spain', in *Spain and Its World*, pp. 241–61 (p. 255). A quarter of a century later, in 1623, Philip IV asserted that 'population and numbers of people represent the single most important foundation of Republics, and great attention should be devoted to them in order to ensure their conservation and increase' (*Novísima recopilación, libro 3, título VI, ley VIII*, p. 297).

9. *Memorial de la política necesaria*, p. 21.

10. *Médico espiritual, en el qual se contiene doctrina muy provechosa para predicadores, confesores y penitentes* (Toledo: Juan Ruiz, 1623), p. 19.

11. *Cortes* of Madrid, 1551, *petición* 34, and *Cortes* of Madrid 1585, *petición* 51, in Colmeiro (ed.), *Cortes de los antiguos reinos*, vol. 5, p. 253.

12. *Novísima recopilación, libro XII, título XVI, ley III*, p. 358.

13. AML, *leg. monográfico sobre gitanos*, doc. 3, cited in Martínez Martínez 'Los gitanos en el sureste', p. 95.

14. *Actas de las Cortes de Castilla, Cortes* of 19 March 1594, vol. XIII, p. 220.

15. The *Casas* or *Colegios de los Niños de la Doctrina*, as these orphanages were known, dated back to the 1540s, their fundamental purpose being to keep orphans from a life of crime and vagabondage. Municipal authorities were required by law to support them.

16. I. A. A. Thompson, 'Oposición política y juicio del gobierno en las Cortes de 1592–98', *Studia Histórica. Historia Moderna*, 17 (1997), 37–62 (pp. 43–4). Thompson notes that royal irritation at the obstructive activities of Jerónimo de Salamanca and his supporters found concrete expression as the *Cortes* closed in the award to him of 40,000 maravedís, less than half the figure of 100,000 awarded to Martín de Porras (p. 45).

17. Kamen, *Philip of Spain*, pp. 131–2.

18. See Chapter 1, n. 53.

19. Feros, *Kingship and Favoritism*, pp. 199–201.

20. Kamen, *Spain 1469–1714*, p. 174.

21. *Tratado acerca de los moriscos de España*, Joaquín Gil Sanjuan (Málaga: Algazara, 1997 [1606]), p. 128.

22. See, for example, Pérez de Herrera, *Amparo de pobres*, p. 133. Citing similar claims by Damián Fonseca in his *Justa expulsión de los moriscos de España*, Trevor Dadson notes that modern studies of Córdoba, Granada, Cáceres, Salamanca and Cuenca suggest that *morisco* families there may in fact have been no larger than the average Old Christian family ('Official Rhetoric Versus Local Reality', p. 19). On the other hand, John Lynch noted that in Valencia and Aragon the relative growth of already large *morisco* communities was indeed outstripping that of Old Christians in those areas (*The Hispanic World in Crisis and Change, 1598–1700*, Oxford: Blackwell, 1994, p. 60). See also Carla Rahn Phillips 'Time and Duration', p. 538, n. 14.

23. *Tratado acerca de los moriscos*, p. 105.

24. *Tratado acerca de los moriscos*, p. 120.

25. *Relaciones de las cosas sucedidas en la corte de España desde 1599 hasta 1614* (Madrid: J. M. Alegría, 1857), p. 30.

26. *Relaciones*, p. 357.

27. Casey, *Early Modern Spain*, p. 24.
28. *Actas de las Cortes de Castilla*, vol. XXI, p. 294, *Cortes* of Valladolid of 7 July 1603.
29. *Actas de las Cortes de Castilla*, vol. XXI, p. 482.
30. Sancho de Moncada, professor of theology at the University of Toledo, wrote in 1619 in 'On the Expulsion of the Gypsies', the eighth discourse of his *Restauración política de España*, that 'although they are given to all kinds of theft, they most often steal animals and livestock, and that is why they are known in law as *abigeos*, and in Spanish as *cuatreros*' (Madrid: Instituto de estudios fiscales, 1974 [1619]), p. 215. See also Julio Caro Baroja, 'Los gitanos en cliché', in *Temas castizos* (Madrid: Istmo, 1980), pp. 118–19.
31. *Actas de las Cortes de Castilla*, vol. XXIII, p. 321.
32. *Actas de las Cortes de Castilla*, vol. XXV, pp. 68–9, *Cortes* of Madrid, 13 February 1609.
33. *Actas de las Cortes de Castilla*, vol. XXV, pp. 68–9, *Cortes* of Madrid, 14 May 1609 and vol. XXVI, p. 151, *Cortes* of Madrid 3 November 1609.
34. *Actas de las Cortes de Castilla*, vol. XXVI, pp. 163–5, *Cortes* of Madrid 8 November 1610.
35. *Actas de las Cortes de Castilla*, vol. XXVI, p. 164.
36. Antonio Domínguez Ortiz, *The Golden Age of Spain: 1516–1659* (London: Weidenfeld and Nicolson, 1971), p. 165.
37. AHN C, *leg.* 4428, *exp.* 118, cited by Gómez Alfaro in 'Anotaciones', p. 254.
38. ARCV, Pleitos criminales, caja 0332.0002.
39. Kamen, *Spain 1469–1714*, pp. 140–1; Constancio Bernaldo de Quirós and Luis Ardila, *El bandolerismo andaluz* (Madrid: Turner, 1988), pp. 24–7.
40. AGP, II/2157, doc. 187, letter from Diego de Recalde y Zúñiga to Diego Sarmiento de Acuña, dated 4 April 1596.
41. AGS E, *leg.* 4126, doc. 6. Undated, the letter nevertheless refers to earlier legislation passed 'last year' (actually on 5 October 1611) ordering that gypsies should henceforth only be permitted to work on the land.
42. For the very high mortality rates experienced by these displaced *moriscos*, especially in the immediate aftermath of the resettlement, see José León Martín Viana, 'Moriscos de Tudela de Duero', *Revista de Folklore*, 47 (1984), 164–70.
43. In his reply from Murcia to Philip II's 1572 census of prisoners, Don Lope de Valenzuela drew the King's attention, as did others, to the problem of vagrant Granadine *moriscos* (AGS CC, *Diversos*, *leg.* 29, doc. 1, fol. 359, letter dated 31 December 1572). See also Serafín Fanjul, 'Gitanos y moriscos', p. 13 and Mary Elizabeth Perry, *The Handless Maiden: Moriscos and the Politics of Religion in Early Modern Spain* (Princeton: Princeton University Press, 2005), pp. 120–1.
44. Vol. I (Madrid: Castalia, 2000), pp. 267–7.
45. Martínez Martínez, 'Los gitanos en el sureste', p. 96.
46. *Vidas mágicas e Inquisición*, 2 vols (Madrid: Istmo, 1992), I, p. 77.
47. José Moreno Casado, 'Los gitanos de España bajo Carlos I', *Chrónica Nova*, 4–5 (1969), p. 197, cited by Martínez Martínez in 'Los gitanos en el sureste', p. 96.
48. In 1629, in his *Libro de las cinco excelencias del español que despueblan a España para su mayor potencia y dilatación*, Benito de Peñalosa y Mondragón

enumerated the five 'excellences' of the Spaniard as religious zeal, military prowess, purity of lineage, the monarchy, and liberality (cited by Hillgarth, 'Spanish Historiography', p. 32). Struggles for rank and access to power, as well, perhaps, as an underlying concern with lineage and identity, are suggested by the introduction here and there of statutes of racial purity (*limpieza de sangre*), most famously by Archbishop Siliceo in Toledo in 1547 as a device for excluding *conversos* from ecclesiastical office. Opposed by many, often at the highest levels (Siliceo's statute was immediately condemned by the Council of Castile), and never formally incorporated in law, such statutes were applied to those seeking membership of a very limited number of religious orders, guilds and universities. Before Siliceo there had been precedents in Salamanca, Seville, Badajoz, and Toledo itself. Given that such restrictions represented the exception rather than the rule, one should be careful, however, not to overstate their importance (see Kamen, 'Limpieza and the Ghost of Américo Castro: Racism as a Tool of Literary Analysis', *Hispanic Review*, 64:1, 1996, 19–29).

49. *The Hispanic World*, pp. 56–7. See also Dadson, 'Official Rhetoric Versus Local Reality', p. 1.
50. Feros, *Kingship and Favoritism*, p. 204.
51. AGS E, *leg.* 228.
52. AHN N, Osuna, *caja* 4256, *libro* 3, doc. 13.
53. *Actas de las Cortes de Castilla*, vol. XXVI, pp. 291–2.
54. In fact, it is now clear that the expulsions of the *moriscos* were far less successful that the Council of Castile claimed, given that many were either not expelled in the first place, or were protected by noble families across Spain, or, if expelled, contrived to return shortly thereafter, as, for example, in the Val de Ricote in Murcia and the Campo de Calatrava (see Dadson 'Official Rhetoric Versus Local Reality', pp. 13–14 and 23). Henry Kamen notes that even after the expulsions, proceedings against *moriscos* accounted for some 9 per cent of Inquisitorial prosecutions between 1615 and 1700 (*The Spanish Inquisition*, p. 229).
55. AGS E, *leg.* 4126, docs 1 and 3.
56. Luis Cabrera de Córdoba wrote of 13 February 1610 that 'with the expulsion of the *moriscos* from Valencia, the order has been given to expel those of Andalusia, the Kingdom of Granada, and Murcia, together with the town of Hornachos (in Extremadura), where many have been punished for the numerous murders and crimes they have committed in that town against the Old Christians' (*Relaciones*, p. 396). Isolated and remote, Hornachos was unusual in the region in that its population of about 5000 consisted almost entirely of *moriscos*, who, despite the Catholic Monarchs' edict of 1502 and the subsequent attentions of the Inquisition, managed determinedly – and not without violence – to follow their traditional religious and cultural practices much as before until the early seventeenth century when they were eventually expelled. Thereafter, the *hornacheros* established themselves in Salé near Rabat in Morocco, where, with the help of Dutch shipbuilders, among others, many took to the sea and became notably successful corsairs. See Antonio Domínguez Ortiz and Bernard Vincent, *Historia de los moriscos* (Madrid: Alianza, 1978), pp. 234–5 and Bennassar, *La España del Siglo de Oro*, pp. 305–7.

57. AGS E, *leg.* 4126, doc. 1.

58. *Tratado acerca de los moriscos*, p. 113.

59. Ringrose, 'The Impact of a New Capital City', p. 766; Carla Rahn Phillips, 'Time and Duration', p. 538. See Casey, *Early Modern Spain*, Chapter 2 for some of the reasons behind the decline in population, which, as Casey points out, are still imperfectly understood. He estimates that there were some five and a quarter million people in Castile in 1591, a figure which by 1631 had dropped to about four and a half million (*Early Modern Spain*, p. 21). Elliott observed that after the plague years of 1596–1602, the sharp increases in wages in the opening decade of the seventeenth century 'suggest something of the gravity of the manpower crisis through which Castile was passing', a crisis further exacerbated thereafter by the expulsion of some 275,000 *moriscos* (J. H. Elliott, 'The Decline of Spain', in *Spain and Its World 1500–1700*, New Haven and London: Yale University Press, 1989, pp. 224–5). The *moriscos* represented some 4 per cent of the total population, though many of them were productive workers and, of course, taxpayers. However, given recent research suggesting that the expulsions were actually anything but complete or definitive, it is likely that their economic impact in some areas may have been felt rather more keenly in the anticipation than in the actual event. In other regions, however, like Aragon and Valencia, which lost about one third of its population, the impact of such losses was inevitably severe.

60. AGS E, *leg.* 1862. The entire text is reproduced in Dóminguez Ortiz and Vincent, *Historia de los moriscos*, pp. 283–4.

61. AGS E, *leg.* 4126, doc. 2.

62. Kamen, *Spain in the Later Seventeenth Century*, p. 282. Kamen describes the figures of 8.1 million in 1591 and 7.5 million in 1717 for Spain's population as 'inspired guesses', adding that estimates for the seventeenth century, which saw a number of serious epidemics, must be regarded as even more speculative (pp. 46–7).

63. Sánchez Ortega, *Los gitanos españoles*, p. 89. J. M., *Historia de los gitanos* (Madrid: Heliodoro, 1980 [orig. Barcelona: A. Bergnes, 1832]), pp. 67–9.

64. AHN, *Sala de Alcaldes de Casa y Corte* 1609, fols 425 and 434.

5 Representations

1. Pinelo, *Anales de Madrid de León Pinelo*, ed. Ricardo Martorell Téllez-Girón (Madrid: Maxtor, 2003), p. 126.

2. Kamen, *Spain in the Later Seventeenth Century*, p. 27. J. H. Elliott noted that on his deathbed Philip III lamented to his son 'over and over again how he had been deceived throughout his life' (*The Count-Duke of Olivares*, p. 103). I am inclined to agree with the recent observation by Alistair Malcolm that revisionist efforts by Antonio Feros and others to rehabilitate Philip III in the eyes of history have on the whole failed to dispel the traditional view of a weak king 'hopelessly dependant on the Duke of Lerma' and, indeed, on the latter's son, the Duke of Uceda, after Lerma's death. See 'Spanish Queens and Aristocratic Women at the Court of Madrid', in *Studies on Medieval and Early Modern Women 4: Victims or Viragos*, eds Christine Meek and Catherine Lawless (Dublin: Four Courts Press, 2005), pp. 160–79 (pp. 167–8).

3. Cited in the notes to Pinelo's *Anales de Madrid*, p. 398. Despite his evident concern with purity of blood (physicians were often assumed to be of *converso* descent), Don Fernando was his own man. He was offered the primacy of all Spain when Lerma's uncle, the Archbishop of Toledo, Cardinal Bernardo Sandoval y Rojas, died, but turned the offer down.

4. The figure, whilst relatively small when compared to the 6, 7, or 8 million ducats raised annually via taxation in Castile, was nevertheless of fundamental importance, since the continuing flow of silver, which represented one of Castile's few non-hypothecated sources of revenue, was considered a *sine qua non* if bankers were to continue to provide credit to the crown. See Elliott, 'The Decline of Spain', in *Spain and Its World*, pp. 217–40 (pp. 236–7).

5. As Henry Kamen has pointed out, other factors like sharp rises in mortality as a result of epidemics, the effect of poor weather on agriculture, and alienation of land also contributed to rural depopulation, though he also notes that even villages completely abandoned were sometimes repopulated when conditions changed for the better (*Spain in the Later Seventeenth Century*, p. 98).

6. *Junta de Reformación: documentos procedentes del Archivo Histórico Nacional y del General de Simancas*, ed. Ángel Gonzalez Palencia (Valladolid: Poncelix, 1932), pp. 13–14.

7. *Restauración política de España*, 4th discourse (Madrid: Instituto de estudios fiscales, 1974), p. 49.

8. Elliott, *The Count-Duke of Olivares*, p. 98.

9. Dubet, *Los arbitristas*, p. 8, n. 5.

10. Dubet, *Los arbitristas*, p. 6.

11. *El diablo cojuelo* (Madrid: Castalia, 1988), p. 112.

12. In the *Viaje del Parnaso*, Chapter 4, ll. 34–6 (Madrid: Castalia, 1973), p. 103. Cervantes's worries about satire related to its more mordant, Juvenalian forms rather than the gentler approach typified by Horace, even if, as Anthony Close has observed, this was a distinction which 'he found easier to uphold in theory than in practice'. See *Cervantes and the Comic Mind of His Age* (Cambridge: Cambridge University Press, 2000), p. 27.

13. *Don Quijote*, 2 vols (Madrid: Castalia, 1978), Part 2, Chapter 1, p. 44, and see also *Coloquio de los perros*, in *Novelas ejemplares* (Madrid: Castalia, 1982), pp. 316–18. For a typically caustic Francisco de Quevedo on the *arbitristas*, see *La hora de todos y la fortuna con seso* (Madrid: Castalia, 1987), pp. 95–9 and his 1622, 'El sueño de la muerte', in *Sueños y discursos* (Madrid: Castalia, 1993), p. 359.

14. Ed. Michael D. Gordon (Madrid: Instituto de Estudios Fiscales, 1982), p. 74. An earlier version entitled *Discursos políticos* appeared in Barcelona five years earlier (Elliott, *The Count-Duke of Olivares*, p. 98, n. 54).

15. *Conservación de monarquías*, p. 73.

16. (Basel: Heinrich Petri, 1550).

17. *Didascalia multiplex* (Leiden: Horace Cardon, 1615); *Disquisitionum magicarum libri sex* (Cologne: Peter Henning?, 1617?), Book 4, Chapter 3, Inquiry 5, 'De Chiromantia', pp. 587–8. Copy consulted BNM, R/39181.

18. (Murcia: Agustín Martínez, 1607). Copy consulted BNM, 3/64915. San Ginés de la Jara was adopted by vintners as their patron and was invoked as protector of those who worked the land, this doubtless explaining why Huélamo saw fit to include his diatribe against gypsies in a work of hagiography.

19. For some of these vivid condemnations of the *zarabanda* see my article 'The Errant Fortunes of "La gitanilla" and Cervantes's Performing Gypsies', *Journal of Iberian and Latin American Studies*, 12:1 (2006), 15–37.

20. *Conservación de monarquías*, pp. 67, 71, 72–4.

21. *Memorial de el hecho de los gitanos*, fol. 1.

22. *Relación verdadera de las crueldades y robos grandes que hacían en Sierra Morena unos gitanos salteadores, los quales mataron un Religioso y le comieron la cabeza cozida.* Cited by Sánchez Ortega, *Los gitanos y la Inquisición*, p. 21.

23. *Discurso contra los gitanos*, fol. 10. In *The Zincali: An Account of the Gypsies of Spain*, George Borrow dismissed Quiñones's claims, adding, however, that he was personally familiar with what he calls the 'forest of Las Gamas, which lies between Jaraicejo and Trujillo' and that it was, at least when he was there in the 1830s, 'frequented occasionally by gypsies' (London: John Murray, 1901 [1843]), pp. 77–8.

24. *Memorial de el hecho de los gitanos*, fol. 6; *Restauración política*, 8th discourse, p. 120.

25. Linda Colley, *Captives: Britain, Empire, and the World, 1600–1850* (New York: Anchor Books, 2004), p. 45. The figure Colley gives of 15,000 relates only to those who, like Cervantes, returned from their captivity. Thousands of others, as she observes, did not live to see Spain again.

26. Del Río, *Disquisitionum*, p. 587.

27. *Didascalia multiplex*, Book 8, Chapter 50, pp. 406–7.

28. *Memorial de el hecho de los gitanos*, fols 12, 13, 17 and 18.

29. The *Siete infantes de Lara* was a medieval epic which celebrated Castile's heroic past.

30. *Memorial de el hecho de los gitanos*, fol. 6.

31. *Memorial de el hecho de los gitanos*, fol. 19.

32. See J. E. Varey, *Town and Country in the Theatre of the Golden Age* (London: Queen Mary and Westfield College, 1994), pp. 5, 7, and 14. The word *farsa* was used in the sixteenth century as a virtual synonym for *comedia* (any play, not just a comedy), but suggested a rather poorly or carelessly constructed piece (see Covarrubias's *Tesoro de la lengua*, p. 586a).

33. *Novelas ejemplares* (Madrid: Castalia, 1982), I, pp. 126 and 145.

34. Martínez Martínez, 'Los gitanos en el sureste', p. 93; Astrana Marín, *Vida*, p. 131; Rafael Ramírez de Arellano, *El teatro en Córdoba* (Córdoba: Diputación de Córdoba, 1997), p. 22; Miguel Garrido Atienza (*Antigüallas Granadinas: Las Fiestas del Corpus*, Granada, 1889), cited by Manuel López Rodríguez, *Tras las huellas del flamenco: el mundo gitano en la obra de Cervantes* (Jerez de la Frontera: Ediciones de la Cátedra de Flamencología y Estudios Folklóricos Andaluces, 1978), p. 15; Mercedes Agulló y Cobo, 'Primera entrega documental sobre teatro en Andalucía', in *En torno al teatro del Siglo de Oro: Actas Jornadas XII–XIII* (Almería: Instituto de Estudios Almerienses, Diputación de Almería, 1996), p. 124; Bartolomé García Jiménez, *Demografía rural andaluza: Rute en el antiguo régimen* (Córdoba: Diputación de Córdoba, 1987), p. 289.

35. Manuel López Molina, 'Gitanos y Corpus Christi en Jaén en la primera mitad del siglo XVII', *Boletín del Instituto de Estudios Giennenses*, 176, tomo II (2000), 737–50 (pp. 738, 741, 743, 746, and 748).
36. AHPJ, Escribano Luis Parral, *leg*. 1229, fol. 508v, cited by López Molina, 'Gitanos y Corpus Christi', p. 739.
37. Martínez Martínez, 'Los gitanos en el sureste', p. 93.
38. (Barcelona: Francisco Seix, 1910), p. 144.
39. C. A. Marsden, 'Entrées et fêtes espagnoles au XVI siècle', in *Les fêtes de la Renaissance*, ed. J. Jacquot, 3 vols (Paris: Centre National de la Recherche Scientifique, 1960), II, pp. 393–7.
40. *Memorial de el hecho de los gitanos*, fol. 5.
41. (Ingoldstadt: Adam Sartorius, 1611), Book 20, Chapter 5.
42. AHN, *Inquisición*, *leg*. 33, *exp*. 32.
43. AHN C, *leg*. 7133.
44. AGS GA, *leg*. 1261.
45. AHN CC, *leg*. 51422, *exp*. 6, letter dated 23 May 1674.
46. Moncada, *Restauración*, p. 213.
47. AGS E, *leg*. 4126, doc. 6.
48. (Rome: ex typographia apostolica Vaticana, 1591).
49. Moncada, *Restauración*, p. 222.
50. Moncada's claim was not entirely correct, in that *morisco* children under the age of four were theoretically permitted to remain in Spain after the expulsions, subject to the consent of their parents. See Domínguez Ortiz and Vincent, *Historia de los moriscos*, p. 181.
51. Moncada, *Restauración*, p. 223.
52. Moncada, *Restauración*, p. 221.
53. *Cortes* of Madrid of 24 December 1610, *Actas de las Cortes de Castilla*, Vol. XXVI, pp. 291–2; *Cortes* of Madrid of 30 July 1618, *Actas de las Cortes de Castilla*, vol. XXXII, pp. 118–19.
54. *Comedia de Calisto y Melibea*, 2 vols (Madrid: Espasa-Calpe, 1968), II, p. 72.
55. *Copilaçam de todalas obras de Gil Vicente*, ed. María Leonor Carvalhão Buescu (Lisbon: Nacional-Casa da Moeda, 1983), pp. 226–8.
56. Julio Caro Baroja noted that the term *gitano* was in the nineteenth century used as virtual synonym for 'flatterer', appearing in this sense in correspondence by Leandro Fernández de Moratín and Manuel Bretón de los Herreros, among others. See 'Los gitanos en cliché', p. 131.
57. Lope de Rueda, *Las cuatro comedias* (Madrid: Cátedra, 2001), p. 217.
58. Lope de Rueda, *Las cuatro comedias*, pp. 238–40.
59. Lope de Rueda, *Las cuatro comedias*, p. 233; *Pasos completos* (Madrid: Austral, 1990), p. 186.
60. Teresa de San Román, 'Kinship, Marriage, Law and Leadership in Two Urban Gypsy Settlements in Spain', in *Gypsies, Tinkers and Other Travellers*, ed. Farnham Refisch (London: Academic Press, 1975), pp. 169–89 (p. 195).
61. Romaní itself, of which there are at least sixty varieties in Europe alone, has been shown to bear certain, remote family resemblances to Sanskrit. For a fuller discussion, the reader is referred to Fraser, *The Gypsies*, pp. 15–18 and 38. The *caló* occasionally employed nowadays by Spain's gypsies, who habitually converse among themselves in ordinary Castilian Spanish, is currently undergoing something of an artificial and, at least in part,

188   *Notes*

commercially motivated revival. For a present-day glimpse of the occasional use of *caló*, and of gypsies performing gypsies, the reader is referred to Dominique Abel's simultaneously engaging and disturbing documentary film *Polígono sur: el arte de las tres mil* (Barcelona: Manga Films, 2003), set in one of Seville's most deprived and problematic gypsy *barrios*.

62. 'Prólogo al lector', in *Cervantes: teatro completo* (Barcelona: Editorial Iberia, 1966), p. 133.
63. (Madrid: Castalia, 1982), I, p. 85.
64. (Madrid: Cátedra, 1986), ll. 1083–1107, pp. 302–3 and ll. 1138–40, p. 304.
65. (Madrid: Castalia), III, p. 94.
66. p. 205.
67. Vol. I, p. 249.
68. (Madrid: Cátedra, 1986), line 2675, p. 371.
69. The relevant passage appears in the second edition of Juan de la Cuesta. See *El ingenioso hidalgo don Quijote de la Mancha*, 2 vols (Madrid: Castalia, 1978), I, p. 380, n. 26.
70. For a much fuller discussion of both Ginés de Pasamonte and the representation and use of gypsies in *La gitanilla*, the reader is referred to my article 'The Errant Fortunes of *La gitanilla* and Cervantes's Performing Gypsies', *Journal of Iberian and Latin American Studies*, 12:1 (2006), 15–37. Lou Charnon-Deutsch's recent study of cultural representations of the gypsy, *The Spanish Gypsy: The History of a European Obsession* (University Park, PA: The Pennsylvania State University Press, 2004) also focuses on *La gitanilla* as well as Antonio Solís y Rivadeneira's derivative play *La gitanilla de Madrid*. The primary focus of Charnon-Deutsch's study nevertheless lies in the eighteenth, nineteenth and twentieth centuries.
71. *La gitanilla*, pp. 118–20; *Coloquio de los perros* (Madrid: Castalia, 1982), III, pp. 306–8; *Pedro de Urdemalas*, lines 550–89, pp. 282–3.
72. *Libro primero...*, p. 113.
73. *La gitanilla*, pp. 111 and 127.
74. (Valladolid: Ediciones Cumbre, 1940), p. 149.
75. (Madrid: Editora Nacional, 1980), p. 189.
76. Ed. José María Micó, 2 vols (Madrid: Cátedra, 1998), I, pp. 61 and 78; II, p. 135.
77. Ed. Pedro M. Piñero (Madrid: Cátedra, 1988 [1620]), pp. 345–7.
78. *Obras de Lope de Vega*, ed. Marcelino Menéndez y Pelayo (Madrid: Atlas, 1963), III, pp. 7–50. Similar, brief references to gypsies are also found in Lope's *El arenal de Sevilla*, *El ganso de oro*, *El primer rey de Castilla*, *Sueños hay que verdad son*, *El tirano castigado* and *La madre de la mejor*; *Obras dramáticas completas de Tirso de Molina*, ed. Blanca de los Ríos (Madrid: Aguilar, 1952), pp. 1390–431.
79. BNM, R/31254 (2).
80. Pedro Calderón de la Barca, *Entremeses, jácaras y mojigangas*, ed. Evangelina Rodríguez and Antonio Tordera (Madrid: Castalia, 1982), pp. 371–84 (see also p. 384, n. 262); *Mojigangas dramáticas (siglos XVII y XVIII)*, ed. Catalina Buezo (Madrid: Cátedra, 2005), p. 113.
81. On seeing his old friend, the *morisco* Ricote, who has returned to Spain disguised as a foreign pilgrim, Sancho Panza asks him who has turned him into a 'franchote' (*Don Quijote*, II, p. 448).

82. *Entremeses, jácaras y mojigangas*, p. 254. The editors, Evangelina Rodríguez and Antonio Tordera, also suggest that the *franchotes* of this *entremés* may in fact be intended to be read as gypsies. See pp. 254, n. 43 and 255, n. 62.
83. *El arenal de Sevilla* (Madrid: Austral), p. 119. The play was published in 1618, though it may have been written as early as 1603.
84. Under *ley* the contemporary lexicographer Covarrubias observed that the term 'sometimes means fidelity, as of a servant who is faithful to [*tiene ley con*] his master' (*Tesoro de la lengua*, p. 758a).
85. *El arenal de Sevilla*, p. 125.
86. *El arenal de Sevilla*, p. 108.
87. p. 202.
88. Ed. Emilio Cotarelo y Mori (Madrid: Librería de la Viuda del Rico, 1907), pp. 22–5.
89. 'Los gitanos en cliché', p. 131; *La gitanilla*, p. 89.
90. *Agudeza y arte de ingenio*, ed. Evaristo Correa Calderón, 2 vols (Madrid: Castalia, 1987), II, p. 257.
91. p. 307.
92. p. 118.
93. 'A "Different" Body?', p. 521.

6   Purging the body politic

1. *Actas de las Cortes de Castilla*, vol. XXVIII, Cortes de Madrid, 3 April 1615, p. 201; 9 April 1615, p. 240.
2. *Actas de las Cortes de Castilla*, vol. XXVIII, Cortes de Madrid, 10 June 1615, p. 396.
3. Carla Rahn Phillips and William D. Phillips, *Spain's Golden Fleece* (Baltimore and London: Johns Hopkins University Press, 1997), p. 63.
4. *Actas de las Cortes de Castilla*, vol. XXXII, pp. 118–19, Cortes de Madrid, 30 July 1618. The voting system in the *Cortes* allowed delegates to express a nuanced opinion on the matter in hand, rather than demanding from them a simple affirmative or negative response. See I. A. A. Thompson, 'Oposición política', p. 44, n. 20.
5. Martín del Río, *Disquisitionum*, p. 584. In a passage inserted in the second Juan de la Cuesta edition of *Don Quijote*, Ginés de Pasamonte appears 'dressed as a gypsy, whose language and many others he knew as if they were his own' (Part 1, Chapter 30, p. 380, n. 26). Del Río's astonishment that a Spanish gypsy should speak Castilian was ridiculed in the eighteenth century by Feijoo in his *Teatro Crítico Universal*, 8 vols (Madrid: Joaquín Ibarra, 1779), II, p. 74.
6. *Cédula de SM tiene por bien, y manda, salgan del Reyno dentro de seis meses los Gitanos, que andan vagando por él* (BNM, MS 13120).
7. Pinelo, *Anales de Madrid*, p. 129; Elliott, *The Count-Duke of Olivares*, p. 40.
8. Lynch, *The Hispanic World*, p. 77.
9. Elliot, 'The Decline of Spain', in *Spain and Its World*, p. 235.
10. Lynch, *The Hispanic World*, pp. 77–8.
11. Kamen, *Spain 1469–1714*, p. 255.
12. Elliott, 'The Decline of Spain', in *Spain and Its World*, p. 236.

13. Elliott, *The Count-Duke of Olivares*, pp. 117–18.
14. Elliott, 'The Decline of Spain', in *Spain and Its World*, p. 260.
15. There is some uncertainty about the date, though that it should have preceded the 1633 legislation on gypsies seems entirely appropriate. Certainly, another playwright, Juan Pérez de Montalbán, claimed in 1632 that 'Don Antonio de Solís is completing a *comedia* called *La gitanilla*', adding three years later that 'Don Antonio de Solís wrote *La gitanilla*'. See J. H. Parker, 'The Versification of the Comedias of Antonio de Solís y Rivadeneyra', 17:4 (1949), 308–15, p. 312, n. 13.
16. AHN C, *leg.* 7133, *Mesta*, 10 February 1633. Cited by Domínguez Ortiz in *Documentos sobre los gitanos españoles en el siglo XVII* in *Homenaje a Julio Caro Baroja*, ed. A. Carreira (Madrid: Centro de Investigaciones Sociológicas, 1978), p. 322.
17. AHN C, *leg.* 7133, *Mesta*, March 1633.
18. The *maravedí* was Castile's money of account from the time of the Catholic Monarchs. The *ducado* (ducat) was officially worth 375 *maravedís*.
19. López Molina, 'Gitanos y Corpus Christi', p. 745.
20. *Pragmática que su Magestad manda se promulgue en razón de los gitanos que andan por el reino* (Madrid: Viuda de Juan González, 1633). For obvious reasons, women were not sent to the galleys, but could instead be sent to an institution known as the *Galera* (Galley) in Madrid which had been founded specifically for them, probably in 1608, by a nun, Magdalena de San Jerónimo, and where conditions were designed to reflect the harshness implied by its name (Pike, *Penal Servitude*, p. 5).
21. I. A. A. Thompson, *War and Government in Habsburg Spain 1560–1620* (London: The Athlone Press, 1976), p. 45.
22. Such lawsuits ran at a rate of approximately 3000 a year. See Phillips and Phillips, *Spain's Golden Fleece*, p. 66.
23. Klein, *The Mesta*, p. 126.
24. Phillips and Phillips, *Spain's Golden Fleece*, pp. 66–7.
25. *Pragmática que su Magestad manda se promulgue en razón de los gitanos que andan por el reino* (Madrid: Viuda de Juan González, 1633).
26. *Actas de las Cortes de Castilla*, Cortes of 19 March 1594, vol. XIII, p. 220.
27. Gómez Alfaro. 'Anotaciones', p. 252.
28. Torcuato Pérez de Guzmán, *Los gitanos herreros de Sevilla* (Sevilla: Servicio de Publicaciones del Ayuntamiento, 1982), p. 64.
29. AHN C, *leg.* 524, and *leg.* 527, both cited by Gómez Alfaro in *Anotaciones*, p. 241, where the author surmises of the name Román that it may well be a naturalized form of *Romaní*.
30. Martínez Martínez, 'Los gitanos en el sureste', pp. 94–5.
31. He in fact merely added 34 towns to the original list of 41 designated by his father Philip V in a royal ordinance of 1717.
32. AMC, 1, 14, 29, cited by Antonio Gómez Alfaro in 'Anotaciones', p. 245.
33. AHN C, *leg.* 257, cited by Gómez Alfaro in 'Anotaciones', pp. 244–5.
34. See, for example, Manuel López Molina, 'Gitanos y Corpus Christi', p. 738.
35. See Leblon, *Los gitanos*, p. 60; San Román, *La diferencia*, pp. 23–4.
36. *Documentos*, p. 325. By the late 1600s, Seville's gypsies were well established in the suburb of Triana, across the River Guadalquivir from the city proper. Before that, however, they had occupied the Santa Catalina area of the city,

whose calle Jáuregui was formerly known as the calle de los Gitanos. See Pérez de Guzmán, *Los gitanos herreros de Sevilla*, p. 63.

37. Juan de la Plata, *Los gitanos de Jerez*, p. 8.
38. AGI, *Contratación*, 5585, no. 86, *bienes de difuntos*.
39. AHN N, Osuna, *leg.* 336, doc. 2, fols 1 and 3.
40. AHN N, Osuna, *leg.* 336, doc. 2, fol. 15.
41. AHN N, Osuna, *leg.* 336, doc. 2, fols 6–8.
42. San Román, *La diferencia*, pp. 34 and 239–45. See also Martínez Martínez, 'Los gitanos en el sureste', pp. 94–5.
43. AHN C, *leg.* 49, fols 691–2, cited by Sánchez Ortega, *Los gitanos españoles*, pp. 140–1; *Documentación selecta sobre la situación de los gitanos españoles en el siglo XVIII* (Madrid: Editora Nacional, 1976), pp. 250–2.
44. AHN C, *leg.* 51442, no. 6, letter dated 13 November 1679.
45. Kamen, *Spain in the Later Seventeenth Century*, pp. 282–3.
46. Domínguez Ortiz, *Documentos*, p. 322.
47. AHN CC, *leg.* 51422, *exp.* 6, letter dated 23 May 1674 in Porcuna, Jaén.
48. Kamen, *Spain in the Later Seventeenth Century*, pp. 207–11 (p. 209).
49. Kamen, *Spain in the Later Seventeenth Century*, p. 211.
50. AHN C, *leg.* 51045, *exp.* 4, letter dated 23 April 1633. Today's Los Hinojosos was then two villages, Hinojoso de la Orden, owned by the Order of Santiago, and Hinojoso del Marquesado, owned by the Marquis of Villena.
51. San Román, *La diferencia*, pp. 30–1.
52. AGS RGS, letter dated January 1639.
53. AGS RGS, letter dated 16 February 1639 in Madrid.
54. AHN C, *libro* 1530; *Sala de Alcaldes, libro* 1201, 3 September 1611.
55. Goodman, *Spanish Naval Power*, p. 219.
56. Hit hard by the crown's various financial crises, so desperate had the needs of the galleys become at one stage that in 1620 the then commander of the galleys of Spain, the marquis of Santa Cruz, even tried to raise funds for them by pawning his own silver. See Goodman, *Spanish Naval Power*, pp. 157–8.
57. Pike, *Penal Servitude*, pp. 4 and 7–8. See also AGS GA, *leg.* 3173, *Junta de galeotes, esclavos, y gitanos*.
58. Félix Sevilla y Solana, *Historia penitenciaria española (la galera), apuntes de archivo* (Segovia: n.p., 1917), p. 96.
59. *Los códigos españoles, libro* 8, *título* 14, p. 383. On 4 December 1655, Jerónimo de Barrionuevo reported in Madrid that Philip IV, responding to representations from the kingdoms, was consulting theologians and other eminent persons, desirous once again of seeing all gypsy males sent to the galleys. The rumour was that those too young to man the oars would serve as ship's boys, while females would be taken in chains to the hospitals. The Duke of Pastrana, it appeared, had already rounded up 52 gypsies, young and old. 'I do not know if they will succeed in getting it done', added Barrionuevo. See *Avisos del Madrid de los Austrias*, ed. José M. Díez Borque (Madrid: Castalia, 1996), p. 260.
60. Henry Kamen, 'Aspects of Spanish Military and Naval Organization During the Ministry of Olivares', in *War and Society in Habsburg Spain* (Aldershot: Variorum, 1992), IV, p. 4.
61. Goodman, *Spanish Naval Power*, p. 215.

62. Goodman, *Spanish Naval Power*, p. 204.
63. Leblon, *Los gitanos*, p. 117; Vassberg, *The Village*, p. 144.
64. AHN C, *leg.* 17834, *exp.* 1, doc. 2.
65. AGS GA, *leg.* 3173, 19 November, 1639.
66. AGS RGS, letter dated 9 February 1639.
67. AGS RGS, letter dated 16 March 1639.
68. AGS RGS, letter dated 23 March 1639.
69. *Los códigos españoles, libro* 8, *título* 14, p. 382.
70. *Avisos históricos* (Madrid: Taurus, 1965), p. 198.
71. Mackay, *The Limits of Royal Authority*, pp. 37–8.
72. AHN C, *leg.* 17834, *exp.* 1, docs 3 and 4.
73. AGS GA, *leg.* 3173, *Junta de galeotes, esclavos, y gitanos.*
74. Antonio Martínez Salazar, *Colección de memorias y noticias del gobierno* (Madrid: A. Sanz, 1764), Copy consulted BNM, R/101558, fol. 356.
75. Domínguez Ortiz, *The Golden Age*, p. 165; Leblon, *Los gitanos*, p. 117.
76. *Avisos históricos* (Madrid: Taurus, 1965), p. 56.
77. Domínguez Ortiz, *Documentos*, p. 320.
78. Goodman, *Spanish Naval Power*, pp. 217–20.

7   The Spanish church and the gypsies

1. Sánchez Ortega, *La Inquisición*, p. 26.
2. Leblon, *Los gitanos*, p. 28.
3. Sánchez Ortega, *La Inquisición*, pp. 27–30.
4. Sánchez Ortega, *La Inquisición*, p. 420.
5. Kamen, *The Spanish Inquisition*, pp. 163–4.
6. Kamen, *The Spanish Inquisition*, p. 140. For 1488 as the date of origin of the *Suprema* see José Antonio Escudero, 'The Origin of the *Suprema*', in *The Spanish Inquisition and the Inquisitorial Mind*, ed. Ángel Alcalá (New York: Columbia University Press, 1987), pp. 89–131 (p. 90).
7. Henry Kamen, 'Notes on Witchcraft, Sexuality, and the Inquisition', in *The Spanish Inquisition and the Inquisitorial Mind*, ed. Ángel Alcalá (New York: Columbia University Press, 1987), pp. 237–47 (p. 244). As Kamen notes elsewhere, in 1550, only 40 per cent of those questioned could recite the basic prayers used by the Church. By the late seventeenth century, however, the level of religious instruction was 'fairly high' (*The Spanish Inquisition*, p. 263).
8. Kamen, *The Spanish Inquisition*, p. 80. See also Stephen Haliczer, *Inquisition and Society in the Kingdom of Valencia 1478–1834* (Berkeley: University of California Press, 1990), pp. 4–5.
9. All the figures are based on those provided by María Helena Sánchez (*La Inquisición*, pp. 399–445). It is, however, difficult to be absolutely precise about them, since some documentary sources refer to those processed by first names only, while others include surnames which may or may not refer to the same individual. Then there are the aliases so often used by the gypsies and which so often frustrated the authorities. In 1705, the Toledo tribunal, for example, is recorded as having processed a Francisca Sánchez, also known as 'la Gitana' *and* a Francisca Pérez, also known as Sánchez. They

were probably one and the same person, the accusation in both cases being one of superstition, but one cannot, of course, be certain.

10. *Libro primero*, p. 113.
11. Even the original 1499 ordinance against gypsies had instructed justices that it should be enforced on 'the persons and goods' of those who contravened it (*Textos y disposiciones legales de Castilla impresos en los siglos XVI y XVII*, p. 12).
12. AHN N, Osuna, *leg.* 336, doc. 2, fol. 27.
13. The Inquisition's records contain only five cases of gypsy men accused of sorcery, Joan Baptista, a native of Játiva in Valencia in 1621, Juan (alias Antonio) Malla in Murcia in 1732, and Manuel Cortés, Agustín Montoya and Juan Escalante, all in Granada in 1715, 1745 and 1747, respectively.
14. Sánchez Ortega, *La Inquisición*, p. 57.
15. Sánchez Ortega, *La Inquisición*, p. 86.
16. Sánchez Ortega, *La Inquisición*, pp. 408, 412, 414, 418, 420, and 445.
17. Kamen, *The Spanish Inquisition*, p. 199.
18. Kamen, *The Spanish Inquisition*, p. 268.
19. Kamen, *The Spanish Inquisition*, p. 268.
20. As Henry Kamen has pointed out, from the Inquisition's point of view, the real offence in such cases was not so much the sexual activity as the disrespect implied by it for the Sacrament of matrimony (*The Spanish Inquisition*, p. 265).
21. Sánchez Ortega, *La Inquisición*, pp. 76–7.
22. Gómez Alfaro, 'Anotaciones', p. 253.
23. *Reprobación de las supersticiones y hechicerías*, ed. Alva V. Ebersole (Valencia: Albatros, 1950), p. 60.
24. Sánchez Ortega, *La Inquisición*, p. 430.
25. This, of course, is precisely the reason why Sancho Panza's *morisco* friend Ricote returns to Spain in disguise (*Don Quijote*, II, pp. 451–2).
26. Domínguez Ortiz and Vincent, *Historia de los moriscos*, p. 182.
27. See Leblon, *Los gitanos*, pp. 120–8.
28. Recent decades have seen historians reassess the Spanish Inquisition as a body considerably less terrible for much of its existence than was once thought to be the case. For a summary of this trend, see Helen Rawlings, *The Spanish Inquisition* (Oxford: Blackwell, 2006), pp. 8–12.
29. Sánchez Ortega, *La Inquisición*, p. 57.
30. AHN I, Toledo, *leg.* 90, *exp.* 9.
31. AHN I, *leg.* 2075.
32. Sánchez Ortega, *La Inquisición*, p. 55.
33. AHN I, *leg.* 2075.
34. AHN I, Toledo, *leg.* 35, no. 5, fol. 12.
35. AHN I, Toledo, *leg.* 35, no. 5, fol. 7.
36. Sánchez Ortega, *La Inquisición*, p. 412.
37. AHN I, Toledo, *leg.* 33, *exp.* 32.
38. Kamen, *The Spanish Inquisition*, p. 199.
39. Sánchez Ortega, *La Inquisición*, p. 62.
40. Sánchez Ortega, *La Inquisición*, p. 402.
41. This was unusual, but by no means unprecedented. In 1576, the gypsy Alonso Mellado, a resident of Loja, was denounced by María Hernández,

also a gypsy, who accused him of stealing clothing from her. ARCG, *cabina* 322, *leg.* 4447, no. 11, cited in Martínez Martínez, 'Los gitanos en el sureste', p. 95.

42. AHN I, Toledo, *leg.* 26, no. 20, dated 5 May 1626. This case is also reported by Sánchez Ortega (*La Inquisición*, pp. 78–81) and Leblon (*Los gitanos*, p. 162).
43. *La Inquisición*, p. 80.
44. AHN I, Toledo, *leg.* 84, no. 5, 'Isabel Cortés gitana. Hechicería'; documents dated 26 August to 1 September 1624.
45. Elliott, *The Count-Duke of Olivares*, pp. 166–7; Gregorio Marañón, *El Conde-Duque de Olivares* (Madrid: Austral, 1990 [1939]), p. 162.
46. Elliott, *The Count-Duke of Olivares*, pp. 275 and 478.
47. *Novísima recopilación, libro II, título I, ley VII*, p. 203.
48. *Novísima recopilación, libro II, título I, ley IX*, p. 203.
49. Elliott, *Imperial Spain*, pp. 101–2.
50. Thompson, 'Castile', p. 83.
51. Pike, Ruth, 'Crime and Criminals', p. 6.
52. *Cortes* of Valladolid 1542, *Petición* 40, Colmeiro (ed.), *Cortes de los antiguos reinos*, vol. 5, p. 240.
53. *Cortes* of Madrid 1551, *Petición* 35, Colmeiro (ed.), *Cortes de los antiguos reinos*, vol. 5, p. 253.
54. *Pragmática que su Magestad manda que se imprima. Sobre los Vagamundos, Ladrones, Blasphemos, Rufianes*...(Alcalá de Henares: En casa de Juan de Villanueva, 1566). Copy consulted BNM R/14090 (26).
55. *Novísima recopilación, libro I, título IV, ley 1*, p. 22.
56. Leblon, *Los gitanos*, p. 42.
57. BNM, MS 18665, *Discurso acerca de si fue lícito que los Alcaldes de la Chancillería de Valladolid señalasen con un hierro candente a varios gitanos.*
58. BNM, R/14090, *petición* 80.
59. AGS GA, *leg.* 3173, dated 19 November 1639.
60. *Discursos jurídicos políticos en razón de que los gitanos bandoleros de estos tiempos no les valga la Iglesia para su inmunidad* (Salamanca: Diego de Cossío, 1644). Copy consulted AHN N, Osuna, caja 4248, doc. 4.
61. AHN C, *leg.* 51442, no. 6, *Premática en que Su Magestad da la orden que se ha de tener en la prisión y castigo de los bandoleros, y gente perdida, y que roban, y saltean en los caminos, y poblados.*
62. Kamen, *Spain in the Later Seventeenth Century*, pp. 208–11.
63. BNM, VC/226/98, *Discurso al Rey don Felipe IV que se sirva dar orden como más convenga para que a ningún género de ladrones les valga la iglesia* (1654?).
64. Leblon, *Los gitanos*, p. 42.
65. AHN C, *leg.* 51442, doc. 6, dated 15 June 1700.
66. AHN C, *Libro* 1290, fol. 262, dated 8 September 1705.
67. AHN C, *leg.* 24, *exp.* 1, November 1722.
68. AHN C, *leg.* 62 contains various eighteenth-century examples of such disputes.
69. Leblon, *Los gitanos*, p. 43.
70. AHN CRC, no. 44, 7 February 1746.
71. María Helena Sánchez Ortega, *Los gitanos españoles* (Barcelona: Castellote, 1977), p. 261.

8 The failure of the laws and the last Habsburg

1. In *Don Quijote*, Cervantes has one of the guards escorting prisoners condemned to serve in the galleys describe Ginés de Pasamonte's ten-year sentence as 'civil death' (*Don Quijote*, I, p. 271).
2. See, for example, I. A. A. Thompson, 'Castile', pp. 69–98 and Ruth Mackay, *The Limits of Royal Authority*, pp. 99–102.
3. *Empresas políticas* (Madrid: Cátedra, 1999 [1643]), p. 359.
4. *Don Quijote*, I, p. 266.
5. (Madrid: Castalia, 1995 [1603]), p. 457.
6. 'Castile', pp. 93–4.
7. *Memorial de el hecho de los gitanos*, fol. 1.
8. *España, un enigma*, II, p. 501.
9. Fol. 3.
10. AHN C, *libro* 1290 (1705), fols 263–4.
11. *Actas de las Cortes de Castilla*, vol. XXVI, p. 164.
12. AHN C, *leg.* 51060.
13. San Román, *La diferencia*, p. 30.
14. AHN C, *leg.* 7133, *Mesta*.
15. AHN CC, *leg.* 51442, fol. 6.
16. Pérez de Guzmán, *Los gitanos herreros de Sevilla*, p. 90.
17. *La Inquisición y los gitanos* (Madrid: Taurus, 1988), p. 132.
18. AHN C, *leg.* 51060.
19. AGS GA, *leg.* 3173.
20. Leblon, *Los gitanos*, p. 117.
21. In Cervantes's *La gitanilla* (p. 124): 'Andrés asked them to move to another place away from Madrid, because he feared being recognized if he remained there; they told him they had already decided to go to the Montes de Toledo, and from there plunder all the surrounding area.'
22. AHN C, *libro* 1290, fol. 260.
23. AGS RGS, letter dated 9 February 1639. Philip II had ordered that sentences for suitably serious crimes should be commuted to galley service in his '*Pragmática de los vagamundos y ladrones*' (1566).
24. AGS RGS, letter dated 16 February 1639.
25. AGS GA, *leg.* 3173.
26. AHN C, *leg.* 51045, *exp.* 4, letter dated 23 April 1633.
27. Kamen, *Spain in the Later Seventeenth Century*, p. 29.
28. Ruth Mackay, *The Limits of Royal Authority*, p. 66; Thompson, 'Castile', pp. 93–4.
29. *Spain in the Later Seventeenth Century*, p. 17.
30. AHN C, *leg.* 54, *exp.* 1, cited by Sánchez Ortega, *Los gitanos españoles*, p. 445.
31. Cited by Gómez Alfaro, in *The Great Gypsy Round-up*, p. 102.
32. Sánchez Ortega, *Los gitanos españoles*, p. 262.
33. Leblon, *Los gitanos*, p. 95.
34. AGS GA, *leg.* 1256.
35. J. H. Elliott, *Imperial Spain 1469–1716* (London: Edward Arnold, 1963), p. 295. In Calderón's *El alcalde de Zalamea*, which explores just such a jurisdictional dispute, the *dénouement* pointedly favours civil authority and is endorsed by no less a figure than Philip II.

36. AGS GA, *leg.* 3173.
37. AGS GA, *leg.* 3173, 19 November 1639.
38. AHN C, *leg.* 51060, 'Quaderno de autos generales'. García de Córdoba's commission included all territory within a 20-league (70-mile) radius of Madrid.
39. Ruth Mackay, *The Limits of Royal Authority*, p. 41.
40. Faustino Gil Ayuso, *Textos y disposiciones*, p. 328, 21 July 1673; AHN C, *libro* 1474, no. 188, 20 November 1692; AHN C, *libro* 1474, no. 196, 26 February 1693; AHN C, *leg.* 51442, no. 6, 12 June 1695.
41. Faustino Gil Ayuso, *Textos y disposiciones*, p. 328.
42. AHN C, *libro* 1474, no. 188.
43. AHN C, *leg.* 51442, no. 6.
44. Kamen, *Spain in the Later Seventeenth Century*, p. 282.
45. Domínguez Ortiz, *Documentos*, p. 320.
46. AHN C, *leg.* 51442, fol. 6.

9   The Bourbon period

1. Elliott, *Imperial Spain*, p. 375.
2. Henry Kamen, *The War of Succession in Spain, 1700–15* (London: Weidenfeld and Nicolson, 1969), pp. 85–6.
3. Kamen, *Spain's Road to Empire*, p. 337.
4. Elliott, *Imperial Spain*, 377; Barton, *A History of Spain*, p. 139.
5. Fraser, *The Gypsies*, p. 95.
6. Paul W. Bamford, *Fighting Ships and Prisons: The Mediterranean Galleys of France in the Age of Louis XIV* (Minneapolis: University of Minnesota Press, 1973), p. 180. Interestingly, Pedro Rodríguez de Campomanes expressed the view in 1763 that France's gypsies had generally been less malignant there than elsewhere (Sánchez Ortega, *Los gitanos españoles*, p. 253).
7. AHN C, *libro* 1290, fols 260–4; *libro* 1475, no. 52.
8. Capdevila y Orozco, *Errantes y expulsados*, p. 55; José Carlos de Luna, *Gitanos de la Bética* (Chiclana: Universidad de Cádiz, 1989 [1951]), p. 85.
9. The reader should note that no English translation adequately captures the ambiguity present here. While the Spanish phrase does not amount to 'so-called gypsies', it does nevertheless convey a subtle and understated scepticism.
10. AHN C, *leg.* 7, *exp.* 7.
11. Gómez Alfaro, *The Great Gypsy Round-up*, p. 26.
12. Sánchez Ortega, *Los gitanos españoles*, p. 119.
13. The law in question was promulgated in 1586. See *Novísima recopilación, libro* XII, *título* XVI, *ley* III, p. 358.
14. Leblon, *Los gitanos*, p. 95.
15. AHN C, *leg.* 7, *exp.* 8, fol. 41.
16. AHN C, *leg.* 7, *exp.* 8, fols 26, 28, 101, and 115.
17. Leblon, *Los gitanos*, pp. 97–9.
18. AHN C, *leg.* 49690.
19. It is, for example, used repeatedly from the late 1660s in parish registers recording the marriages or deaths of gypsies in Illora, Granada (API, *libro* 7b, fol. 149, 1676; *libro* 4d, fol. 36, 1678; *libro* 4d, fol. 120, 1680).

20. Leblon, *Los gitanos*, p. 95.
21. AHN CRC, nos 43 and 44.
22. AHN CRC, no. 44, 7 February 1746.
23. Sánchez Ortega, *Los gitanos españoles*, p. 138.
24. Sánchez Ortega, *Los gitanos españoles*, p. 136.
25. Sánchez Ortega, *Los gitanos españoles*, p. 134.
26. Sánchez Ortega, *Los gitanos españoles*, p. 452.
27. Sánchez Ortega, *Los gitanos españoles*, p. 145.
28. Sánchez Ortega, *Los gitanos españoles*, pp. 152–3.
29. AHN CRC, no. 44, 7 February 1746.
30. Sánchez Ortega, *Documentos*, pp. 64–5.
31. Gómez Alfaro, *The Great Gypsy Round-up*, p. 20.
32. Gil Ayuso, *Textos y disposiciones*, p. 328, 21 July 1673.
33. Gómez Alfaro, *The Great Gypsy Round-up*, pp. 11–12.
34. Bachiller Revoltoso, El, *Libro de la gitanería de Triana de los años 1740 a 1750 que escribió el Bachiller Revoltoso para que no se imprimiera* (Sevilla: Junta Municipal de Triana, 1995), pp. 2–3.
35. Gómez Alfaro, *The Great Gypsy Round-up*, p. 35.
36. Gómez Alfaro, *The Great Gypsy Round-up*, p. 25.
37. Sánchez Ortega, *Los gitanos españoles*, p. 211; Fraser, *The Gypsies*, p. 164.
38. Sánchez Ortega, *Los gitanos españoles*, p. 210.
39. Gómez Alfaro, *The Great Gypsy Round-up*, pp. 65–6.
40. Sánchez Ortega, *Los gitanos españoles*, p. 215.
41. Gómez Alfaro, *The Great Gypsy Round-up*, pp. 66–7.
42. AGS M, *Arsenales*, leg. 723, cited by Sánchez Ortega, *Los gitanos españoles*, p. 231.
43. Gómez Alfaro, *The Great Gypsy Round-up*, p. 74.
44. Cited by Sánchez Ortega, *Los gitanos españoles*, p. 211.
45. Gómez Alfaro, *The Great Gypsy Round-up*, pp. 90–2.
46. Sánchez Ortega, *Los gitanos españoles*, pp. 213–14.
47. Sánchez Ortega, *Los gitanos españoles*, p. 262.
48. *King Charles III of Spain: An Enlightened Despot* (London: Constable, 1971), pp. 1–2.
49. Cited by Sánchez Ortega in *Los gitanos españoles*, p. 254.
50. Cited by Sánchez Ortega in *Los gitanos españoles*, p. 265.
51. Leblon, *Los gitanos*, pp. 52–3.
52. Leblon, *Los gitanos*, pp. 66–7.
53. AGS GJ, leg. 1004, cited by Sánchez Ortega in *Los gitanos españoles*, p. 268.
54. Sánchez Ortega, *Los gitanos españoles*, p. 274.
55. *Pragmática-Sanción en fuerza de ley, en que se dan nuevas reglas para contener y castigar la vagancia de los que hasta aquí se han conocido con el nombre de gitanos, o castellanos nuevos, con lo demás que expresa* (Madrid: Pedro Marín, 1783). Copy consulted AHN CRC, *Sala de Alcaldes de Casa y Corte*, 1783, fols 938–57.
56. The hostilities represented an attempt by Spain to exploit to its advantage England's preoccupation with the War of American Independence (1775–83). Some small territorial gains were made in Florida and with the recovery of Minorca, but Gibraltar stood its ground under the leadership of its Governor George Eliott of Stobs, of whom Petrie memorably wrote, 'He was

a Scot, but although he was a vegetarian and a teetotaller he possessed a
sense of humour, and it is unquestionably due to him that Britain continued
to hold the Rock' (*King Charles III of Spain*, p. 187).

57. Gómez Alfaro, 'Anotaciones', p. 244.
58. AHN C, *leg*. 526, AMC, 1, 14, 10, and AHN C, *leg*. 527, cited by Gómez Alfaro
   in 'Anotaciones', p. 245.
59. 'Anotaciones', p. 250.
60. Sánchez Ortega, *Los gitanos españoles*, p. 453.
61. 'Anotaciones', p. 249.
62. John Lynch, *Bourbon Spain, 1700–1808* (Oxford: Blackwell, 1989), p. 196.
63. San Román, *La diferencia*, p. 62.
64. Bachiller Revoltoso, El, *Libro de la gitanería*, p. 2.
65. Leblon, *Los gitanos*, pp. 67 and 75.

Conclusion

1. *Informe sobre la cuestión gitana: orientaciones para un plan estatal de acciones
   prioritarias respecto a la problemática de la comunidad gitana española* (Madrid:
   Editorial Presencia Gitana, 1991), p. 8.
2. Thompson, *War and Government*, p. 47. Thompson notes that jurisdictional
   disputes between local and military authorities were also frequent in Portugal,
   Aragon, and Navarre.

Bibliography

Manuscript sources

ACA   Archivo de la Corona de Aragón, Barcelona
ACRV   Archivo de la Chancillería Real, Valladolid
AGI   Archivo General de Indias, Seville
AGP   Archivo General de Palacio, Madrid
AGS   Archivo General de Simancas
         AGS CC Cámara de Castilla
         AGS E Estado
         AGS GA Guerra Antigua
         AGS GJ Gracia y Justicia
         AGS GM Guerra y Marina
         AGS M Secretaría de Marina
         AGS RGS Registro General del Sello
AHN   Archivo Histórico Nacional, Madrid
         AHN C Consejos
         AHN CC Cámara de Castilla
         AHN CRC Consejo de Castilla
         AHN I Inquisición
         AHN N Archivo Histórico Nacional, Sección Nobleza, Toledo
AHPJ   Archivo Histórico Provincial de Jaén
AMC   Archivo Municipal de Córdoba
AML   Archivo Municipal de Lorca
API   Archivo Parroquial de Illora
ARCG   Archivo de la Real Chancillería de Granada
BNM   Biblioteca Nacional, Madrid

Additional primary sources

Alcalá Yáñez, Jerónimo de, *Alonso, mozo de muchos amos o el donado hablador* (Madrid: Aguilar, 1980 [1624–6]).

Alemán, Mateo, *Guzmán de Alfarache*, ed. José María Micó (Madrid: Cátedra, 2000 [1599]).

Alfaro, Fray Gregorio de, *La vida ejemplar de don Franciso de Reinoso, Abad de Husillos y Obispo de Córdoba* (Valladolid: Cumbre, 1940 [1617]).

Anonymous, *Hechos del Condestable don Miguel Lúcas de Iranzo (crónica del siglo XV)*, ed. Juan de Mata Carriazo (Madrid: Espasa-Calpe, 1940).

Anonymous, *Vida y hechos de Estebanillo González*, ed. María Soledad Carrasco Urgoiti (Madrid: Castalia, 1978 [1646]).

Ariño, Francisco de, *Sucesos de Sevilla de 1592 a 1604* (Sevilla: Servicio de Publicaciones, Ayuntamiento, 1993 [1873]).

Bachiller Revoltoso, El, *Libro de la gitanería de Triana de los años 1740 a 1750 que escribió el Bachiller Revoltoso para que no se imprimiera* (Sevilla: Junta Municipal de Triana, 1995 [1781?]).

Barrionuevo, Jerónimo de, *Avisos del Madrid de los Austrias*, ed. José M. Díez Borque (Madrid: Castalia, 1996).

Bisciola, Lelio, *Horarum subsecuiarum* (Ingoldstadt: Adam Sartorius, 1611).

Cabrera de Córdoba, Luis, *Relaciones de las cosas sucedidas en la corte de España desde 1599 hasta 1614* (Madrid: J. M. Alegría, 1857).

Cadalso, José, *Cartas marruecas; Noches lúgubres*, ed. Joaquín Arce (Madrid: Cátedra, 1998 [1775]).

Calderón de la Barca, Pedro, *La franchota* and *Las visiones de la muerte*, in *Entremeses, jácaras y mojigangas*, eds Evangelina Rodríguez and Antonio Tordera (Madrid: Castalia, 1982 [1642]), pp. 251–61 and 369–84.

——, *Mojiganga de la negra, que se hizo en fiesta de sus Magestades*, in *Mojigangas dramáticas (siglos XVII y XVIII)*, ed. Catalina Buezo (Madrid: Cátedra, 2005), pp. 106–18.

Castillo de Bobadilla, Jerónimo, *Política para Corregidores y señores de vasallos en tiempo de paz, y de guerra* (Antwerp: Hermanos de Tournes, 1659 [1597]).

Caxa de Leruela, Miguel, *Restauración de la antigua abundancia de España*, ed. J. P. Le Flem (Madrid: Instituto de Estudios Fiscales, 1975 [1631]).

Cervantes, Miguel de, *El ingenioso hidalgo don Quijote de La Mancha*, ed. Luis Andrés Murillo (Madrid: Castalia, 1978 [1605 and 1615]), available in various translations including *Don Quixote*, translated by J. M. Cohen (Harmondsworth: Penguin, 1950).

——, *Novelas ejemplares*, ed. Juan Bautista Avalle-Arce, 3 vols (Madrid: Castalia, 1982 [1613]); *Exemplary Stories*, translated by C. A. Jones (London: Penguin, 1972).

——, *Viaje del Parnaso*, ed. Vicente Gaos (Madrid: Castalia, 1973 [1614]).

——, *El Rufián dichoso/Pedro de Urdemalas*, eds Jenaro Talens and Nicholas Spadaccini (Madrid: Cátedra, 1986[1615]).

——, *Entremés de la elección de los alcaldes de Daganzo*, in *Entremeses*, ed. Eugenio Asensio (Madrid: Castalia, 1970).

——, *Comedias y entremeses* 'Prólogo al lector', in *Cervantes: teatro completo* (Barcelona: Editorial Iberia, 1966), pp. 133–6.

Céspedes y Meneses, Gonzalo de, *Varia fortuna del soldado Pindaro* (Madrid: S. A. de Promoción y Ediciones, 1980 [1626]).

Ciruelo, Pedro, *Reprobación de las supersticiones y hechicerías*, ed. Alva V. Ebersole (Valencia: Ediciones Albatros, 1950 [c.1530]).

Covarrubias, Sebastián de, *Tesoro de la lengua castellana o española*, ed. Martín de Riquer (Barcelona: Alta Fulla, 1998 [1611]).

Espinel, Vicente, *Vida del escudero Marcos de Obregón*, ed. María Soledad Carrasco Urgoiti (Madrid: Castalia, 2002 [1618]).

Feijoo, Benito Jerónimo, *Teatro crítico universal*, 8 vols (Madrid: Joaquín Ibarra, 1779).

Fernández, Francisco Manuel, *Escudo de la justicia en desagravio de la Iglesia: defensa jurídica de la Real jurisdicción*, AHN Nobleza, 1747?, Osuna, caja 4269, doc. 4.

Fernández de Córdoba, Francisco, *Didascalia multiplex*, 1615 (Copy consulted in Bodleian Library, Oxford 80 F 22 Art. Seld).

Fernández Navarrete, *Conservación de monarquías y discursos políticos*, ed. Michael D. Gordon (Madrid: Instituto de Estudios Fiscales, 1982 [1626]).

Figueroa, Pedro de, *Aviso de príncipes en aphorismos políticos y morales* (Madrid: Diego Díaz de la Carrera, 1647), copy consulted BNM, 3/20037.

González de Cellorigo, Martín, *Memorial de la política necesaria y útil restauración a la república de España y estados de ella y del desempeño universal de estos reinos*, ed. José L. Pérez de Ayala (Madrid: Instituto de Estudios Fiscales, 1991 [1600]).

Huarte de San Juan, *Examen de ingenios*, ed. Guillermo Serés (Madrid: Cátedra, 1989 [1575]).

Huélamo, Fray Melchor de, *Libro primero de la vida y milagros del glorioso Confessor Sant Ginés de la Xara* (Murcia: Agustín Martínez, 1607).

Krantz, Albert, *Rerum Germanicarum historici clariss. Saxonia* (Cologne: n. p., 1530).

Liñan y Verdugo, Antonio, *Guía y avisos de forasteros que vienen a la Corte* (Madrid: Editora Nacional, 1980 [1620]).

Luna, Juan de, *Segunda parte del Lazarillo*, ed. Pedro M. Piñero (Madrid: Cátedra, 1988).

Martínez Salazar, Antonio, *Colección de memorias y noticias del gobierno* (Madrid: A. Sanz, 1764).

Moncada, Sancho de, *Restauración política de España*, ed. Jean Vilar (Madrid: Instituto de estudios fiscales, 1974 [1619]).

Münster, Sebastian, *Cosmographia universalis* (Basel: Heinrich Petri, 1550).

Novísima recopilación de las leyes de España (Madrid: n.p., 1805 [1567]).

Pellicer, José de, *Avisos históricos* (Madrid: Taurus, 1965).

Pérez de Herrera, Cristobál, *Amparo de pobres*, ed. Michel Cavillac (Madrid: Espasa-Calpe, 1975 [1598]).

Piña, Juan de, *Casos prodigiosos y cueva encantada*, ed. Emilio Cotarelo y Mori (Madrid: Librería de la Viuda del Rico, 1907 [1628]).

Pinelo, León, *Anales de Madrid: Años 1598 a 1621*, ed. Ricardo Martorell Téllez Girón (Valladolid: Maxtor, 2003 [1658]).

Pragmática que su Magestad manda se promulgue en razón de los gitanos que andan por el reino (Madrid: Viuda de Juan González, 1633).

Pragmática que su Magestad manda publicar, dando la forma en que deven vivir los gitanos que se hallaren en estos Reynos, con expresión de las penas en que incurren contraviniendo a ella (Valladolid: Joseph de Rueda, 1695).

Pragmatica que su Magestad manda promulgar, dando regla, y estableciendo nueva forma en que desde aora en adelante han de vivir los que se dizen Gitanos y Gitanas (Madrid: Jerónimo de Estrada, 1717).

Pragmática-Sanción en fuerza de ley, en que se dan nuevas reglas para contener y castigar la vagancia de los que hasta aquí se han conocido con el nombre de gitanos, o castellanos nuevos, con lo demás que expresa (Madrid: Pedro Marín, 1783).

Quiñones, Juan de, *Discurso contra los gitanos* (Madrid: Juan González, 1631) Copy consulted BNM R/31436.

Río, Martín del, *Disquisitionum magicarum libri sex* (Cologne?: Petri Henningi?, 1617), copy consulted BNM, R/39181.

Rivadeneyra, Pedro de, *Tratado de la religión y virtudes que debe tener el príncipe cristiano para gobernar y conservar sus estados contra lo que Nicolás Maquiavelo y los políticos desde tiempo enseñan* (Barcelona: Viuda e Hijos de J. Subirana, 1881).

Rocca, Angelo, *Bibliotheca apostolica Vaticana* (Rome: Ex typographia apostolica Vaticana, 1591).

Rojas, Fernando de, *Comedia de Calisto y Melibea*, ed. Julio Cejador y Frauca, 2 vols (Madrid: Espasa-Calpe, 1968 [1499]).

Rojas Villandrando, Agustín de, *El viaje entretenido*, ed. Jean Pierre Ressot (Madrid: Castalia, 1995 [1603]).

Rueda, Lope de, *Comedia llamada Eufemia* and *Comedia llamada Medora*, in *Las cuatro comedias*, ed. Alfredo Hermenegildo (Madrid: Cátedra, 2001 [1567]), pp. 73–127 and 215–55.

——, *La gitana ladrona*, in *Pasos completos*, ed. Juan María Marín Martínez (Madrid: Austral, 1990), pp. 185–9.

Salazar de Mendoza, Pedro, *Memorial de el hecho de los gitanos* (Toledo?: n.p., 1618), AGP, VII/357.

Solís y Rivadeneira, Antonio de, *La gitanilla de Madrid*, in *Comedias de Antonio de Solís*, 2 vols, ed. Manuela Sánchez Regueira (Madrid: Consejo Superior de Investigaciones Científicas, 1984 [1632]), II, pp. 609–81.

Valencia, Pedro de, *Tratado acerca de los moriscos de España*, ed. Joaquín Gil Sanjuan (Málaga: Algazara, 1997 [1606]).

Vega, Lope de, *El arenal de Sevilla* (Madrid: Austral, 1977 [1618]).

——, *El robo de Dina*, in *Obras de Lope de Vega*, ed. Marcelino Menéndez y Pelayo (Madrid: Atlas, 1963), pp. 131–74.

Vélez de Guevara, Luis, *El diablo cojuelo*, eds Ángel R. Fernández and Ignacio Arellano (Madrid: Castalia, 1988 [1641]).

Vicente, Gil, *Farsa das ciganas*, in *Copilaçam de todalas obras de Gil Vicente*, ed. María Leonor Carvalhão Buescu (Lisbon: Nacional-Casa da Moeda, 1983 [1521]), pp. 226–8.

Villalobos, Pedro de, *Discursos jurídicos políticos en razón de que los gitanos bandoleros de estos tiempos no les valga la Iglesia para su inmunidad* (Salamanca: Diego de Cossío, 1644). Copy consulted AHN N, Osuna, caja 4248, doc. 4.

Secondary sources

Abel, Dominique (dir.), *Polígono sur: el arte de las tres mil* (Barcelona: Manga Films, 2003).

Agulló y Cobo, Mercedes, 'Primera entrega documental sobre teatro en Andalucía', in *En torno al teatro del Siglo de Oro: Actas jornadas XII-XII* (Almería: Instituto de Estudios Almerienses, Diputación de Almería, 1996), pp. 39–45.

Astrana Marín, Luis, *Vida ejemplar y heroica de Miguel de Cervantes Saavedra con mil documentos hasta ahora inéditos y numerosas ilustraciones y grabados de época*, 7 vols (Madrid: Editorial Reus, 1948–58).

Aydelotte, Frank, *Elizabethan Rogues and Vagabonds* (Oxford: Clarendon Press, 1913).

Babinger, Franz, *Mehmed the Conqueror and His Time* (Princeton, NJ: Princeton University Press, 1978).

Bamford, Paul W., *Fighting Ships and Prisons: The Mediterranean Galleys of France in the Age of Louis XIV* (Minneapolis: University of Minnesota Press, 1973).

Barton, Simon, *A History of Spain* (Basingstoke: Palgrave Macmillan, 2004).

Beier, A. L., *Masterless Men: The Vagrancy Problem In England 1560–1640* (London: Methuen, 1985).

Benítez Alba, Manuel Jesús, 'Grupos marginados e instituciones piadosas en la Málaga de Felipe V', *Jábega*, 60 (1988), 7–14.

Bernaldo de Quirós, Constancio and Luis Ardila, *El bandolerismo andaluz* (Madrid: Turner, 1998).

Borrow, George, *The Zincali: An Account of the Gypsies of Spain* (London: John Murray, 1901 [1843]).

Brandes, Stanley, *Metaphors of Masculinity: Sex and Status in Andalusian Folklore* (Philadelphia: University of Pennsylvania Press, 1971).

Braudel, Fernand, *The Mediterranean and the Mediterranean World in the Age of Philip II*, 2 vols (Glasgow: Fontana/Collins, 1972).

Campuzano, E., *De los jitanos, y diccionario de su dialecto* (Madrid: Maxtor, 2004 [1848]).

Canavaggio, Jean, *Cervantes* (Madrid: Austral, 2003 [1986]).

Capdevila y Orozco, José, *Errantes y expulsados: normativas jurídicas contra gitanos, judíos, y moriscos* (Córdoba: Francisco Baena, 1991).

Cardaillac, Louis, 'Vision simplificatrice des groupes marginaux', in *Les problèmes de l'exclusion en Espagne (XVIᵉ–XVIIᵉ siècles)*, ed. Augustin Redondo (Paris: Publications de la Sorbonne, 1983), pp. 43–64.

Caro Baroja, Julio, *Los moriscos del Reino de Granada* (Madrid: Istmo, 2000).

——, 'Magia y grupo étnico o la tribu mágica', in *Vidas mágicas e Inquisición*, 2 vols (Madrid: Istmo, 1992), I, pp. 75–93.

——, 'Los gitanos en cliché', in *Temas castizos* (Madrid: Istmo, 1980), pp. 103–40.

Casey, James, *Early Modern Spain: A Social History* (London: Routledge, 1999).

Castro, Américo, *España en su historia: cristianos, moros y judíos* (Buenos Aires: Editorial Losada, 1948), translated into English by Edmund L. King as *The Structure of Spanish History* (Princeton, NJ: Princeton University Press, 1954).

Chamberlain, Robert S., 'The Corregidor in Castile in the Sixteenth Century and the Residencia as Applied to the Corregidor', *The Hispanic American Historical Review*, 23:2 (1943), 222–57.

Charnon-Deutsch, Lou, *The Spanish Gypsy: The History of a European Obsession* (University Park, PA: Pennsylvania State University Press, 2004).

——, 'Travels of the Imaginary Spanish Gypsy' in *Constructing Identity in Modern Spain: Theoretical Debates and Cultural Practice*, ed. Jo Labanyi (Oxford, 2002), pp. 22–40.

Close, Athony, *Cervantes and the Comic Mind of His Age* (Oxford: Oxford University Press, 2000).

Clébert, J. P., *Los gitanos* (Barcelona: Orbis, 1965).

Colley, Linda, *Captives: Britain, Empire, and the World, 1600–1850* (New York: Anchor Books, 2004 [2002]).

Colmeiro, Manuel (ed.), *Cortes de los antiguos Reinos de León y de Castilla*, 5 vols (Madrid: Rivadeneyra, 1861–1903).

Dadson, T. J., 'Un Ricote verdadero: el licenciado Alonso Herrador de Villarubia de los Ojos de Guadiana – morisco que vuelve', in *Actas del VI Congreso de la Asociación Internacional Siglo de Oro*, eds María Luisa Lobato and Francisco Domínguez Matito (Burgos-La Rioja: Iberoamericana-Vervuert, 2004), pp. 601–12.

——, 'Convivencia y cooperación entre moriscos y cristianos del Campo de Calatrava: de nuevo con Cervantes y Ricote', in *Siglos dorados: Homenaje a Augustin Redondo*, ed. Pierre Civil, 2 vols (Madrid: Castalia, 2004), I, pp. 301–14.

——, 'Literacy and Education in Early Modern Rural Spain: The Case of Villarubia de los Ojos', *Bulletin of Spanish Studies*, LXXXI: 7–8 (2004), 1011–37.

——, 'Official Rhetoric Versus Local reality: Propaganda and the Expulsion of the *Moriscos*', in *Rhetoric and Reality in Early Modern Spain*, ed. Richard J. Pym (Woodbridge: Tamesis, 2006), pp. 1–24.

Danvila y Collado, Manuel, 'Nuevos datos para escribir la historia de las Cortes de Castilla en el reinado de Felipe IV', *Boletín de la Real Academia de la Historia*, 15 (1889), 385–433.

Deleite y Piñuelo, *La vida mala en la España de Felipe II* (Madrid: Alianza, 1986).

——, *El rey se divierte* (Madrid: Alianza, 1988).

Domínguez Ortiz, Antonio, *Documentos sobre los gitanos españoles en el siglo XVII* in *Homenaje a Julio Caro Baroja*, ed. A. Carreira (Madrid: Centro de Investigaciones Sociológicas, 1978), pp. 319–26.

——, *El antiguo regimen: los Reyes Católicos y los Austrias* (Madrid: Alianza Universidad, 1974).

——, 'Social Outcasts' in *The Golden Age of Spain: 1516–1659* (London: Weidenfeld and Nicolson, 1971), pp. 162–72.

Domínguez Ortiz, Antonio and Bernard Vincent, *Historia de los moriscos: Vida y tragedia de una minoría*, 2 edn (Madrid: Alianza, 1980).

Dubet, Anne, 'Los arbitristas entre discurso y acción política: propuestas para un análisis de la negociación política', *Tiempos Modernos*, 9 (1999), 1–14.

Edwards, John, *The Spain of the Catholic Monarchs 1474–1520* (Oxford: Blackwell, 2000).

Elliot, J. H., ' "Máquina insigne": la monarquía hispana en el reinado de Felipe II', in *España en tiempos del Quijote*, eds Antonio Feros and Juan Gelabert, Juan (Madrid: Taurus, 2004), pp. 41–60.

——, *Spain and Its World 1500–1700* (New Haven and London: Yale University Press, 1989).

——, *The Count-Duke of Olivares: The Statesman in an Age of Decline* (New Haven and London: Yale University Press, 1986).

——, *The Revolt of the Catalans: A Study in the Decline of Spain* (Cambridge: Cambridge University Press, 1963).

——, *Imperial Spain 1469–1716* (Harmondsworth: Penguin, 1963).

Escudero, José Antonio, 'The Origin of the *Suprema*', in *The Spanish Inquisition and the Inquisitorial Mind*, ed. Ángel Alcalá (New York: Columbia University Press, 1987), pp. 89–131.

Fanjul, Serafín, 'Gitanos y moriscos: verdad y ficción', in *VIII Simposio Internacional de Mudejarismo. De Mudéjares a moriscos: una conversión forzada*, 2 vols (Teruel, 2002) I, pp. 7–25.

Fernández Álvarez, Manuel, *Felipe II y su tiempo* (Madrid: Espasa-Calpe, 1999).

Fernández-Armesto, Felipe, *Ferdinand and Isabella* (New York: Taplinger Publishing Company, 1975).

Fernández-Santamaría, J. A., *The State, War and Peace: Spanish Political Thought in the Renaissance, 1516–1559* (Cambridge: Cambridge University Press, 1977).

Feros, Antonio, *Kingship and Favoritism in the Spain of Philip III: 1598–1621* (Cambridge: Cambridge University Press, 2000).

Fraser, Angus, *The Gypsies* (Oxford: Blackwell, 1992).

——, 'Juridical Autonomy among Fifteenth and Sixteenth Century Gypsies', *The American Journal of Comparative Law*, 45:2 (1997), 291–304.

Fuchs, Barbara, 'Virtual Spaniards: The *Moriscos* and the Fictions of Spanish Identity', *Journal of Spanish Cultural Studies*, 2:1 (2001), 13–25.

García Jiménez, Bartolomé, *Demografía rural andaluza: Rute en el antiguo régimen* (Córdoba: Diputación de Córdoba, 1987).

García Martínez, S., 'Los gitanos en Valencia', in *I Congreso Histórico. País Valenciano* (Valencia, 1976), vol. III, pp. 251–69.

Gay y Blasco, Paloma, 'A "Different" Body? Desire and Virginity Among Gitanos', *The Journal of the Royal Anthropological Institute*, 1:3 (1997), 517–35.

——, 'Gitano Evangelism: The Emergence of a Politico-Religious Diaspora' (paper presented at the 6th EASA Conference, Krakow, 26–9 July 2000).

Gil Ayuso, Faustino (ed.), *Textos y disposiciones legales de Castilla impresos en los siglos XVI y XVII* (Madrid: S. Aguirre, 1935).

Glick, Thomas F., *Islamic and Christian Spain in the Early Middle Ages* (Princeton, NJ: Princeton University Press, 1979).

Gmelch, Sharon Bohn, 'Groups that Don't Want In: Gypsies and Other Artisan, Trader, and Entertainer Minorities', *Annual Review of Anthropology*, 15 (1986), 307–30.

Gómez Alfaro, *The Great Gypsy Round-up* (Madrid: Editorial Presencia Gitana, 1993).

——, 'Anotaciones a los censos gitanos de Andalucía', in *Actas I Congreso de Historia de Andalucía: Andalucía Moderna, Siglo XVIII* (Córdoba: Monte de Piedad, 1978), pp. 239–56.

González Palencia, Angel, *Junta de Reformación: Documentos procedentes del Archivo Histórico Nacional y del General de Simancas* (Valladolid: Poncelix, 1932).

Goodman, David, *Spanish Naval Power, 1589–1665* (Cambridge: Cambridge University Press, 1997).

Goytisolo, Juan, 'Fuenteovejuna, señor', *Journal of Spanish Cultural Studies*, 3:1 (2002), 9–13.

Guilmartin, John Francis, *Gunpowder and Galleys: Changing Technology and Mediterranean Warfare at Sea in the Sixteenth Century* (Cambridge: Cambridge University Press, 1974).

——, 'The Galley in Combat', *MHQ: The Quarterly Journal of Military History*, 9:2 (Winter, 1997), 20–1.

Haliczer, Stephen, *Inquisition and Society in the Kingdom of Valencia 1478–1834* (Berkeley: University of California Press, 1990).

Hamilton, Bernice, *Political Thought in Sixteenth-Century Spain* (Oxford: Clarendon Press, 1963).

Hamilton, Earl J., 'The Decline of Spain', *The Economic History Review*, 8:2 (1938), 168–79.

Hebdige, Dick, 'The Function of Subculture', in *The Cultural Studies Reader*, ed. Simon During (London and New York: Routledge, 1999), pp. 441–50.

Herrero García, Miguel, *Ideas de los españoles del siglo XVII* (Madrid: Gredos, 1966).

Herrera Puga, Pedro, *Sociedad y delincuencia en el Siglo de Oro* (Madrid: La Editorial Católica, 1974).

Hess, A. S., 'The Moriscos. An Ottoman Fifth Column in Sixteenth-Century Spain', *American Historical Review*, 74 (1968), 1–21.

Hillgarth, J. N., *The Spanish Kingdoms 1250–1516*, vol. II, *Castilian Hegemony 1410–1516* (Oxford: Clarendon Press, 1978).

——, 'Spanish Historiography and Iberian Reality', *History and Theory*, 24:1 (1985), 23–43.

Huizinga, J., *The Waning of the Middle Ages* (Harmondsworth: Penguin, 1968 [1924]).

Hull, Anthony H., *Charles III and the Revival of Spain* (Washington: University Press of America, 1981).

Hume, Martin, *The Court of Philip IV* (London: Eveleigh Nash, 1907).

——, *Spain 1479–1788* (Cambridge: Cambridge University Press, 1899).

Hutchinson, Stephen, 'Arbitrating the National *Oikos*', *Journal of Spanish Cultural Studies*, 2:1 (2001), 69–80.

Informe sobre la cuestión gitana (Madrid: Editorial Presencia Gitana, 1991).

J. M., *Historia de los gitanos* (Madrid: Heliodoro, 1980 [1832]).

Justinus, Marcus Junianus, *Epitome to the Philippic History of Pompeius Trogus*, trans. John Selby Watson (London: George Bell and Sons, 1886).

Kamen, Henry, *Spain's Road to Empire: The Making of a World Power 1492–1763* (London: Penguin, 2003).

——, *Philip of Spain* (New Haven and London: Yale University Press, 1997).

——, *The Spanish Inquisition: An Historical Revision* (London: Phoenix, 1997).

——, 'Limpieza and the Ghost of Américo Castro: Racism as a Tool of Literary Analysis', *Hispanic Review*, 64:1, 1996, 19–29.

——, *Spain 1469–1714* (London: Longman, 1993).

——, 'Notes on Witchcraft, Sexuality, and the Inquisition', in *The Spanish Inquisition and the Inquisitorial Mind*, ed. Ángel Alcalá (New York: Columbia University Press, 1987), pp. 237–47.

——, *Spain in the Later Seventeenth Century* (London and New York: Longman, 1980).

——, 'The Decline of Spain: A Historical Myth', *Past and Present*, 81 (1978), 24–50.

——, *The War of Succession in Spain, 1700–15* (London: Weidenfeld and Nicolson, 1969).

Klein, Julius, *The Mesta* (Port Washington, NY: Kennikat Press, 1964).

Koenigsberger, H. G., 'National Consciousness in Early Modern Spain', in *Politicians and Virtuosi: Essays in Early Modern History* (London: The Hambledon Press, 1986), pp. 121–47.

Leblon, Bernard, *Los gitanos de España* (Barcelona: Gedisa, 2001 [1985]).

——, *Inventario de los documentos sobre gitanos de los archivos de Simancas, Madrid, Barcelona y Cuenca* (Perpignan: Universidad de Perpignan, 1980).

——, *Les gitans dans la littérature espagnole* (Toulouse: Université de Toulouse-Le Mirail, 1982).

——, *Gypsies and Flamenco* (Hatfield: University of Hertfordshire Press, 2003)

Lomax, D. W., *The Reconquest of Spain* (London: Longman, 1978).

López de Meneses, Amada, 'La inmigración gitana en España en el siglo XV', in *Martínez Ferrando, Archivero. Miscelánea de estudios dedicados a su memoria* (Madrid: Asociación Nacional de Bibliotecarios, Archiveros y Arqueólogos, 1968), pp. 239–63.

López Molina, Manuel, 'Gitanos y Corpus Christi en Jaén en la primera mitad del siglo XVII', *Boletín del Instituto de Estudios Giennenses*, 176 (2000), 737–50.

Los códigos españoles concordados y anotados, 12 vols (Madrid: M. Rivedeneyra, 1847–51).

Luna, José Carlos de, *Gitanos de la Bética* (Chiclana: Universidad de Cádiz, 1989 [1951]).

Lynch, John, *The Hispanic World in Crisis and Change: 1598–1700* (Oxford: Blackwell, 1992).

——, *Spain 1516–1598: From Nation State to World Empire* (Oxford: Blackwell, 1991).

——, *Bourbon Spain, 1700–1808* (Oxford: Blackwell, 1989).

Mackay, Angus, *Spain in the Middle Ages: From Frontier to Empire, 1000–1500* (Basingstoke: Macmillan, 1977).

——, 'The Late Middle Ages, 1250–1500', in *A History of Spain*, ed. Raymond Carr (Oxford: Oxford University Press, 2000), pp. 90–115.

Mackay, Ruth, *The Limits of Royal Authority: Resistance and Obedience in Seventeenth-Century Castile* (Cambridge: Cambridge University Press, 1999).

Malcolm, Alistair, 'Spanish Queens and Aristocratic Women at the Court of Madrid', in *Studies on Medieval and Early Modern Women 4: Victims or Viragos*, eds Christine Meek and Catherine Lawless (Dublin: Four Courts Press, 2005), pp. 160–79.

Marañón, Gregorio, *El Conde-Duque de Olivares* (Madrid: Austral, 1990 [1939]).

Maravall, José Antonio, *Poder, Honor y élites en el siglo XVII* (Madrid: Siglo Veintiuno, 1984).

Marsden, C. A., 'Entrées et fêtes espagnoles au XVI siècle', in *Les fêtes de la Renaissance*, ed. J. Jacquot, 3 vols (Paris: Centre National de la Recherche Scientifique, 1960), II, pp. 393–7.

Martin, Elisa and Juan F. Gamella, 'Marriage Practices and Ethnic Differentiation: The Case of Spanish Gypsies (1870–2000)', *The History of the Family*, 10 (2005), 45–63.

Martínez Martínez, Manuel, 'Los gitanos en el sureste peninsular de los siglos XV y XVI', *Boletín del Instituto de Estudios Almerienses*, 14 (1995), 91–101.

Martz, Linda, *Poverty and Welfare in Habsburg Spain: The Example of Toledo* (Cambridge: Cambridge University Press, 1983).

——, *A Network of Converso Families in Early Modern Toledo* (Ann Arbor: University of Michigan Press, 2003).

Mitchell, Timothy, *Flamenco Deep Song* (New Haven and London: Yale University Press, 1994).

Navarro García, José Luis, 'Bailes de gitanos de los siglos XVI y XVII', *Revista de Flamencología*, 13 (2001), 27–32.

Okely, Judith, *The Traveller-Gypsies* (Cambridge: Cambridge University Press, 1983).

Pabanó, F. M., *Historia y costumbres de los gitanos* (Barcelona: Montañer y Simón, 1915).

Parker, J. H., 'The Versification of the Comedias of Antonio de Solís y Rivadeneyra', *Hispanic Review*, 17:4 (1949), 308–15.

Pérez de Guzmán, Torcuato, *Los gitanos herreros de Sevilla* (Sevilla: Servicio de Publicaciones del Ayuntamiento, 1982).

Peristiany, J. G., *Honour and Shame: The Values of Mediterranean Society* (London: Weidenfeld and Nicholson, 1965).

Perry, Mary Elizabeth, *The Handless Maiden: Moriscos and the Politics of Religion in Early Modern Spain* (Princeton: Princeton University Press, 2005).

Petrie, Sir Charles, *King Charles III: An Enlightened Despot* (London: Constable, 1971).

Phillips, Carla Rahn, 'Time and Duration: A Model for the Economy of Early Modern Spain', *The American Historical Review*, 92:3 (1987), 531–62.

Phillips, Carla Rahn and William D. Phillips, *Spain's Golden Fleece: Wool Production and the Wool Trade from the Middle Ages to the Nineteenth Century* (Baltimore and London: The Johns Hopkins University Press, 1997).

Pike, Ruth, *Aristocrats and Traders: Sevillian Society in the Sixteenth Century* (Ithaca and London: Cornell University Press, 1972).

——, 'Crime and Criminals in Sixteenth-Century Seville', *Sixteenth Century Journal*, 6:1 (1975), 3–18.

——, *Penal Servitude in Early Modern Spain* (Madison, WI: University of Wisconsin Press, 1983).

Pitt-Rivers, Julian, *The People of the Sierra* (Chicago: University of Chicago Press, 1971).

——, *The Fate of Shechem or the Politics of Sex: Essays in the Anthropology of the Mediterranean* (Cambridge: Cambridge University Press, 1977).

Plata, Juan de la, *Los gitanos de Jerez: historias, dinastías, oficios y tradiciones* (Jerez: Cátedra de Flamencología y Estudios Folklóricos Andaluces, 2001).

Presencia Gitana (Equipo de Estudios), *Informe sobre la cuestión gitana: orientaciones para un plan estatal de acciones prioritarias respecto a la problemática de la comunidad gitana española* (Madrid: Editorial Presencia Gitana, 1991).

Pym, Richard J., 'The Pariah Within: Early Modern Spain's Gypsies', *Journal of Romance Studies*, 4:2 (2004), 21–35.

——, 'The Errant Fortunes of *La gitanilla* and Cervantes's Performing Gypsies', *Journal of Iberian and Latin American Studies*, 12:1 (2006), 15–37.

Ramírez de Arellano, Rafael, *El teatro en Córdoba* (Córdoba: Diputación de Córdoba, 1997 [1912]).

Ramírez Heredia, Juan de Dios, *Nosotros, los gitanos* (Barcelona: Bruguera, 1974).

Rawlings, Helen, '*Arbitrismo* and the Early Seventeenth-Century Spanish Church: The Theory and Practice of Anti-Clericalist Philosophy', in *Rhetoric and Reality in Early Modern Spain*, ed. Richard J. Pym (Woodbridge: Tamesis, 2006), pp. 25–40.

——, *The Spanish Inquisition* (Oxford: Blackwell, 2006).

Rincón Atienza, Pedro, *Rasgos culturales y organización social de la comunidad gitana española (síntesis para educadores)* (Madrid: Asociación Secretariado General Gitano, 1995).

Ringrose, David R., *Madrid and the Spanish Economy, 1560–1850* (Berkeley: University of California Press, 1983).

——, 'The Impact of a New Capital City: Madrid, Toledo, and New Castile, 1560–1660', *The Journal of Economic History*, 33:4 (1973), 761–91.

Río Ruiz, Manuel Ángel, *Violencia étnica y destierro: dinámicas de cuatro disturbios antigitanos en Andalucía* (Granada: Maristán, 2003).

Said, Edward W., *Orientalism: Western Conceptions of the Orient* (London: Penguin, 1995).

Sánchez-Albornoz, Claudio, *España: un enigma histórico* (Buenos Aires: Sudamericana, 1956).

Sánchez Ortega, María Helena, *Documentación selecta sobre la situación de los gitanos españoles en el siglo XVIII* (Madrid: Editora Nacional, 1976).

——, *La Inquisición y los gitanos* (Madrid: Taurus, 1988).

——, *Los gitanos españoles: el período borbónico* (Madrid: Castellote, 1977).

——, 'El problema gitano desde una perspectiva histórica', lecture given at the Instituto Internacional de Antropología, 9 February 1981.

San Román Espinosa, Teresa, *La diferencia inquietante: Viejas y nuevas estrategias culturales de los gitanos* (Madrid: Siglo Veintiuno, 1997).

——, 'Kinship, Marriage, Law and Leadership in Two Urban Gypsy Settlements in Spain', in *Gypsies, Tinkers and Other Travellers*, ed. Farnham Refisch (London: Academic Press, 1975), pp. 169–89.

——, *Gitanos de Madrid y Barcelona: Ensayos sobre aculturación y etnicidad* (Barcelona: Servicio de Publicaciones de la Universidad de Barcelona, 1984).

Santolaria Sierra, Félix (ed.), *El gran debate sobre los pobres en el siglo XVI: Domingo de Soto y Juan de Robles, 1545* (Barcelona: Ariel, 2003).

Sevilla y Solana, Félix, *Historia penitenciaria española (la galera)* (Segovia: n.p., 1917).

Slack, Paul A., 'Vagrants and Vagrancy in England, 1598–1664', *The Economic History Review*, New Series, 27:3 (1974), 360–79.

Sliwa, Krysztof and Daniel Eisenberg, 'El licenciado Juan de Cervantes, abuelo de Miguel de Cervantes Saavedra', *Cervantes*, 17:2 (1997), 106–14.

Stradling, R. A., *Philip IV and the Government of Spain, 1621–1665* (Cambridge: Cambridge University Press, 1988).

Suárez Fernández, Luis, *Nobleza y monarquía: Puntos de vista sobre la historia política castellana del siglo XV* (Valladolid: Universidad de Valladolid, 1975)

Thompson, I. A. A., 'Oposición política y juicio del gobierno en las Cortes de 1592–98', *Studia Historica. Historia Moderna*, 17 (1997), 37–62.

——, *Crown and Cortes: Government, Institutions and Representation in Early-Modern Castile* (Aldershot: Variorum, 1993).

——, 'A Map of Crime in Sixteenth-Century Spain', in *The Economic History Review*, 21:2 (1968), 244–67.

——, 'Aspects of Spanish Military and Naval Organization During the Ministry of Olivares', in *War and Society in Habsburg Spain* (Aldershot: Variorum, 1992), IV, pp. 1–26.

——, 'Castile', in *Absolutism in Seventeenth-Century Europe*, ed. John Miller (London: Macmillan, 1990), pp. 69–98.

——, *War and Government in Habsburg Spain* (London: The Athlone Press, 1976).

Unamuno, Miguel de, *En torno al casticismo* (Madrid: Austral, 1991).

UN International Convention on the Elimination of All Forms of Racial Discrimination (CERD), 'Thirteenth Periodic Reports of States Parties Due in 1994: Spain', 3 May 1995, http://www.unhchr.ch/tbs/doc.nsf/0/4540ad81d312afd78025654f00519c73? Opendocument.

Varey, J. E., *Town and Country in the Theatre of the Golden Age* (London: Queen Mary and Westfield College, 1994).

Vassberg, David E., *The Village and the Outside World in Golden Age Castile* (Cambridge: Cambridge University Press, 1996).

Vincent, Bernard, *Minorías y marginados en la España del siglo XVI* (Granada: Diputación Provincial de Granada, 1987).

Weber, Max, *Economy & Society* (New York: Bedminster Press, 1968).

Williams, Patrick, 'Philip III and the Restoration of Spanish Government, 1598–1603', *The English Historical Review*, 88:349 (1973), 751–69.

Index

Printed in Great Britain
by Amazon